Hard Press

THE HISTORY OF ROME

The Period Anterior to the Abolition of the Monarchy

by

THEODOR MOMMSEN

Translated with the Sanction of the Author

by

William Purdie Dickson, D.D., LL.D.
Professor of Divinity in the University of Glasgow

A New Edition Revised throughout and Embodying Recent Additions

Preparer's Note

This work contains many literal citations of and references to foreign
words, sounds, and alphabetic symbols drawn from many languages,
including Gothic and Phoenician, but chiefly Latin and Greek. This
English Gutenberg edition, constrained to the characters of 7-bit
ASCII code, adopts the following orthographic conventions:

1) Except for Greek, all literally cited non-English words that
do not refer to texts cited as academic references, words that in
the source manuscript appear italicized, are rendered with a single
preceding, and a single following dash; thus, -xxxx-.

2) Greek words, first transliterated into Roman alphabetic equivalents,
are rendered with a preceding and a following double-dash; thus,
—xxxx—. Note that in some cases the root word itself is a compound
form such as xxx-xxxx, and is rendered as —xxx-xxx—

3) Simple unideographic references to vocalic sounds, single
letters, or alphabeic dipthongs; and prefixes, suffixes, and syllabic
references are represented by a single preceding dash; thus, -x,
or -xxx.

4) (Especially for the complex discussion of alphabetic evolution
in Ch. XIV: Measuring And Writing). Ideographic references,
meaning pointers to the form of representation itself rather than

3

to its content, are represented as -"id:xxxx"-. "id:" stands for "ideograph", and indicates that the reader should form a picture based on the following "xxxx"; which may be a single symbol, a word, or an attempt at a picture composed of ASCII characters. E. g. —"id:GAMMA gamma"— indicates an uppercase Greek gamma-form followed by the form in lowercase. Some such exotic parsing as this is necessary to explain alphabetic development because a single symbol may have been used for a number of sounds in a number of languages, or even for a number of sounds in the same language at different times. Thus, -"id:GAMMA gamma" might very well refer to a Phoenician construct that in appearance resembles the form that eventually stabilized as an uppercase Greek "gamma" juxtaposed to one of lowercase. Also, a construct such as —"id:E" indicates a symbol that with ASCII resembles most closely a Roman uppercase "E", but, in fact, is actually drawn more crudely.

5) Dr. Mommsen has given his dates in terms of Roman usage, A.U.C.; that is, from the founding of Rome, conventionally taken to be 753 B. C. The preparer of this document, has appended to the end of each volume a table of conversion between the two systems.

PREFACE BY THE TRANSLATOR

When the first portion of this translation appeared in 1861, it was accompanied by a Preface, for which I was indebted to the kindness of the late Dr. Schmitz, introducing to the English reader the work of an author whose name and merits, though already known to scholars, were far less widely familiar than they are now. After thirty-three years such an introduction is no longer needed, but none the less gratefully do I recall how much the book owed at the outset to Dr. Schmitz's friendly offices.

The following extracts from my own "Prefatory Note" dated "December 1861" state the circumstances under which I undertook the translation, and give some explanations as to its method and aims:—

"In requesting English scholars to receive with indulgence this first portion of a translation of Dr. Mommsen's 'Romische Geschichte,' I am somewhat in the position of Albinus; who, when appealing to his readers to pardon the imperfections of the Roman History which he had written in indifferent Greek, was met by Cato with the rejoinder that he was not compelled to write at all—that, if the Amphictyonic Council had laid their commands on him, the case would have been different—but that it was quite out of place to ask the indulgence of his readers when his task had been self-imposed. I may state, however, that I did not undertake this task, until I had sought to ascertain whether it was likely to be taken up by

4

any one more qualified to do justice to it. When Dr. Mommsen's work accidentally came into my hands some years after its first appearance, and revived my interest in studies which I had long laid aside for others more strictly professional, I had little doubt that its merits would have already attracted sufficient attention amidst the learned leisure of Oxford to induce some of her great scholars to clothe it in an English dress. But it appeared on inquiry that, while there was a great desire to see it translated, and the purpose of translating it had been entertained in more quarters than one, the projects had from various causes miscarried. Mr. George Robertson published an excellent translation (to which, so far as it goes, I desire to acknowledge my obligations) of the introductory chapters on the early inhabitants of Italy; but other studies and engagements did not permit him to proceed with it. I accordingly requested and obtained Dr. Mommsen's permission to translate his work.

"The translation has been prepared from the third edition of the original, published in the spring of the present year at Berlin. The sheets have been transmitted to Dr. Mommsen, who has kindly communicated to me such suggestions as occurred to him. I have thus been enabled, more especially in the first volume, to correct those passages where I had misapprehended or failed to express the author's meaning, and to incorporate in the English work various additions and corrections which do not appear in the original.

"In executing the translation I have endeavoured to follow the original as closely as is consistent with a due regard to the difference of idiom. Many of our translations from the German are so literal as to reproduce the very order of the German sentence, so that they are, if not altogether unintelligible to the English reader, at least far from readable, while others deviate so entirely from the form of the original as to be no longer translations in the proper sense of the term. I have sought to pursue a middle course between a mere literal translation, which would be repulsive, and a loose paraphrase, which would be in the case of such a work peculiarly unsatisfactory. Those who are most conversant with the difficulties of such a task will probably be the most willing to show forbearance towards the shortcomings of my performance, and in particular towards the too numerous traces of the German idiom, which, on glancing over the sheets, I find it still to retain.

"The reader may perhaps be startled by the occurrence now and then of modes of expression more familiar and colloquial than is usually the case in historical works. This, however, is a characteristic feature of the original, to which in fact it owes not a little of its charm. Dr. Mommsen often uses expressions that are not

to be found in the dictionary, and he freely takes advantage of
the unlimited facilities afforded by the German language for the
coinage or the combination of words. I have not unfrequently, in
deference to his wishes, used such combinations as 'Carthagino-Sicilian,'
'Romano-Hellenic,' although less congenial to our English idiom,
for the sake of avoiding longer periphrases.

"In Dr. Mommsen's book, as in every other German work that has
occasion to touch on abstract matters, there occur sentences couched
in a peculiar terminology and not very susceptible of translation.
There are one or two sentences of this sort, more especially in
the chapter on Religion in the 1st volume, and in the critique of
Euripides as to which I am not very confident that I have seized
or succeeded in expressing the meaning. In these cases I have
translated literally.

"In the spelling of proper names I have generally adopted the Latin
orthography as more familiar to scholars in this country, except
in cases where the spelling adopted by Dr. Mommsen is marked by any
special peculiarity. At the same time entire uniformity in this
respect has not been aimed at.

"I have ventured in various instances to break up the paragraphs of
the original and to furnish them with additional marginal headings,
and have carried out more fully the notation of the years B.C. on
the margin.

"It is due to Dr. Schmitz, who has kindly encouraged me in
this undertaking, that I should state that I alone am responsible
for the execution of the translation. Whatever may be thought of
it in other respects, I venture to hope that it may convey to the
English reader a tolerably accurate impression of the contents and
general spirit of the book."

In a new Library edition, which appeared in 1868, I incorporated all
the additions and alterations which were introduced in the fourth
edition of the German, some of which were of considerable importance;
and I took the opportunity of revising the translation, so as to
make the rendering more accurate and consistent.

Since that time no change has been made, except the issue in 1870
of an Index. But, as Dr. Mommsen was good enough some time ago
to send to me a copy in which he had taken the trouble to mark the
alterations introduced in the more recent editions of the original,
I thought it due to him and to the favour with which the translation
had been received that I should subject it to such a fresh revision
as should bring it into conformity with the last form (eighth

6

edition) of the German, on which, as I learn from him, he hardly contemplates further change. As compared with the first English edition, the more considerable alterations of addition, omission, or substitution amount, I should think, to well-nigh a hundred pages. I have corrected various errors in renderings, names, and dates (though not without some misgiving that others may have escaped notice or been incurred afresh); and I have still further broken up the text into paragraphs and added marginal headings.

The Index, which was not issued for the German book till nine years after the English translation was published, has now been greatly enlarged from its more recent German form, and has been, at the expenditure of no small labour, adapted to the altered paging of the English. I have also prepared, as an accompaniment to it, a collation of pagings, which will materially facilitate the finding of references made to the original or to the previous English editions.

I have had much reason to be gratified by the favour with which my translation has been received on the part alike of Dr. Mommsen himself and of the numerous English scholars who have made it the basis of their references to his work.(1) I trust that in the altered form and new dress, for which the book is indebted to the printers, it may still further meet the convenience of the reader.

September 1894.

Notes for Preface

1. It has, I believe, been largely in use at Oxford for the last thirty years; but it has not apparently had the good fortune to have come to the knowledge of the writer of an article on "Roman History" published in the Encyclopedia Britannica in 1886, which at least makes no mention of its existence, or yet of Mr. Baring-Gould, who in his Tragedy of the Caesars (vol. 1. p. 104f.) has presented Dr. Mommsen's well-known "character" of Caesar in an independent version. His rendering is often more spirited than accurate. While in several cases important words, clauses, or even sentences, are omitted, in others the meaning is loosely or imperfectly conveyed—e.g. in "Hellenistic" for "Hellenic"; "success" for "plenitude of power"; "attempts" or "operations" for "achievements"; "prompt to recover" for "ready to strike"; "swashbuckler" for "brilliant"; "many" for "unyielding"; "accessible to all" for "complaisant towards every one"; "smallest fibre" for "Inmost core"; "ideas" for "ideals"; "unstained with blood" for "as bloodless as possible"; "described" for "apprehended"; "purity" for "clearness"; "smug" for "plain" (or homely); "avoid" for "avert"; "taking his dark course" for "stealing towards his aim by paths of darkness"; "rose" for "transformed

himself"; "checked everything like a praetorian domination" for "allowed no hierarchy of marshals or government of praetorians to come into existence"; and in one case the meaning is exactly reversed, when "never sought to soothe, where he could not cure, intractable evils" stands for "never disdained at least to mitigate by palliatives evils that were incurable."

INTRODUCTORY NOTE BY DR. MOMMSEN

The Varronian computation by years of the City is retained in the text; the figures on the margin indicate the corresponding year before the birth of Christ.

In calculating the corresponding years, the year 1 of the City has been assumed as identical with the year 753 B.C., and with Olymp. 6, 4; although, if we take into account the circumstance that the Roman solar year began with the 1st day of March, and the Greek with the 1st day of July, the year 1 of the City would, according to more exact calculation, correspond to the last ten months of 753 and the first two months of 752 B.C., and to the last four months of Ol. 6, 3 and the first eight of Ol. 6, 4.

The Roman and Greek money has uniformly been commuted on the basis of assuming the libral as and sestertius, and the denarius and Attic drachma, respectively as equal, and taking for all sums above 100 denarii the present value in gold, and for all sums under 100 denarii the present value in silver, of the corresponding weight. The Roman pound (=327.45 grammes) of gold, equal to 4000 sesterces, has thus, according to the ratio of gold to silver 1:15.5, been reckoned at 304 1/2 Prussian thalers [about 43 pounds sterling], and the denarius, according to the value of silver, at 7 Prussian groschen [about 8d.].(1)

Kiepert's map will give a clearer idea of the military consolidation of Italy than can be conveyed by any description.

1. I have deemed it, in general, sufficient to give the value of the Roman money approximately in round numbers, assuming for that purpose 100 sesterces as equivalent to 1 pound sterling.—TR.

DEDICATIONS

The First Volume of the original bears the inscription:—

To My Friend

MORIZ HAUPT Of Berin

The Second:—

To My Dear Associates

FERDINAND HITZIG Of Zurich

And

KARL LUDWIG Of Vienna 1852, 1853, 1854

And the Third:—

Dedicated With Old And Loyal Affection To

OTTO JAHN Of Bonn

CONTENTS

BOOK FIRST

The Period Anterior to the Abolition of the Monarchy

—Ta palaiotera saphos men eurein dia chronou pleithos adunata ein ek de tekmeirion on epi makrotaton skopounti moi pisteusai xumbainei ou megala nomizo genesthai oute kata tous polemous oute es ta alla.—

Thucydides.

CHAPTER I

Introduction

Ancient History

The Mediterranean Sea with its various branches, penetrating far into the great Continent, forms the largest gulf of the ocean, and, alternately narrowed by islands or projections of the land and expanding to considerable breadth, at once separates and connects the three divisions of the Old World. The shores of this inland sea were in ancient times peopled by various nations belonging in an ethnographical and philological point of view to different races, but constituting in their historical aspect one whole. This historic whole has been usually, but not very appropriately, entitled the history of the ancient world. It is in reality the history of civilization among the Mediterranean nations; and, as it passes before us in its successive stages, it presents four great phases of development—the history of the Coptic or Egyptian stock dwelling on the southern shore, the history of the Aramaean or Syrian nation which occupied the east coast and extended into the interior of Asia as far as the Euphrates and Tigris, and the histories of the twin-peoples, the Hellenes and Italians, who received as their heritage the countries on the European shore. Each of these histories was in its earlier stages connected with other regions and with other cycles of historical evolution; but each soon entered on its own distinctive career. The surrounding nations of alien or even of kindred extraction—the Berbers and Negroes of Africa, the Arabs, Persians, and Indians of Asia, the Celts and Germans of Europe—came into manifold contact with the peoples inhabiting the borders of the Mediterranean, but they neither imparted unto them nor received from them any influences exercising decisive effect on their respective destinies. So far, therefore, as cycles of culture admit of demarcation at all, the cycle which has its culminating points denoted by the names Thebes, Carthage, Athens, and Rome, may be regarded as an unity. The four nations represented by these names, after each of them had attained in a path of its own a peculiar and noble civilization, mingled with one another in the most varied relations of reciprocal intercourse, and skilfully elaborated and richly developed all the elements of human nature. At length their cycle was accomplished. New peoples who hitherto had only laved the territories of the states of the Mediterranean, as waves lave the beach, overflowed both its shores, severed the history of its south coast from that of the north, and transferred the centre of civilization from the Mediterranean to the Atlantic Ocean. The distinction between ancient and modern history, therefore, is no mere accident, nor yet a mere matter of chronological convenience. What is called modern history is in reality the formation of a new cycle of culture, connected in several stages of its development with the perishing or perished civilization of the Mediterranean states, as this was connected with the primitive civilization of the Indo-Germanic stock, but destined, like the earlier cycle, to traverse an orbit of its own. It too is destined to experience in full measure the vicissitudes of national weal and woe, the periods of growth, of maturity, and of age, the blessedness of creative effort in religion, polity, and art, the comfort of enjoying the material and intellectual acquisitions which it has won, perhaps also, some day, the decay of productive power in the satiety of contentment with the goal attained. And yet this goal will only be temporary: the grandest system of civilization has its orbit, and may complete its course but not so the human race, to which, just when it seems to have reached its goal, the old task is ever set anew with a wider range and with a deeper meaning.

Italy

Our aim is to exhibit the last act of this great historical drama, to relate the ancient history of the central peninsula projecting from the northern continent into the Mediterranean. It is formed by the mountain-system of the Apennines branching off in a southern direction from the western Alps. The Apennines take in the first instance a south-eastern course between the broader gulf of the Mediterranean on the west, and the narrow one on the east; and in the close vicinity of the latter they attain their greatest elevation, which, however, scarce reaches the line of perpetual snow, in the Abruzzi. From the Abruzzi the chain continues in a southern direction, at first undivided and of considerable height; after a depression which formsa hill-country, it splits into a somewhat flattened succession of heights towards the south-east and a more rugged chain towards the south, and in both directions terminates in the formation of narrow peninsulas.

The flat country on the north, extending between the Alps and the Apennines as far down as the Abruzzi, does not belong geographically, nor until a very late period even historically, to the southern land of mountain and hill, the Italy whose history is here to engage our attention. It was not till the seventh century of the city that the coast-district from Sinigaglia to Rimini, and not till the eighth that the basin of the Po, became incorporated with Italy. The ancient boundary of Italy on the north was not the Alps but the Apennines. This mountain-system nowhere rises abruptly into a precipitous chain, but, spreading broadly over the land and enclosing many valleys and table-lands connected by easy passes, presents conditions which well adapt it to become the settlement of man. Still more suitable in this respect are the adjacent slopes and the coast-districts on the east, south, and west. On the east coast the plain of Apulia, shut in towards the north by the mountain-block of the Abruzzi and only broken by the steep isolated ridge of Garganus, stretches in a uniform level with but a scanty development of coast and stream. On the south coast, between the two peninsulas in which the Apennines terminate, extensive lowlands, poorly provided with harbours but well watered and fertile, adjoin the hill-country of the interior. The west coast presents a far-stretching domain intersected by considerable streams, in particular by the Tiber, and shaped by the action of the waves and of the once numerous volcanoes into manifold variety of hill and valley, harbour and island. Here the regions of Etruria, Latium, and Campania form the very flower of the land of Italy. South of Campania, the land in front of the mountains gradually diminishes, and the Tyrrhenian Sea almost washes their base. Moreover, as the Peloponnesus is attached to Greece, so the island of Sicily is attached to Italy—the largest and fairest isle of the Mediterranean, having a mountainous and partly desert interior, but girt, especially on the east and south, by a broad belt of the finest coast-land, mainly the result of volcanic action. Geographically the Sicilian mountains are a continuation of the Apennines, hardly interrupted by the narrow "rent" —Pegion—of the straits; and in its historical relations Sicily was in earlier times quite as decidedly a part of Italy as the Peloponnesus was of Greece, a field for the struggles of the same races, and the seat of a similar superior civilization.

The Italian peninsula resembles the Grecian in the temperate climate and wholesome air that prevail on the hills of moderate height, and on the whole, also, in the valleys and plains. In development of coast it is inferior; it wants, in particular, the island-studded sea which made the Hellenes a seafaring nation. Italy on the other hand excels its neighbour in the rich alluvial plains and the fertile and grassy mountain-slopes, which are requisite for agriculture and the rearing of cattle. Like Greece, it is a noble land which calls forth and rewards the energies of man, opening up alike for restless adventure the way to distant lands and for quiet exertion modes of peaceful gain at home.

But, while the Grecian peninsula is turned towards the east, the Italian is turned towards the west. As the coasts of Epirus and Acarnania had but a subordinate importance in the case of Hellas, so had the Apulian and Messapian coasts in that of Italy; and, while the regions on which the historical development of Greece has been mainly dependent—Attica and Macedonia—look to the east, Etruria, Latium, and Campania look to the west. In this way the two peninsulas, so close neighbours and almost sisters, stand as it were averted from each other. Although the naked eye can discern from Otranto the Acroceraunian mountains, the Italians and Hellenes came into earlier and closer contact on every other pathway rather than on the nearest across the Adriatic Sea, In their instance, as has happened so often, the historical vocation of the nations was prefigured in the relations of the ground which they occupied; the two great stocks, on which the civilization of the ancient world grew, threw their shadow as well as their seed, the one towards the east, the other towards the west.

Italian History

We intend here to relate the history of Italy, not simply the history of the city of Rome. Although, in the formal sense of political law, it was the civic community of Rome which gained the sovereignty first of Italy and then of the world, such a view cannot be held to express the higher and real meaning of history. What has been called the subjugation of Italy by the Romans appears rather, when viewed in its true light, as the consolidation into an united state of the whole Italian stock—a stock of which the Romans were doubtless the most powerful branch, but still were only a branch.

The history of Italy falls into two main sections: (1) its internal history down to its union under the leadership of the Latin stock, and (2) the history of its sovereignty over the world. Under the first section, which will occupy the first two books, we shall have to set forth the settlement of the Italian stock in the peninsula; the imperilling of its national and political existence, and its partial subjugation, by nations of other descent and older civilization, Greeks and Etruscans; the revolt of the Italians against the strangers, and the annihilation or subjection of the latter; finally, the struggles between the two chief Italian stocks, the Latins and the Samnites, for the hegemony of the peninsula, and the victory of the Latins at the end of the fourth century before the birth of Christ—or of the fifth century of the city. The second section opens with the Punic wars; it embraces the rapid extension of the dominion of Rome up to and beyond the natural boundaries of Italy, the long status quo of the imperial period, and the collapse of the mighty empire. These events will be narrated in the third and following books.

Notes for Book I Chapter I

1. The dates as hereafter inserted in the text are years of the City (A.U.C.); those in the margin give the corresponding years B.C.

CHAPTER II

The Earliest Migrations into Italy

Primitive Races of Italy

We have no information, not even a tradition, concerning the first migration of the human race into Italy. It was the universal belief of antiquity that in Italy, as well as elsewhere, the first population had sprung from the soil. We leave it to the province of the naturalist to decide the question of the origin of different races, and of the influence of climate in producing their diversities. In a historical point of view it is neither possible, nor is it of any importance, to determine whether the oldest recorded population of a country were autochthones or immigrants. But it is incumbent on the historical inquirer to bring to light the successive strata of population in the country of which he treats, in order to trace, from as remote an epoch as possible, the gradual progress of civilization to more perfect forms, and the suppression of races less capable of, or less advanced in, culture by nations of higher standing.

Italy is singularly poor in memorials of the primitive period, and presents in this respect a remarkable contrast to other fields of civilization. The results of German archaeological research lead to the conclusion that in England, France, the North of Germany and Scandinavia, before the settlement of the Indo-Germans in those lands, there must have dwelt, or rather roamed, a people, perhaps of Mongolian race, gaining their subsistence by hunting and fishing, making their implements of stone, clay, or bones, adorning themselves with the teeth of animals and with amber, but unacquainted with agriculture and the use of the metals. In India, in like manner, the Indo-Germanic settlers were preceded by a dark-coloured population less susceptible of culture. But in Italy we neither meet with fragments of a supplanted nation, such as the Finns and Lapps in the Celto-Germanic domain and the black tribes in the Indian mountains; nor have any remains of an extinct primitive people been hitherto pointed out there, such as appear to be revealed in the peculiarly-formed skeletons, the places of assembling, and the burial mounds of what is called the stone-period of Germanic antiquity. Nothing has hitherto been brought to light to warrant the supposition that mankind existed in Italy at a period anterior to the knowledge of agriculture and of the smelting of the metals; and if the human race ever within the bounds of Italy really occupied the level of that primitive stage of culture which we are accustomed to call the savage state, every trace of such a fact has disappeared.

Individual tribes, or in other words, races or stocks, are the constituent elements of the earliest history. Among the stocks which in later times we meet with in Italy, the immigration of some, of the Hellenes for instance, and the denationalization of others, such as the Bruttians and the inhabitants of the Sabine territory, are historically attested. Setting aside both these classes, there remain a number of stocks whose wanderings can no longer be traced by means of historical testimony, but only by a priori inference, and whose nationality cannot be shown to have undergone any radical change from external causes. To establish the national individuality of these is the first aim of our inquiry. In such an inquiry, had we nothing to fall back upon but the chaotic mass of names of tribes and the confusion of what professes to be historical tradition, the task might well be abandoned as hopeless. The conventionally received tradition, which assumes the name of history, is composed of a few serviceable notices by civilized travellers, and a mass of mostly worthless legends, which have usually been combined with little discrimination of the true character either of legend or of history. But there is another source of tradition to which we may resort, and which yields information fragmentary but authentic; we mean the indigenous languages of the stocks settled in Italy from time immemorial. These languages, which have grown with the growth of the peoples themselves, have had the stamp of their process of growth impressed upon them too deeply to be wholly effaced by subsequent civilization. One only of the Italian languages is known to us completely; but the remains which have been preserved of several of the others are sufficient to afford a basis for historical inquiry regarding the existence, and the degrees, of family relationship among the several languages and peoples.

In this way philological research teaches us to distinguish three primitive Italian stocks, the Iapygian, the Etruscan, and that which we shall call the Italian. The last is divided into two main branches,—the Latin branch, and that to which the dialects of the Umbri, Marsi, Volsci, and Samnites belong.

Iapygians

As to the Iapygian stock, we have but little information. At the south-eastern extremity of Italy, in the Messapian or Calabrian peninsula, inscriptions in a peculiar extinct language(1) have been found in considerable numbers; undoubtedly remains of the dialect of the Iapygians, who are very distinctly pronounced by tradition also to have been different from the Latin and Samnite stocks. Statements deserving of credit and numerous indications lead to the conclusion that the same language and the same stock were indigenous also in Apulia. What we at present know of this people suffices to show clearly that they were distinct from the other Italians, but does not suffice to determine what position should be assigned to them and to their language in the history of the human race. The inscriptions have not yet been, and it is scarcely to be expected that they ever will be, deciphered. The genitive forms, -aihi- and -ihi-, corresponding to the Sanscrit -asya- and the Greek —oio—, appear to indicate that the dialect belongs to the Indo-Germanic family. Other indications, such as the use of the aspirated consonants and the avoiding of the letters m and t as terminal sounds, show that this Iapygian dialect was essentially different from the Italian and corresponded in some respects to the Greek dialects. The supposition of an especially close affinity between the Iapygian nation and the Hellenes finds further support in the frequent occurrence of the names of Greek divinities in the inscriptions, and in the surprising facility with which that people became Hellenized, presenting a striking contrast to the shyness in this respect of the other Italian nations. Apulia, which in the time of Timaeus (400) was still described as a barbarous land, had in the sixth century of the city become a province thoroughly Greek, although no direct colonization from Greece had taken place; and even among the ruder stock of the Messapii there are various indications of a similar tendency. With the recognition of such a general family relationship or peculiar affinity between the Iapygians and Hellenes (a recognition, however, which by no means goes so far as to warrant our taking the Iapygian language to be a rude dialect of Greek), investigation must rest content, at least in the meantime, until some more precise and better assured result be attainable.(2) The lack of information, however, is not much felt; for this race, already on the decline at the period when our history begins, comes before us only when it is giving way and disappearing. The character of the Iapygian people, little capable of resistance, easily merging into other nationalities, agrees well with the hypothesis, to which their geographical position adds probability, that they were the oldest immigrants or the historical autochthones of Italy. There can be no doubt that all the primitive migrations of nations took place by land; especially such as were directed towards Italy, the coast of which was accessible by sea only to skilful sailors and on that account was still in Homer's time wholly unknown to the Hellenes. But if the earlier settlers came over the Apennines, then, as the geologist infers the origin of mountains from their stratification, the historical inquirer may hazard the conjecture that the stocks pushed furthest towards the south were the oldest inhabitants of Italy; and it is just at its extreme south-eastern verge that we meet with the Iapygian nation.

Italians

The middle of the peninsula was inhabited, as far back as trustworthy tradition reaches, by two peoples or rather two branches of the same people, whose position in the Indo-Germanic family admits of being determined with greater precision than that of the Iapygian nation. We may with propriety call this people the Italian, since upon it rests the historical significance of the peninsula. It is divided into the two branch-stocks of the Latins and the Umbrians; the latter including their southern offshoots, the Marsians and Samnites, and the colonies sent forth by the Samnites in historical times. The philological analysis of the idioms of these stocks has shown that they together constitute a link in the Indo-Germanic chain of languages, and that the epoch in which they still formed an unity is a comparatively late one. In their system of sounds there appears the peculiar spirant -f, in the use of which they agree with the Etruscans, but decidedly differ from all Hellenic and Helleno-barbaric races as well as from the Sanscrit itself. The aspirates, again, which are retained by the Greeks throughout, and the harsher of them also by the Etruscans, were originally foreign to the Italians, and are represented among them by one of their elements—either by the media, or by the breathing alone -f or -h. The finer spirants, -s, -w, -j, which the Greeks dispense with as much as possible, have been retained in the Italian languages almost unimpaired, and have been in some instances still further developed. The throwing back of the accent and the consequent destruction of terminations are common to the Italians with some Greek stocks and with the Etruscans; but among the Italians this was done to a greater extent than among the former, and to a lesser extent than among the latter. The excessive disorder of the terminations in the Umbrian certainly had no foundation in the original spirit of the language, but was a corruption of later date, which appeared in a similar although weaker tendency also at Rome. Accordingly in the Italian languages short vowels are regularly dropped in the final sound, long ones frequently: the concluding consonants, on the other hand, have been tenaciously retained in the Latin and still more so in the Samnite; while the Umbrian drops even these. In connection with this we find that the middle voice has left but slight traces in the Italian languages, and a peculiar passive formed by the addition of -r takes its place; and further that the majority of the tenses are formed by composition with the roots -es and -fu, while the richer terminational system of the Greeks along with the augment enables them in great part to dispense with auxiliary verbs. While the Italian languages, like the Aeolic dialect, gave up the dual, they retained universally the ablative which the Greeks lost, and in great part also the locative. The rigorous logic of the Italians appears to have taken offence at the splitting of the idea of plurality into that of duality and of multitude; while they have continued with much precision to express the relations of words by inflections. A feature peculiarly Italian, and unknown even to the Sanscrit, is the mode of imparting a substantive character to the verb by gerunds and supines,—a process carried out more completely here than in any other language.

Relation of the Italians to the Greeks

These examples selected from a great abundance of analogous phenomena suffice to establish the individuality of the Italian stock as distinguished from the other members of the Indo-Germanic family, and at the same time show it to be linguistically the nearest relative, as it is geographically the next neighbour, of the Greek. The Greek and the Italian are brothers; the Celt, the German, and the Slavonian are their cousins. The essential unity of all the Italian as of all the Greek dialects and stocks must have dawned early and clearly on the consciousness of the two great nations themselves; for we find in the Roman language a very ancient word of enigmatical origin, -Graius-or -Graicus-, which is applied to every Greek, and in like manner amongst the Greeks the analogous appellation —Opikos— which is applied to all the Latin and Samnite stocks known to the Greeks in earlier times, but never to the Iapygians or Etruscans.

Relation of the Latins to the Umbro-Samnites

Among the languages of the Italian stock, again, the Latin stands in marked contrast with the Umbro-Samnite dialects. It is true that of these only two, the Umbrian and the Samnite or Oscan, are in some degree known to us, and these even in a manner extremely defective and uncertain. Of the rest some, such as the Marsian and the Volscian, have reached us in fragments too scanty to enable us to form any conception of their individual peculiarities or to classify the varieties of dialect themselves with certainty and precision, while others, like the Sabine, have, with the exception of a few traces preserved as dialectic peculiarities in provincial Latin, completely disappeared. A conjoint view, however, of the facts of language and of history leaves no doubt that all these dialects belonged to the Umbro-Samnite branch of the great Italian stock, and that this branch, although much more closely related to Latin than to Greek, was very decidedly distinct from the Latin. In the pronoun and other cases frequently the Samnite and Umbrian used -p where the Roman used -q, as -pis- for -quis-; just as languages otherwise closely related are found to differ; for instance, -p is peculiar to the Celtic in Brittany and Wales, -k to the Gaelic and Erse. Among the vowel sounds the diphthongs in Latin, and in the northern dialects generally, appear very much destroyed, whereas in the southern Italian dialects they have suffered little; and connected with this is the fact, that in composition the Roman weakens the radical vowel otherwise so strictly preserved,—a modification which does not take place in the kindred group of languages. The genitive of words in -a is in this group as among the Greeks -as, among the Romans in the matured language -ae; that of words in -us is in the Samnite -eis, in the Umbrian -es, among the Romans -ei; the locative disappeared more and more from the language of the latter, while it continued in full use in the other Italian dialects; the dative plural in -bus is extant only in Latin. The Umbro-Samnite infinitive in -um is foreign to the Romans; while the Osco-Umbrian future formed from the root -es after the Greek fashion (-her-est- like —leg-so—) has almost, perhaps altogether, disappeared in Latin, and its place is supplied by the optative of the simple verb or by analogous formations from -fuo-(-amabo-). In many of these instances, however—in the forms of the cases, for example—the differences only exist in the two languages when fully formed, while at the outset they coincide. It thus appears that, while the Italian language holds an independent position by the side of the Greek, the Latin dialect within it bears a relation to the Umbro-Samnite somewhat similar to that of the Ionic to the Doric; and the differences of the Oscan and Umbrian and kindred dialects may be compared with the differences between the Dorism of Sicily and the Dorism of Sparta.

Each of these linguistic phenomena is the result and the attestation of an historical event. With perfect certainty they guide us to the conclusion, that from the common cradle of peoples and languages there issued a stock which embraced in common the ancestors of the Greeks and the Italians; that from this, at a subsequent period, the Italians branched off; and that these again divided into the western and eastern stocks, while at a still later date the eastern became subdivided into Umbrians and Oscans.

When and where these separations took place, language of course cannot tell; and scarce may adventurous thought attempt to grope its conjectural way along the course of those revolutions, the earliest of which undoubtedly took place long before that migration which brought the ancestors of the Italians across the Apennines. On the other hand the comparison of languages, when conducted with accuracy and caution, may give us an approximate idea of the degree of culture which the people had reached when these separations took place, and so furnish us with the beginnings of history, which is nothing but the development of civilization. For language, especially in the period of its formation, is the true image and organ of the degree of civilization attained; its archives preserve evidence of the great revolutions in arts and in manners, and from its records the future will not fail to draw information as to those times regarding which the voice of direct tradition is dumb.

Indo-Germanic Culture

During the period when the Indo-Germanic nations which are now separated still formed one stock speaking the same language, they attained a certain stage of culture, and they had a vocabulary corresponding to it. This vocabulary the several nations carried along with them, in its conventionally established use, as a common dowry and a foundation for further structures of their own. In it we find not merely the simplest terms denoting existence, actions, perceptions, such as -sum-, -do-, -pater-, the original echo of the impression which the external world made on the mind of man, but also a number of words indicative of culture (not only as respects their roots, but in a form stamped upon them by custom) which are the common property of the Indo-Germanic family, and which cannot be explained either on the principle of an uniform development in the several languages, or on the supposition of their having subsequently borrowed one from another. In this way we possess evidence of the development of pastoral life at that remote epoch in the unalterably fixed names of domestic animals; the Sanscrit -gaus- is the Latin -bos-, the Greek —-bous—; Sanscrit -avis- is the Latin -ovis-, Greek —ois—; Sanscrit -asvas-, Latin -equus-, Greek —ippos—; Sanscrit -hansas-, Latin -anser-, Greek —chein—; Sanscrit -atis-, Latin -anas-, Greek —neissa—; in like manner -pecus-, -sus-, -porcus-, -taurus-, -canis-, are Sanscrit words. Even at this remote period accordingly the stock, on which from the days of Homer down to our own time the intellectual development of mankind has been dependent, had already advanced beyond the lowest stage of civilization, the hunting and fishing epoch, and had attained at least comparative fixity of abode. On the other hand, we have as yet no certain proofs of the existence of agriculture at this period. Language rather favours the negative view. Of the Latin-Greek names of grain none occurs in Sanscrit with the single exception of —zea—, which philologically represents the Sanscrit -yavas-, but denotes in the Indian barley, in Greek spelt. It must indeed be granted that this diversity in the names of cultivated plants, which so strongly contrasts with the essential agreement in the appellations of domestic animals, does not absolutely preclude the supposition of a common original agriculture. In the circumstances of primitive times transport and acclimatizing are more difficult in the case of plants than of animals; and the cultivation of rice among the Indians, that of wheat and spelt among the Greeks and Romans, and that of rye and oats among the Germans and Celts, may all be traceable to a common system of primitive tillage. On the other hand the name of one cereal common to the Greeks and Indians only proves, at the most, that before the separation of the stocks they gathered and ate the grains of barley and spelt growing wild in Mesopotamia,(3) not that they already cultivated grain. While, however, we reach no decisive result in this way, a further light is thrown on the subject by our observing that a number of the most important words bearing on this province of culture occur certainly in Sanscrit, but all of them in a more general signification. -Agras-among the Indians denotes a level surface in general; -kurnu-, anything pounded; -aritram-, oar and ship; -venas-, that which is pleasant in general, particularly a pleasant drink. The words are thus very ancient; but their more definite application to the field (-ager-), to the grain to be ground (-granum-), to the implement which furrows the soil as the ship furrows the surface of the sea (-aratrum-), to the juice of the grape (-vinum-), had not yet taken place when the earliest division of the stocks occurred, and it is not to be wondered at that their subsequent applications came to be in some instances very different, and that, for example, the corn intended to be ground, as well as the mill for grinding it (Gothic -quairinus-, Lithuanian -girnos-,(4)) received their names from the Sanscrit -kurnu-. We may accordingly assume it as probable, that the primeval Indo-Germanic people were not yet acquainted with agriculture, and as certain, that, if they were so, it played but a very subordinate part in their economy; for had it at that time held the place which it afterwards held among the Greeks and Romans, it would have left a deeper impression upon the language.

On the other hand the building of houses and huts by the Indo-Germans is attested by the Sanscrit -dam(as)-, Latin -domus-, Greek —domos—; Sanscrit -vesas-, Latin -vicus-, Greek —oikos—; Sanscrit -dvaras-, Latin -fores-, Greek —thura—; further, the building of oar-boats by the names of the boat, Sanscrit -naus-, Latin -navis-, Greek —naus—, and of the oar, Sanscrit -aritram-, Greek —eretmos—, Latin -remus-, -tri-res-mis-; and the use of waggons and the breaking in of animals for draught and transport by the Sanscrit -akshas-(axle and cart), Latin -axis-, Greek —-axon—, —am-axa—; Sanscrit -iugam-, Latin -iugum-, Greek —zugon—. The words that denote clothing- Sanscrit -vastra-, Latin -vestis-, Greek —esthes—; as well as those that denote sewing and spinning-Sanscrit -siv-, Latin -suo-; Sanscrit -nah-, Latin -neo-, Greek —netho—, are alike in all Indo-Germanic languages. This cannot, however, be equally affirmed of the higher art of weaving.(5) The knowledge of the use of fire in preparing food, and of salt for seasoning it, is a primeval heritage of the Indo-Germanic nations; and the same may be affirmed regarding the knowledge of the earliest metals employed as implements or ornaments by man. At least the names of copper (-aes-) and silver (-argentum-), perhaps also of gold, are met with in Sanscrit, and these names can scarcely have originated before man had learned to separate and to utilize the ores; the Sanscrit -asis-, Latin -ensis-, points in fact to the primeval use of metallic weapons.

No less do we find extending back into those times the fundamental ideas on which the development of all Indo-Germanic states ultimately rests; the relative position of husband and wife, the arrangement in clans, the priesthood of the father of the household and the absence of a special sacerdotal class as well as of all distinctions of caste in general, slavery as a legitimate institution, the days of publicly dispensing justice at the new and full moon. On the other hand the positive organization of the body politic, the decision of the questions between regal sovereignty and the sovereignty of the community, between the hereditary privilege of royal and noble houses and the unconditional legal equality of the citizens, belong altogether to a later age.

Even the elements of science and religion show traces of a community of origin. The numbers are the same up to one hundred (Sanscrit -satam-, -ekasatam-, Latin -centum-, Greek —e-katon—, Gothic -hund-); and the moon receives her name in all languages from the fact that men measure time by her (-mensis-). The idea of Deity itself (Sanscrit -devas-, Latin -deus-, Greek —theos—), and many of the oldest conceptions of religion and of natural symbolism, belong to the common inheritance of the nations. The conception, for example, of heaven as the father and of earth as the mother of being, the festal expeditions of the gods who proceed from place to place in their own chariots along carefully levelled paths, the shadowy continuation of the soul's existence after death, are fundamental ideas of the Indian as well as of the Greek and Roman mythologies. Several of the gods of the Ganges coincide even in name with those worshipped on the Ilissus and the Tiber:—thus the Uranus of the Greeks is the Varunas, their Zeus, Jovis pater, Diespiter is the Djaus pita of the Vedas. An unexpected light has been thrown on various enigmatical forms in the Hellenic mythology by recent researches regarding the earlier divinities of India. The hoary mysterious forms of the Erinnyes are no Hellenic invention; they were immigrants along with the oldest settlers from the East. The divine greyhound Sarama, who guards for the Lord of heaven the golden herd of stars and sunbeams and collects for him the nourishing rain-clouds as the cows of heaven to the milking, and who moreover faithfully conducts the pious dead into the world of the blessed, becomes in the hands of the Greeks the son of Sarama, Sarameyas, or Hermeias; and the enigmatical Hellenic story of the stealing of the cattle of Helios, which is beyond doubt connected with the Roman legend about Cacus, is now seen to be a last echo (with the meaning no longer understood) of that old fanciful and significant conception of nature.

Graeco-Italian Culture

The task, however, of determining the degree of culture which the Indo-Germans had attained before the separation of the stocks properly belongs to the general history of the ancient world. It is on the other hand the special task of Italian history to ascertain, so far as it is possible, what was the state of the Graeco-Italian nation when the Hellenes and the Italians parted. Nor is this a superfluous labour; we reach by means of it the stage at which Italian civilization commenced, the starting-point of the national history.

Agriculture

While it is probable that the Indo-Germans led a pastoral life and were acquainted with the cereals, if at all, only in their wild state, all indications point to the conclusion that the Graeco-Italians were a grain-cultivating, perhaps even a vine-cultivating, people. The evidence of this is not simply the knowledge of agriculture itself common to both, for this does not upon the whole warrant the inference of community of origin in the peoples who may exhibit it. An historical connection between the Indo-Germanic agriculture and that of the Chinese, Aramaean, and Egyptian stocks can hardly be disputed; and yet these stocks are either alien to the Indo-Germans, or at any rate became separated from them at a time when agriculture was certainly still unknown. The truth is, that the more advanced races in ancient times were, as at the present day, constantly exchanging the implements and the plants employed in cultivation; and when the annals of China refer the origin of Chinese agriculture to the introduction of five species of grain that took place under a particular king in a particular year, the story undoubtedly depicts correctly, at least in a general way, the relations subsisting in the earliest epochs of civilization. A common knowledge of agriculture, like a common knowledge of the alphabet, of war chariots, of purple, and other implements and ornaments, far more frequently warrants the inference of an ancient intercourse between nations than of their original unity. But as regards the Greeks and Italians, whose mutual relations are comparatively well known, the hypothesis that agriculture as well as writing and coinage first came to Italy by means of the Hellenes may be characterized as wholly inadmissible. On the other hand, the existence of a most intimate connection between the agriculture of the one country and that of the other is attested by their possessing in common all the oldest expressions relating to it; -ager-, —agros—; -aro aratrum-, —aroo arotron—; -ligo-alongside of —lachaino—; -hortus-, —chortos—; -hordeum-, —krithei—; -milium-, —melinei—; -rapa-, —raphanis-; -malva-, —malachei—; -vinum-, —oinos—. It is likewise attested by the agreement of Greek and Italian agriculture in the form of the plough, which appears of the same shape on the old Attic and the old Roman monuments; in the choice of the most ancient kinds of grain, millet, barley, spelt; in the custom of cutting the ears with the sickle and having them trodden out by cattle on the smooth-beaten threshing-floor; lastly, in the mode of preparing the grain -puls-—poltos—, -pinso- —ptisso—, -mola- —mulei—; for baking was of more recent origin, and on that account dough or pap was always used in the Roman ritual instead of bread. That the culture of the vine too in Italy was anterior to the earliest Greek immigration, is shown by the appellation "wine-land" (—Oinotria—), which appears to reach back to the oldest visits of Greek voyagers. It would thus appear that the transition from pastoral life to agriculture, or, to speak more correctly, the combination of agriculture with the earlier pastoral economy, must have taken place after the Indians had departed from the common cradle of the nations, but before the Hellenes and Italians dissolved their ancient communion. Moreover, at the time when agriculture originated, the Hellenes and Italians appear to have been united as one national whole not merely with each other, but with other members of the great family; at least, it is a fact, that the most important of those terms of cultivation, while they are foreign to the Asiatic members of the Indo-Germanic family, are used by the Romans and Greeks in common with the Celtic as well as the Germanic, Slavonic, and Lithuanian stocks.(6)

The distinction between the common inheritance of the nations and their own subsequent acquisitions in manners and in language is still far from having been wrought out in all the variety of its details and gradations. The investigation of languages with this view has scarcely begun, and history still in the main derives its representation of primitive times, not from the rich mine of language, but from what must be called for the most part the rubbish-heap of tradition. For the present, therefore, it must suffice to indicate the differences between the culture of the Indo-Germanic family in its oldest undivided form, and the culture of that epoch when the Graeco-Italians still lived together. The task of discriminating the results of culture which are common to the European members of this family, but foreign to its Asiatic members, from those which the several European groups, such as the Graeco-Italian and the Germano-Slavonic, have wrought out for themselves, can only be accomplished, if at all, after greater progress has been made in linguistic and historical inquiries. But there can be no doubt that, with the Graeco-Italians as with all other nations, agriculture became and in the mind of the people remained the germ and core of their national and of their private life. The house and the fixed hearth, which the husbandman constructs instead of the light hut and shifting fireplace of the shepherd, are represented in the spiritual domain and idealized in the goddess Vesta or —Estia— almost the only divinity not Indo-Germanic yet from the first common to both nations. One of the oldest legends of the Italian stock ascribes to king Italus, or, as the Italians must have pronounced the word, Vitalus or Vitulus, the introduction of the change from a pastoral to an agricultural life, and shrewdly connects with it the original Italian legislation. We have simply another version of the same belief in the legend of the Samnite stock which makes the ox the leader of their primitive colonies, and in the oldest Latin national names which designate the people as reapers (-Siculi-, perhaps also -Sicani-), or as field-labourers (-Opsci-). It is one of the characteristic incongruities which attach to the so-called legend of the origin of Rome, that it represents a pastoral and hunting people as founding a city. Legend and faith, laws and manners, among the Italians as among the Hellenes are throughout associated with agriculture.(7)

Cultivation of the soil cannot be conceived without some measurement of it, however rude. Accordingly, the measures of surface and the mode of setting off boundaries rest, like agriculture itself, on a like basis among both peoples. The Oscan and Umbrian -vorsus-of one hundred square feet corresponds exactly with the Greek —plethron—. The principle of marking off boundaries was also the same. The land-measurer adjusted his position with reference to one of the cardinal points, and proceeded to draw in the first place two lines, one from north to south, and another from east to west, his station being at their point of intersection (-templum-, —temenos— from —temno—); then he drew at certain fixed distances lines parallel to these, and by this process produced a series of rectangular pieces of ground, the corners of which were marked by boundary posts (-termini-, in Sicilian inscriptions -termones-, usually —oroi—). This mode of defining boundaries, which is probably also Etruscan but is hardly of Etruscan origin, we find among the Romans, Umbrians, Samnites, and also in very ancient records of the Tarentine Heracleots, who are as little likely to have borrowed it from the Italians as the Italians from the Tarentines: it is an ancient possession common to all. A peculiar characteristic of the Romans, on the other hand, was their rigid carrying out of the principle of the square; even where the sea or a river formed a natural boundary, they did not accept it, but wound up their allocation of the land with the last complete square.

Other Features of Their Economy

It is not solely in agriculture, however, that the especially close relationship of the Greeks and Italians appears; it is unmistakably manifest also in the other provinces of man's earliest activity. The Greek house, as described by Homer, differs little from the model which was always adhered to in Italy. The essential portion, which originally formed the whole interior accommodation of the Latin house, was the -atrium-, that is, the "blackened" chamber, with the household altar, the marriage bed, the table for meals, and the hearth; and precisely similar is the Homeric —-megaron—, with its household altar and hearth and smoke-begrimed roof. We cannot say the same of ship-building. The boat with oars was an old common possession of the Indo-Germans; but the advance to the use of sailing vessels can scarcely be considered to have taken place during the Graeco-Italian period, for we find no nautical terms originally common to the Greeks and Italians except such as are also general among the Indo-Germanic family. On the other hand the primitive Italian custom of the husbandmen having common midday meals, the origin of which the myth connects with the introduction of agriculture, is compared by Aristotle with the Cretan Syssitia; and the earliest Romans further agreed with the Cretans and Laconians in taking their meals not, as was afterwards the custom among both peoples, in a reclining, but in a sitting posture. The mode of kindling fire by the friction of two pieces of wood of different kinds is common to all peoples; but it is certainly no mere accident that the Greeks and Italians agree in the appellations which they give to the two portions of the touch-wood, "the rubber" (—trypanon—, -terebra-), and the "under-layer" (—storeus—, —eschara—, -tabula-, probably from -tendere-, —tetamai—). In like manner the dress of the two peoples is essentially identical, for the -tunica- quite corresponds with the —chiton—, and the -toga- is nothing but a fuller —himation—. Even as regards weapons of war, liable as they are to frequent change, the two peoples have this much at least in common, that their two principal weapons of attack were the javelin and the bow,—a fact which is clearly expressed, as far as Rome is concerned, in the earliest names for warriors (-pilumni—arquites-),(8) and is in keeping with the oldest mode of fighting which was not properly adapted to a close struggle. Thus, in the language and manners of Greeks and Italians, all that relates to the material foundations of human existence may be traced back to the same primary elements; the oldest problems which the world proposes to man had been jointly solved by the two peoples at a time when they still formed one nation.

Difference of the Italian and the Greek Character

It was otherwise in the mental domain. The great problem of man—how to live in conscious harmony with himself, with his neighbour, and with the whole to which he belongs—admits of as many solutions as there are provinces in our Father's kingdom; and it is in this, and not in the material sphere, that individuals and nations display their divergences of character. The exciting causes which gave rise to this intrinsic contrast must have been in the Graeco-Italian period as yet wanting; it was not until the Hellenes and Italians had separated that that deep-seated diversity of mental character became manifest, the effects of which continue to the present day. The family and the state, religion and art, received in Italy and in Greece respectively a development so peculiar and so thoroughly national, that the common basis, on which in these respects also the two peoples rested, has been so overgrown as to be almost concealed from our view. That Hellenic character, which sacrificed the whole to its individual elements, the nation to the township, and the township to the citizen; which sought its ideal of life in the beautiful and the good, and, but too often, in the enjoyment of idleness; which attained its political development by intensifying the original individuality of the several cantons, and at length produced the internal dissolution of even local authority; which in its view of religion first invested the gods with human attributes, and then denied their existence; which allowed full play to the limbs in the sports of the naked youth, and gave free scope to thought in all its grandeur and in all its awfulness;—and that Roman character, which solemnly bound the son to reverence the father, the citizen to reverence the ruler, and all to reverence the gods; which required nothing and honoured nothing but the useful act, and compelled every citizen to fill up every moment of his brief life with unceasing work; which made it a duty even in the boy modestly to cover the body; which deemed every one a bad citizen who wished to be different from his fellows; which regarded the state as all in all, and a desire for the state's extension as the only aspiration not liable to censure,—who can in thought trace back these sharply-marked contrasts to that original unity which embraced them both, prepared the way for their development, and at length produced them? It would be foolish presumption to desire to lift this veil; we shall only endeavour to indicate in brief outline the beginnings of Italian nationality and its connections with an earlier period—to direct the guesses of the discerning reader rather than to express them.

The Family and the State

All that may be called the patriarchal element in the state rested in Greece and Italy on the same foundations. Under this head comes especially the moral and decorous arrangement of social life,(9) which enjoined monogamy on the husband and visited with heavy penalties the infidelity of the wife, and which recognized the equality of the sexes and the sanctity of marriage in the high position which it assigned to the mother within the domestic circle. On the other hand the rigorous development of the marital and still more of the paternal authority, regardless of the natural rights of persons as such, was a feature foreign to the Greeks and peculiarly Italian; it was in Italy alone that moral subjection became transformed into legal slavery. In the same way the principle of the slave being completely destitute of legal rights—a principle involved in the very nature of slavery—was maintained by the Romans with merciless rigour and carried out to all its consequences; whereas among the Greeks alleviations of its harshness were early introduced both in practice and in legislation, the marriage of slaves, for example, being recognized as a legal relation.

On the household was based the clan, that is, the community of the descendants of the same progenitor; and out of the clan among the Greeks as well as the Italians arose the state. But while under the weaker political development of Greece the clan-bond maintained itself as a corporate power in contradistinction to that of the state far even into historical times, the state in Italy made its appearance at once complete, in so far as in presence of its authority the clans were quite neutralized and it exhibited an association not of clans, but of citizens. Conversely, again, the individual attained, in presence of the clan, an inward independence and freedom of personal development far earlier and more completely in Greece than in Rome—a fact reflected with great clearness in the Greek and Roman proper names, which, originally similar, came to assume very different forms. In the more ancient Greek names the name of the clan was very frequently added in an adjective form to that of the individual; while, conversely, Roman scholars were aware that their ancestors bore originally only one name, the later -praenomen-. But while in Greece the adjectival clan-name early disappeared, it became, among the Italians generally and not merely among the Romans, the principal name; and the distinctive individual name, the -praenomen-, became subordinate. It seems as if the small and ever diminishing number and the meaningless character of the Italian, and particularly of the Roman, individual names, compared with the luxuriant and poetical fulness of those of the Greeks, were intended to illustrate the truth that it was characteristic of the one nation to reduce all to a level, of the other to promote the free development of personality. The association in communities of families under patriarchal chiefs, which we may conceive to have prevailed in the Graeco-Italian period, may appear different enough from the later forms of Italian and Hellenic polities; yet it must have already contained the germs out of which the future laws of both nations were moulded. The "laws of king Italus," which were still applied in the time of Aristotle, may denote the institutions essentially common to both. These laws must have provided for the maintenance of peace and the execution of justice within the community, for military organization and martial law in reference to its external relations, for its government by a patriarchal chief, for a council of elders, for assemblies of the freemen capable of bearing arms, and for some sort of constitution. Judicial procedure (-crimen-, —krinein—, expiation (-poena-, —-poinei—), retaliation (-talio-, —talao—, —tleinai—, are Graeco-Italian ideas. The stern law of debt, by which the debtor was directly responsible with his person for the repayment of what he had received, is common to the Italians, for example, with the Tarentine Heracleots. The fundamental ideas of the Roman constitution—a king, a senate, and an assembly entitled simply to ratify or to reject the proposals which the king and senate should submit to it—are scarcely anywhere expressed so distinctly as in Aristotle's account of the earlier constitution of Crete. The germs of larger state-confederacies in the political fraternizing or even amalgamation of several previously independent stocks (symmachy, synoikismos) are in like manner common to both nations. The more stress is to be laid on this fact of the common foundations of Hellenic and Italian polity, that it is not found to extend to the other Indo-Germanic stocks; the organization of the Germanic community, for example, by no means starts, like that of the Greeks and Romans, from an elective monarchy. But how different the polities were that were constructed on this common basis in Italy and Greece, and how completely the whole course of their political development belongs to each as its distinctive property,(10) it will be the business of the sequel to show.

Religion

It is the same in religion. In Italy, as in Hellas, there lies at the foundation of the popular faith the same common treasure of symbolic and allegorical views of nature: on this rests that general analogy between the Roman and the Greek world of gods and of spirits, which was to become of so much importance in later stages of development. In many of their particular conceptions also,—in the already mentioned forms of Zeus-Diovis and Hestia-Vesta, in the idea of the holy space (—temenos—, -templum-), in various offerings and ceremonies—the two modes of worship do not by mere accident coincide. Yet in Hellas, as in Italy, they assumed a shape so thoroughly national and peculiar, that but little even of the ancient common inheritance was preserved in a recognizable form, and that little was for the most part misunderstood or not understood at all. It could not be otherwise; for, just as in the peoples themselves the great contrasts, which during the Graeco-Italian period had lain side by side undeveloped, were after their division distinctly evolved, so in their religion also a separation took place between the idea and the image, which had hitherto been but one whole in the soul. Those old tillers of the ground, when the clouds were driving along the sky, probably expressed to themselves the phenomenon by saying that the hound of the gods was driving together the startled cows of the herd. The Greek forgot that the cows were really the clouds, and converted the son of the hound of the gods—a form devised merely for the particular purposes of that conception—into the adroit messenger of the gods ready for every service. When the thunder rolled among the mountains, he saw Zeus brandishing his bolts on Olympus; when the blue sky again smiled upon him, he gazed into the bright eye of Athenaea, the daughter of Zeus; and so powerful over him was the influence of the forms which he had thus created, that he soon saw nothing in them but human beings invested and illumined with the splendour of nature's power, and freely formed and transformed them according to the laws of beauty. It was in another fashion, but not less strongly, that the deeply implanted religious feeling of the Italian race manifested itself; it held firmly by the idea and did not suffer the form to obscure it. As the Greek, when he sacrificed, raised his eyes to heaven, so the Roman veiled his head; for the prayer of the former was contemplation, that of the latter reflection. Throughout the whole of nature he adored the spiritual and the universal. To everything existing, to the man and to the tree, to the state and to the store-room, was assigned a spirit which came into being with it and perished along with it, the counterpart of the natural phenomenon in the spiritual domain; to the man the male Genius, to the woman the female Juno, to the boundary Terminus, to the forest Silvanus, to the circling year Vertumnus, and so on to every object after its kind. In occupations the very steps of the process were spiritualized: thus, for example, in the prayer for the husbandman there was invoked the spirit of fallowing, of ploughing, of furrowing, sowing, covering-in, harrowing, and so forth down to that of the in-bringing, up-storing, and opening of the granaries. In like manner marriage, birth, and every other natural event were endowed with a sacred life. The larger the sphere embraced in the abstraction, the higher rose the god and the reverence paid by man. Thus Jupiter and Juno are the abstractions of manhood and womanhood; Dea Dia or Ceres, the creative power; Minerva, the power of memory; Dea Bona, or among the Samnites Dea Cupra, the good deity. While to the Greek everything assumed a concrete and corporeal shape, the Roman could only make use of abstract, completely transparent formulae; and while the Greek for the most part threw aside the old legendary treasures of primitive times, because they embodied the idea in too transparent a form, the Roman could still less retain them, because the sacred conceptions seemed to him dimmed even by the lightest veil of allegory. Not a trace has been preserved among the Romans even of the oldest and most generally diffused myths, such as that current among the Indians, the Greeks, and even the Semites, regarding a great flood and its survivor, the common ancestor of the present human race. Their gods could not marry and beget children, like those of the Hellenes; they did not walk about unseen among mortals; and they needed no nectar. But that they, nevertheless, in their spirituality—which only appears tame to dull apprehension—gained a powerful hold on men's minds, a hold more powerful perhaps than that of the gods of Hellas created after the image of man, would be attested, even if history were silent on the subject, by the Roman designation of faith (the word and the idea alike foreign to the Hellenes), -Religlo-, that is to say, "that which binds." As India and Iran developed from one and the same inherited store, the former, the richly varied forms of its sacred epics, the latter, the abstractions of the Zend-Avesta; so in the Greek mythology the person is predominant, in the Roman the idea, in the former freedom, in the latter necessity.

Art

Lastly, what holds good of real life is true also of its counterfeit in jest and play, which everywhere, and especially in the earliest period of full and simple existence, do not exclude the serious, but veil it. The simplest elements of art are in Latium and Hellas quite the same; the decorous armed dance, the "leap" (-triumpus-, —thriambos—, —di-thyrambos—); the masquerade of the "full people" (—satyroi—, -satura-), who, wrapped in the skins of sheep and goats, wound up the festival with their jokes; lastly, the pipe, which with suitable strains accompanied and regulated the solemn as well as the merry dance. Nowhere, perhaps, does the especially close relationship of the Hellenes and Italians come to light so clearly as here; and yet in no other direction did the two nations manifest greater divergence as they became developed. The training of youth remained in Latium strictly confined to the narrow limits of domestic education; in Greece the yearning after a varied yet harmonious training of mind and body created the sciences of Gymnastics and Paideia, which were cherished by the nation and by individuals as their highest good. Latium in the poverty of its artistic development stands almost on a level with uncivilized peoples; Hellas developed with incredible rapidity out of its religious conceptions the myth and the worshipped idol, and out of these that marvellous world of poetry and sculpture, the like of which history has not again to show. In Latium no other influences were powerful in public and private life but prudence, riches, and strength; it was reserved for the Hellenes to feel the blissful ascendency of beauty, to minister to the fair boy-friend with an enthusiasm half sensuous, half ideal, and to reanimate their lost courage with the war-songs of the divine singer.

Thus the two nations in which the civilization of antiquity culminated stand side by side, as different in development as they were in origin identical. The points in which the Hellenes excel the Italians are more universally intelligible and reflect a more brilliant lustre; but the deep feeling in each individual that he was only a part of the community, a rare devotedness and power of self-sacrifice for the common weal, an earnest faith in its own gods, form the rich treasure of the Italian nation. Both nations underwent a one-sided, and therefore each a complete, development; it is only a pitiful narrow-mindedness that will object to the Athenian that he did not know how to mould his state like the Fabii and the Valerii, or to the Roman that he did not learn to carve like Pheidias and to write like Aristophanes. It was in fact the most peculiar and the best feature in the character of the Greek people, that rendered it impossible for them to advance from national to political unity without at the same time exchanging their polity for despotism. The ideal world of beauty was all in all to the Greeks, and compensated them to some extent for what they wanted in reality. Wherever in Hellas a tendency towards national union appeared, it was based not on elements directly political, but on games and art: the contests at Olympia, the poems of Homer, the tragedies of Euripides, were the only bonds that held Hellas together. Resolutely, on the other hand, the Italian surrendered his own personal will for the sake of freedom, and learned to obey his father that he might know how to obey the state. Amidst this subjection individual development might be marred, and the germs of fairest promise in man might be arrested in the bud; the Italian gained in their stead a feeling of fatherland and of patriotism such as the Greek never knew, and alone among all the civilized nations of antiquity succeeded in working out national unity in connection with a constitution based on self-government—a national unity, which at last placed in his hands the mastery not only over the divided Hellenic stock, but over the whole known world.

Notes for Book I Chapter II

1. Some of the epitaphs may give us an idea of its sound; as -theotoras artahiaihi bennarrihino- and -dasiihonas platorrihi bollihi-.

2. The hypothesis has been put forward of an affinity between the Iapygian language and the modern Albanian; based, however, on points of linguistic comparison that are but little satisfactory in any case, and least of all where a fact of such importance is involved. Should this relationship be confirmed, and should the Albanians on the other hand—a race also Indo-Germanic and on a par with the Hellenic and Italian races—be really a remnant of that Hellene-barbaric nationality traces of which occur throughout all Greece and especially in the northern provinces, the nation that preceded the Hellenes would be demonstrated as identical with that which preceded the Italians. Still the inference would not immediately follow that the Iapygian immigration to Italy had taken place across the Adriatic Sea.

3. Barley, wheat, and spelt were found growing together in a wild state on the right bank of the Euphrates, north-west from Anah (Alph. de Candolle, Geographie botanique raisonnee, ii. p. 934). The growth of barley and wheat in a wild state in Mesopotamia had already been mentioned by the Babylonian historian Berosus (ap. Georg. Syncell. p. 50 Bonn.).

4. Scotch -quern-. Mr. Robertson.

5. If the Latin -vieo-, -vimen-, belong to the same root as our weave (German -weben-) and kindred words, the word must still, when the Greeks and Italians separated, have had the general meaning "to plait," and it cannot have been until a later period, and probably in different regions independently of each other, that it assumed that of "weaving." The cultivation of flax, old as it is, does not reach back to this period, for the Indians, though well acquainted with the flax-plant, up to the present day use it only for the preparation of linseed-oil. Hemp probably became known to the Italians at a still later period than flax; at least -cannabis-looks quite like a borrowed word of later date.

6. Thus -aro-, -aratrum- reappear in the old German -aran-(to plough, dialectically -eren-), -erida-, in Slavonian -orati-, -oradlo-, in Lithuanian -arti-, -arimnas-, in Celtic -ar-, -aradar-. Thus alongside of -ligo- stands our rake (German -rechen-), of -hortus- our garden (German -garten-), of -mola- our mill (German -muhle-, Slavonic -mlyn-, Lithuanian -malunas-, Celtic -malin-).

With all these facts before us, we cannot allow that there ever was a time when the Greeks in all Hellenic cantons subsisted by purely pastoral husbandry. If it was the possession of cattle, and not of land, which in Greece as in Italy formed the basis and the standard of all private property, the reason of this was not that agriculture was of later introduction, but that it was at first conducted on the system of joint possession. Of course a purely agricultural economy cannot have existed anywhere before the separation of the stocks; on the contrary, pastoral husbandry was (more or less according to locality) combined with it to an extent relatively greater than was the case in later times.

7. Nothing is more significant in this respect than the close connection of agriculture with marriage and the foundation of cities during the earliest epoch of culture. Thus the gods in Italy immediately concerned with marriage are Ceres and (or?) Tellus (Plutarch, Romul. 22; Servius on Aen. iv. 166; Rossbach, Rom. Ehe, 257, 301), in Greece Demeter (Plutarch, Conjug. Praec. init.); in old Greek formulas the procreation of children is called —arotos—(ii. The Family and the State, note); indeed the oldest Roman formof marriage, -confarreatio-, derives its name and its ceremony from the cultivation of corn. The use of the plough in the founding of cities is well known.

8. Among the oldest names of weapons on both sides scarcely any can be shown to be certainly related; -lancea-, although doubtless connected with -logchei-, is, as a Roman word, recent, and perhaps borrowed from the Germans or Spaniards.

9. Even in details this agreement appears; *e.g.*, in the designation of lawful wedlock as "marriage concluded for the obtaining of lawful children" (—gauos epi paidon gneision aroto—, -matrimonium liberorum quaerendorum causa-).

10. Only we must, of course, not forget that like pre-existing conditions lead everywhere to like institutions. For instance, nothing is more certain than that the Roman plebeians were a growth originating within the Roman commonwealth, and yet they everywhere find their counterpart where a body of -metoeci- has arisen alongside of a body of burgesses. As a matter of course, chance also plays in such cases its provoking game.

CHAPTER III

The Settlements of the Latins

Indo-Germanic Migrations

The home of the Indo-Germanic stock lay in the western portion of central Asia; from this it spread partly in a south-eastern direction over India, partly in a northwestern over Europe. It is difficult to determine the primitive seat of the Indo-Germans more precisely: it must, however, at any rate have been inland and remote from the sea, as there is no name for the sea common to the Asiatic and European branches. Many indications point more particularly to the regions of the Euphrates; so that, singularly enough, the primitive seats of the two most important civilized stocks, —the Indo-Germanic and the Aramaean,—almost coincide as regards locality. This circumstance gives support to the hypothesis that these races also were originally connected, although, if there was such a connection, it certainly must have been anterior to all traceable development of culture and language. We cannot define more exactly their original locality, nor are we able to accompany the individual stocks in the course of their migrations. The European branch probably lingered in Persia and Armenia for some considerable time after the departure of the Indians; for, according to all appearance, that region has been the cradle of agriculture and of the culture of the vine. Barley, spelt, and wheat are indigenous in Mesopotamia, and the vine tothe south of the Caucasus and of the Caspian Sea: there too the plum, the walnut, and others of the more easily transplanted fruit trees are native. It is worthy of notice that the name for the sea is common to most of the European stocks—Latins, Celts, Germans, and Slavonians; they must probably therefore before their separation have reached the coast of the Black Sea or of the Caspian. By what route from those regions the Italians reached the chain of the Alps, and where in particular they were settled while still united with the Hellenes alone, are questions that can only be answered when the problem is solved by what route—whether from Asia Minor or from the regions of the Danube—the Hellenes arrived in Greece. It may at all events be regarded as certain that the Italians, like the Indians, migrated into their peninsula from the north.(1)

The advance of the Umbro-Sabellian stock along the central mountain-ridge of Italy, in a direction from north to south, can still be clearly traced; indeed its last phases belong to purely historical times. Less is known regarding the route which the Latin migration followed. Probably it proceeded in a similar direction along the west coast, long, in all likelihood, before the first Sabellian stocks began to move. The stream only overflows the heights when the lower grounds are already occupied; and only through the supposition that there were Latin stocks already settled on the coast are we able to explain why the Sabellians should have contented themselves with the rougher mountain districts, from which they afterwards issued and intruded, wherever it was possible, between the Latin tribes.

Extension of the Latins in Italy

It is well known that a Latin stock inhabited the country from the left bank of the Tiber to the Volscian mountains; but these mountains themselves, which appear to have been neglected on occasion of the first immigration when the plains of Latium and Campania still lay open to the settlers, were, as the Volscian inscriptions show, occupied by a stock more nearly related to the Sabellians than to the Latins. On the other hand, Latins probably dwelt in Campania before the Greek and Samnite immigrations; for the Italian names Novla or Nola (newtown), Campani Capua, Volturnus (from -volvere-, like -Iuturna- from -iuvare-), Opsci (labourers), are demonstrably older than the Samnite invasion, and show that, at the time when Cumae was founded by the Greeks, an Italian and probably Latin stock, the Ausones, were in possession of Campania. The primitive inhabitants of the districts which the Lucani and Bruttii subsequently occupied, the Itali proper (inhabitants of the land of oxen), are associated by the best observers not with the Iapygian, but with the Italian stock; and there is nothing to hinder our regarding them as belonging to its Latin branch, although the Hellenizing of these districts which took place even before the commencement of the political development of Italy, and their subsequent inundation by Samnite hordes, have in this instance totally obliterated the traces of the older nationality. Very ancient legends bring the similarly extinct stock of the Siculi into relation with Rome. For instance, the earliest historian of Italy Antiochus of Syracuse tells us that a man named Sikelos came a fugitive from Rome to Morges king of Italia (i. e. the Bruttian peninsula). Such stories appear to be founded on the identity of race recognized by the narrators as subsisting between the Siculi (of whom there were some still in Italy in the time of Thucydides) and the Latins. The striking affinity of certain dialectic peculiarities of Sicilian Greek with the Latin is probably to be explained rather by the old commercial connections subsisting between Rome and the Sicilian Greeks, than by the ancient identity of the languages of the Siculi and the Romans. According to all indications, however, not only Latium, but probably also the Campanian and Lucanian districts, the Italia proper between the gulfs of Tarentum and Laus, and the eastern half of Sicily were in primitive times inhabited by different branches of the Latin nation.

Destinies very dissimilar awaited these different branches. Those settled in Sicily, Magna Graecia, and Campania came into contact with the Greeks at a period when they were unable to offer resistance to their civilization, and were either completely Hellenized, as in the case of Sicily, or at any rate so weakened that they succumbed without marked resistance to the fresh energy of the Sabine tribes. In this way the Siculi, the Itali and Morgetes, and the Ausonians never came to play an active part in the history of the peninsula. It was otherwise with Latium, where no Greek colonies were founded, and the inhabitants after hard struggles were successful in maintaining their ground against the Sabines as well as against their northern neighbours. Let us cast a glance at this district, which was destined more than any other to influence the fortunes of the ancient world.

Latium

The plain of Latium must have been in primeval times the scene of the grandest conflicts of nature, while the slowly formative agency of water deposited, and the eruptions of mighty volcanoes upheaved, the successive strata of that soil on which was to be decided the question to what people the sovereignty of the world should belong. Latium is bounded on the east by the mountains of the Sabines and Aequi which form part of the Apennines; and on the south by the Volscian range rising to the height of 4000 feet, which is separated from the main chain of the Apennines by the ancient territory of the Hernici, the tableland of the Sacco (Trerus, a tributary of the Liris), and stretching in a westerly direction terminates in the promontory of Terracina. On the west its boundary is the sea, which on this part of the coast forms but few and indifferent harbours. On the north it imperceptibly merges into the broad hill-land of Etruria. The region thus enclosed forms a magnificent plain traversed by the Tiber, the "mountain-stream" which issues from the Umbrian, and by the Anio, which rises in the Sabine mountains. Hills here and there emerge, like islands, from the plain; some of them steep limestone cliffs, such as that of Soracte in the north-east, and that of the Circeian promontory on the south-west, as well as the similar though lower height of the Janiculum near Rome; others volcanic elevations, whose extinct craters had become converted into lakes which in some cases still exist; the most important of these is the Alban range, which, free on every side, stands forth from the plain between the Volscian chain and the river Tiber.

Here settled the stock which is known to history under the name of the Latins, or, as they were subsequently called by way of distinction from the Latin communities beyond the bounds of Latium, the "Old Latins" (-prisci Latini-). But the territory occupied by them, the district of Latium, was only a small portion of the central plain of Italy. All the country north of the Tiber was to the Latins a foreign and even hostile domain, with whose inhabitants no lasting alliance, no public peace, was possible, and such armistices as were concluded appear always to have been for a limited period. The Tiber formed the northern boundary from early times; and neither in history nor in the more reliable traditions has any reminiscence been preserved as to the period or occasion of the establishment of a frontier line so important in its results. We find, at the time when our history begins, the flat and marshy tracts to the south of the Alban range in the hands of Umbro-Sabellian stocks, the Rutuli and Volsci; Ardea and Velitrae are no longer in the number of originally Latin towns. Only the central portion of that region between the Tiber, the spurs of the Apennines, the Alban Mount, and the sea—a district of about 700 square miles, not much larger than the present canton of Zurich—was Latium proper, the "plain,"(2) as it appears to the eye of the observer from the heights of Monte Cavo. Though the country is a plain, it is not monotonously flat. With the exception of the sea-beach which is sandy and formed in part by the accumulations of the Tiber, the level is everywhere broken by hills of tufa moderate in height though often somewhat steep, and by deep fissures of the ground. These alternating elevations and depressions of the surface lead to the formation of lakes in winter; and the exhalations proceeding in the heat of summer from the putrescent organic substances which they contain engender that noxious fever-laden atmosphere, which in ancient times tainted the district as it taints it at the present day. It is a mistake to suppose that these miasmata were first occasioned by the neglect of cultivation, which was the result of the misgovernment in the last century of the Republic and under the Papacy. Their cause lies rather in the want of natural outlets for the water; and it operates now as it operated thousands of years ago. It is true, however, that the malaria may to a certain extent be banished by thoroughness of tillage—a fact which has not yet received its full explanation, but may be partly accounted for by the circumstance that the working of the surface accelerates the drying up of the stagnant waters. It must always remain a remarkable phenomenon, that a dense agricultural population should have arisen in regions where no healthy population can at present subsist, and where the traveller is unwilling to tarry even for a single night, such as the plain of Latium and the lowlands of Sybaris and Metapontum. We must bear in mind that man in a low stage of civilization has generally a quicker perception of what nature demands, and a greater readiness in conforming to her requirements; perhaps, also, a more elastic physical constitution, which accommodates itself more readily to the conditions of the soil where he dwells. In Sardinia agriculture is prosecuted under physical conditions precisely similar even at the present day; the pestilential atmosphere exists, but the peasant avoids its injurious effects by caution in reference to clothing, food, and the choice of his hours of labour. In fact, nothing is so certain a protection against the "aria cattiva" as wearing the fleece of animals and keeping a blazing fire; which explains why the Roman countryman went constantly clothed in heavy woollen stuffs, and never allowed the fire on his hearth to be extinguished. In other respects the district must have appeared attractive to an immigrant agricultural people: the soil is easily laboured with mattock and hoe and is productive even without being manured, although, tried by an Italian standard, it does not yield any extraordinary return: wheat yields on an average about five-fold.(3) Good water is not abundant; the higher and more sacred on that account was the esteem in which every fresh spring was held by the inhabitants.

Latin Settlements

No accounts have been preserved of the mode in which the settlements of the Latins took place in the district which has since borne their name; and we are left to gather what we can almost exclusively from a posteriori inference regarding them. Some knowledge may, however, in this way be gained, or at any rate some conjectures that wear an aspect of probability.

Clan-Villages

The Roman territory was divided in the earliest times into a number of clan-districts, which were subsequently employed in the formation of the earliest "rural wards" (-tribus rusticae-). Tradition informs us as to the -tribus Claudia-, that it originated from the settlement of the Claudian clansmen on the Anio; and that the other districts of the earliest division originated in a similar manner is indicated quite as certainly by their names. These names are not, like those of the districts added at a later period, derived from the localities, but are formed without exception from the names of clans; and the clans who thus gave their names to the wards of the original Roman territory are, so far as they have not become entirely extinct (as is the case with the -Camilii-, -Galerii-, -Lemonii-, -Pollii-, -Pupinii-, -Voltinii-), the very oldest patrician families of Rome, the -Aemilii-, -Cornelii-, -Fabii-, -Horatii-, -Menenii-, -Papirii-, -Romilii-, -Sergii-, -Voturii-. It is worthy of remark, that not one of these clans can be shown to have taken up its settlement in Rome only at a later epoch. Every Italian, and doubtless also every Hellenic, canton must, like the Roman, have been divided into a number of groups associated at once by locality and by clanship; such a clan-settlement is the "house" (—oikia—) of the Greeks, from which very frequently the —komai— and —demoi— originated among them, like the tribus in Rome. The corresponding Italian terms "house" -vicus-or "district" (-pagus-, from -pangere-) indicate, in like manner, the joint settlement of the members of a clan, and thence come by an easily understood transition to signify in common use hamlet or village. As each household had its own portion of land, so the clan-household or village had a clan-land belonging to it, which, as will afterwards be shown, was managed up to a comparatively late period after the analogy of household—land, that is, on the system of joint-possession. Whether it was in Latium itself that the clan-households became developed into clan-villages, or whether the Latins were already associated in clans when they immigrated into Latium, are questions which we are just as little able to answer as we are to determine what was the form assumed by the management on joint account, which such an arrangement required,(4) or how far, in addition to the original ground of common ancestry, the clan may have been based on the incorporation or co-ordination from without of individuals not related to it by blood.

Cantons

These clanships, however, were from the beginning regarded not as independent societies, but as the integral parts of a political community (-civitas-, -populus-). This first presents itself as an aggregate of a number of clan-villages of the same stock, language, and manners, bound to mutual observance of law and mutual legal redress and to united action in aggression and defence. A fixed local centre was quite as necessary in the case of such a canton as in that of a clanship; but as the members of the clan, or in other words the constituent elements of the canton, dwelt in their villages, the centre of the canton cannot have been a place of joint settlement in the strict sense—a town. It must, on the contrary, have been simply a place of common assembly, containing the seat of justice and the common sanctuary of the canton, where the members of the canton met every eighth day for purposes of intercourse and amusement, and where, in case of war, they obtained for themselves and their cattle a safer shelter from the invading enemy than in the villages: in ordinary circumstances this place of meeting was not at all or but scantily inhabited. Ancient places of refuge, of a kind quite similar, may still be recognized at the present day on the tops of several of the hills in the highlands of east Switzerland. Such a place was called in Italy "height" (-capitolium-, like —akra—, the mountain-top), or "stronghold" (-arx-, from -arcere-); it was not a town at first, but it became the nucleus of one, as houses naturally gathered round the stronghold and were afterwards surrounded with the "ring" (-urbs-, connected with -urvus-, -rurvus-, perhaps also with -orbis-). The stronghold and town were visibly distinguished from each other by the number of gates, of which the stronghold has as few as possible, and the town many, the former ordinarily but one, the latter at least three. Such fortresses were the bases of that cantonal constitution which prevailed in Italy anterior to the existence of towns: a constitution, the nature of which may still be recognized with some degree of clearness in those provinces of Italy which did not until a late period reach, and in some cases have not yet fully reached, the stage of aggregation in towns, such as the land of the Marsi and the small cantons of the Abruzzi. The country if the Aequiculi, who even in the imperial period dwelt not in towns, but in numerous open hamlets, presents a number of ancient ring-walls, which, regarded as "deserted towns" with their solitary temples, excited the astonishment of the Roman as well as of modern archaeologists, who have fancied that they could find accommodation there, the former for their "primitive inhabitants" (-aborigines-), the latter for their Pelasgians. We shall certainly be nearer the truth in recognizing these structures not as walled towns, but as places of refuge for the inhabitants of the district, such as were doubtless found in more ancient times over all Italy, although constructed in less artistic style. It was natural that at the period when the stocks that had made the transition to urban life were surrounding their towns with stone walls, those districts whose inhabitants continued to dwell in open hamlets should replace the earthen ramparts and palisades of their strongholds with buildings of stone. When peace came to be securely established throughout the land and such fortresses were no longer needed, these places of refuge were abandoned and soon became a riddle to after generations.

Localities of the Oldest Cantons

These cantons accordingly, having their rendezvous in some stronghold, and including a certain number of clanships, form the primitive political unities with which Italian history begins. At what period, and to what extent, such cantons were formed in Latium, cannot be determined with precision; nor is it a matter of special historical interest The isolated Alban range, that natural stronghold of Latium, which offered to settlers the most wholesome air, the freshest springs, and the most secure position, would doubtless be first occupied by the new comers.

Alba

Here accordingly, along the narrow plateau above Palazzuola, between the Alban lake (-Lago di Castello-) and the Alban mount (-Monte Cavo-), extended the town of Alba, which was universally regarded as the primitive seat of the Latin stock, and the mother-city of Rome as well as of all the other Old Latin communities; here, too, on the slopes lay the very ancient Latin canton-centres of Lanuvium, Aricia, and Tusculum. Here are found some of those primitive works of masonry, which usually mark the beginnings of civilization and seem to stand as a witness to posterity that in reality Pallas Athena when she does appear, comes into the world full grown. Such is the escarpment of the wall of rock below Alba in the direction of Palazzuola, whereby the place, which is rendered naturally inaccessible by the steep declivities of Monte Cavo on the south, is rendered equally unapproachable on the north, and only the two narrow approaches on the east and west, which are capable of being easily defended, are left open for traffic. Such, above all, is the large subterranean tunnel cut—so that a man can stand upright within it—through the hard wall of lava, 6000 feet thick, by which the waters of the lake formed in the old crater of the Alban Mount were reduced to their present level and a considerable space was gained for tillage on the mountain itself.

The summits of the last offshoots of the Sabine range form natural fastnesses of the Latin plain; and the canton-strongholds there gave rise at a later period to the considerable towns of Tibur and Praeneste. Labici too, Gabii, and Nomentum in the plain between the Alban and Sabine hills and the Tiber, Rome on the Tiber, Laurentum and Lavinium on the coast, were all more or less ancient centres of Latin colonization, not to speak of many others less famous and in some cases almost forgotten.

The Latin League

All these cantons were in primitive times politically sovereign, and each of them was governed by its prince with the co-operation of the council of elders and the assembly of warriors. Nevertheless the feeling of fellowship based on community of descent and of language not only pervaded the whole of them, but manifested itself in an important religious and political institution—the perpetual league of the collective Latin cantons. The presidency belonged originally, according to the universal Italian as well as Hellenic usage, to that canton within whose bounds lay the meeting-place of the league; in this case it was the canton of Alba, which, as we have said, was generally regarded as the oldest and most eminent of the Latin cantons. The communities entitled to participate in the league were in the beginning thirty—a number which we find occurring with singular frequency as the sum of the constituent parts of a commonwealth in Greece and Italy. What cantons originally made up the number of the thirty old Latin communities or, as with reference to the metropolitan rights of Alba they are also called, the thirty Alban colonies, tradition has not recorded, and we can no longer ascertain. The rendezvous of this union was, like the Pamboeotia and the Panionia among the similar confederacies of the Greeks, the "Latin festival" (-feriae Latinae-), at which, on the "Mount of Alba" (-Mons Albanus-, -Monte Cavo-), upon a day annually appointed by the chief magistrate for the purpose, an ox was offered in sacrifice by the assembled Latin stock to the "Latin god" (-Jupiter Latiaris-). Each community taking part in the ceremony had to contribute to the sacrificial feast its fixed proportion of cattle, milk, and cheese, and to receive in return a portion of the roasted victim. These usages continued down to a late period, and are well known: respecting the more important legal bearings of this association we can do little else than institute conjectures.

From the most ancient times there were held, in connection with the religious festival on the Mount of Alba, assemblies of the representatives of the several communities at the neighbouring Latin seat of justice at the source of the Ferentina (near Marino). Indeed such a confederacy cannot be conceived to exist without having a certain power of superintendence over the associated body, and without possessing a system of law binding on all. Tradition records, and we may well believe, that the league exercised jurisdiction in reference to violations of federal law, and that it could in such cases pronounce even sentence of death. The later communion of legal rights and, in some sense, of marriage that subsisted among the Latin communities may perhaps be regarded as an integral part of the primitive law of the league, so that any Latin man could beget lawful children with any Latin woman and acquire landed property and carry on trade in any part of Latium. The league may have also provided a federal tribunal of arbitration for the mutual disputes of the cantons; on the other hand, there is no proof that the league imposed any limitation on the sovereign right of each community to make peace or war. In like manner there can be no doubt that the constitution of the league implied the possibility of its waging defensive or even aggressive war in its own name; in which case, of course, it would be necessary to have a federal commander-in-chief. But we have no reason to suppose that in such an event each community was compelled by law to furnish a contingent for the army, or that, conversely, any one was interdicted from undertaking a war on its own account even against a member of the league. There are, however, indications that during the Latin festival, just as was the case during the festivals of the Hellenic leagues, "a truce of God" was observed throughout all Latium;(5) and probably on that occasion even tribes at feud granted safe-conducts to each other.

It is still less in our power to define the range of the privileges of the presiding canton; only we may safely affirm that there is no reason for recognizing in the Alban presidency a real political hegemony over Latium, and that possibly, nay probably, it had no more significance in Latium than the honorary presidency of Elis had in Greece.(6) On the whole it is probable that the extent of this Latin league, and the amount of its jurisdiction, were somewhat unsettled and fluctuating; yet it remained throughout not an accidental aggregate of various communities more or less alien to each other, but the just and necessary expression of the relationship of the Latin stock. The Latin league may not have at all times included all Latin communities, but it never at any rate granted the privilege of membership to any that were not Latin. Its counterpart in Greece was not the Delphic Amphictyony, but the Boeotian or Aetolian confederacy.

These very general outlines must suffice: any attempt to draw the lines more sharply would only falsify the picture. The manifold play of mutual attraction and repulsion among those earliest political atoms, the cantons, passed away in Latium without witnesses competent to tell the tale. We must now be content to realise the one great abiding fact that they possessed a common centre, to which they did not sacrifice their individual independence, but by means of which they cherished and increased the feeling of their belonging collectively to the same nation. By such a common possession the way was prepared for their advance from that cantonal individuality, with which the history of every people necessarily begins, to the national union with which the history of every people ends or at any rate ought to end.

Notes for Book I Chapter III

1. I. II. Italians

2. Like -latus- (side) and —platus— (flat); it denotes therefore the flat country in contrast to the Sabine mountain-land, just as Campania, the "plain," forms the contrast to Samnium. Latus, formerly -stlatus-, has no connection with Latium.

3. A French statist, Dureau de la Malle (-Econ. Pol. des Romains-, ii. 226), compares with the Roman Campagna the district of Limagne in Auvergne, which is likewise a wide, much intersected, and uneven plain, with a superficial soil of decomposed lava and ashes—the remains of extinct volcanoes. The population, at least 2500 to the square league, is one of the densest to be found in purely agricultural districts: property is subdivided to an extraordinary extent. Tillage is carried on almost entirely by manual labour, with spade, hoe, or mattock; only in exceptional cases a light plough is substituted drawn by two cows, the wife of the peasant not unfrequently taking the place of one of them in the yoke. The team serves at once to furnish milk and to till the land. They have two harvests in the year, corn and vegetables; there is no fallow. The average yearly rent for an arpent of arable land is 100 francs. If instead Of such an arrangement this same land were to be divided among six or seven large landholders, and a system of management by stewards and day labourers were to supersede the husbandry of the small proprietors, in a hundred years the Limagne would doubtless be as waste, forsaken, and miserable as the Campagna di Roma is at the present day.

4. In Slavonia, where the patriarchal economy is retained up to the present day, the whole family, often to the number of fifty or even a hundred persons, remains together in the same house under the orders of the house-father (Goszpodar) chosen by the whole family for life. The property of the household, which consists chiefly in cattle, is administered by the house-father; the surplus is distributed according to the family-branches. Private acquisitions by industry and trade remain separate property. Instances of quitting the household occur, in the case even of men, e. g. by marrying into a stranger household (Csaplovies, -Slavonien-, i. 106, 179). —Under such circumstances, which are probably not very widely different from the earliest Roman conditions, the household approximates in character to the community.

5. The Latin festival is expressly called "armistice" (-indutiae-, Macrob. Sat. i. 16; —ekecheipiai—, Dionys. iv. 49); and a war was not allowed to be begun during its continuance (Macrob. l. c.)

6. The assertion often made in ancient and modern times, that Alba once ruled over Latium under the forms of a symmachy, nowhere finds on closer investigation sufficient support. All history begins not with the union, but with the disunion of a nation; and it is very improbable that the problem of the union of Latium, which Rome finally solved after some centuries of conflict, should have been already solved at an earlier period by Alba. It deserves to be remarked too that Rome never asserted in the capacity of heiress of Alba any claims of sovereignty proper over the

Latin communities, but contented herself with an honorary presidency; which no doubt, when it became combined with material power, afforded a handle for her pretensions of hegemony. Testimonies, strictly so called, can scarcely be adduced on such a question; and least of all do such passages as Festus -v. praetor-, p. 241, and Dionys. iii. 10, suffice to stamp Alba as a Latin Athens.

CHAPTER IV

The Beginnings of Rome

Ramnes

About fourteen miles up from the mouth of the river Tiber hills of moderate elevation rise on both banks of the stream, higher on the right, lower on the left bank. With the latter group there has been closely associated for at least two thousand five hundred years the name of the Romans. We are unable, of course, to tell how or when that name arose; this much only is certain, that in the oldest form of it known to us the inhabitants of the canton are called not Romans, but Ramnians (Ramnes); and this shifting of sound, which frequently occurs in the older period of a language, but fell very early into abeyance in Latin,(1) is an expressive testimony to the immemorial antiquity of the name. Its derivation cannot be given with certainty; possibly "Ramnes" may mean "the people on the stream."

Tities, Luceres

But they were not the only dwellers on the hills by the bank of the Tiber. In the earliest division of the burgesses of Rome a trace has been preserved of the fact that that body arose out of the amalgamation of three cantons once probably independent, the Ramnians, Tities, and Luceres, into a single commonwealth—in other words, out of such a —synoikismos— as that from which Athens arose in Attica.(2) The great antiquity of this threefold division of the community(3) is perhaps best evinced by the fact that the Romans, in matters especially of constitutional law, regularly used the forms -tribuere- ("to divide into three") and -tribus-("a third") in the general sense of "to divide" and "a part," and the latter expression (-tribus-), like our "quarter," early lost its original signification of number. After the union each of these three communities—once separate, but now forming subdivisions of a single community—still possessed its third of the common domain, and had its proportional representation in the burgess-force and in the council of the elders. In ritual also, the number divisible by three of the members of almost all the oldest colleges—of the Vestal Virgins, the Salii, the Arval Brethren, the Luperci, the Augurs— probably had reference to that three-fold partition. These three elements into which the primitive body of burgesses in Rome was divided have had theories of the most extravagant absurdity engrafted upon them. The irrational opinion that the Roman nation was a mongrel people finds its support in that division, and its advocates have striven by various means to represent the three great Italian races as elements entering into the composition of the primitive Rome, and to transform a people which has exhibited in language, polity, and religion, a pure and national development such as few have equalled, into a confused aggregate of Etruscan and Sabine, Hellenic and, forsooth! even Pelasgian fragments.

Setting aside self-contradictory and unfounded hypotheses, we may sum up in a few words all that can be said respecting the nationality of the component elements of the primitive Roman commonwealth. That the Ramnians were a Latin stock cannot be doubted, for they gave their name to the new Roman commonwealth and therefore must have substantially determined the nationality of the united community. Respecting the origin of the Luceres nothing can be affirmed, except that there is no difficulty in the way of our assigning them, like the Ramnians, to the Latin stock. The second of these communities, on the other hand, is with one consent derived from Sabina; and this view can at least be traced to a tradition preserved in the Titian brotherhood, which represented that priestly college as having been instituted, on occasion of the Tities being admitted into the collective community, for the preservation of their distinctive Sabine ritual. It may be, therefore, that at a period very remote, when the Latin and Sabellian stocks were beyond question far less sharply contrasted in language, manners, and customs than were the Roman and the Samnite of a later age, a Sabellian community entered into a Latin canton-union; and, as in the older and more credible traditions without exception the Tities take precedence of the Ramnians, it is probable that the intruding Tities compelled the older Ramnians to accept the —synoikismos—. A mixture of different nationalities certainly therefore took place; but it hardly exercised an influence greater than the migration, for example, which occurred some centuries afterwards of the Sabine

Attus Clauzus or Appius Claudius and his clansmen and clients to Rome. The earlier admission of the Tities among the Ramnians does not entitle us to class the community among mongrel peoples any more than does that subsequent reception of the Claudii among the Romans. With the exception, perhaps, of isolated national institutions handed down in connection with ritual, the existence of Sabellian elements can nowhere be pointed out in Rome; and the Latin language in particular furnishes absolutely no support to any such hypothesis.(4) It would in fact be more than surprising, if the Latin nation should have had its nationality in any sensible degree affected by the insertion of a single community from a stock so very closely related to it; and, besides, it must not be forgotten that at the time when the Tides settled beside the Ramnians, Latin nationality rested on Latium as its basis, and not on Rome. The new tripartite Roman commonwealth was, notwithstanding some incidental elements which were originally Sabellian, just what the community of the Ramnians had previously been—a portion of the Latin nation.

Rome the Emporium of Latium

Long, in all probability, before an urban settlement arose on the Tiber, these Ramnians, Tities, and Luceres, at first separate, afterwards united, had their stronghold on the Roman hills, and tilled their fields from the surrounding villages. The "wolf-festival" (Lupercalia) which the gens of the Quinctii celebrated on the Palatine hill, was probably a tradition from these primitive times—a festival of husbandmen and shepherds, which more than any other preserved the homely pastimes of patriarchal simplicity, and, singularly enough, maintained itself longer than all the other heathen festivals in Christian Rome,

Character of Its Site

From these settlements the later Rome arose. The founding of a city in the strict sense, such as the legend assumes, is of course to be reckoned altogether out of the question: Rome was not built in a day. But the serious consideration of the historian may well be directed to the inquiry, in what way Rome can have so early attained the prominent political position which it held in Latium—so different from what the physical character of the locality would have led us to anticipate. The site of Rome is less healthy and less fertile than that of most of the old Latin towns. Neither the vine nor the fig succeed well in the immediate environs, and there is a want of springs yielding a good supply of water; for neither the otherwise excellent fountain of the Camenae before the Porta Capena, nor the Capitoline well, afterwards enclosed within the Tullianum, furnish it in any abundance. Another disadvantage arises from the frequency with which the river overflows its banks. Its very slight fall renders it unable to carry off the water, which during the rainy season descends in large quantities from the mountains, with sufficient rapidity to the sea, and in consequence it floods the low-lying lands and the valleys that open between the hills, and converts them into swamps. For a settler the locality was anything but attractive. In antiquity itself an opinion was expressed that the first body of immigrant cultivators could scarce have spontaneously resorted in search of a suitable settlement to that unhealthy and unfruitful spot in a region otherwise so highly favoured, and that it must have been necessity, or rather some special motive, which led to the establishment of a city there. Even the legend betrays its sense of the strangeness of the fact: the story of the foundation of Rome by refugees from Alba under the leadership of the sons of an Alban prince, Romulus and Remus, is nothing but a naïve attempt of primitive quasi-history to explain the singular circumstance of the place having arisen on a site so unfavourable, and to connect at the same time the origin of Rome with the general metropolis of Latium. Such tales, which profess to be historical but are merely improvised explanations of no very ingenious character, it is the first duty of history to dismiss; but it may perhaps be allowed to go a step further, and after weighing the special relations of the locality to propose a positive conjecture not regarding the way in which the place originated, but regarding the circumstances which occasioned its rapid and surprising prosperity and led to its occupying its peculiar position in Latium.

Earliest Limits of the Roman Territory

Let us notice first of all the earliest boundaries of the Roman territory. Towards the east the towns of Antemnae, Fidenae, Caenina, and Gabii lie in the immediate neighbourhood, some of them not five miles distant from the Servian ring-wall; and the boundary of the canton must have been in the close vicinity of the city gates. On the south we find at a distance of fourteen miles the powerful communities of Tusculum and Alba; and the Roman territory appears not to have extended in this direction beyond the -Fossa Cluilia-, five miles from Rome. In like manner, towards the south-west, the boundary betwixt Rome and Lavinium was at the sixth milestone. While in a landward direction the Roman canton was thus everywhere confined within the narrowest possible limits, from the earliest times, on the other hand, it extended without hindrance on both banks of the Tiber towards the sea. Between Rome and the coast there occurs no locality that is mentioned as an ancient canton-centre, and no trace of any ancient canton-boundary. The legend indeed, which has its definite explanation of the origin of everything, professes to tell us that the Roman possessions on the right bank of the Tiber, the "seven hamlets" (-septem pagi-), and the important salt-works at its mouth, were taken by king Romulus from the Veientes, and that king Ancus fortified on the right bank the -tete de pont-, the "mount of Janus" (-Janiculum-), and founded on the left the Roman Peiraeus, the seaport at the river's "mouth" (-Ostia-). But in fact we have evidence more trustworthy than that of legend, that the possessions on the Etruscan bank of the Tiber must have belonged to the original territory of Rome; for in this very quarter, at the fourth milestone on the later road to the port, lay the grove of the creative goddess (-Dea Dia-), the primitive chief seat of the Arval festival and Arval brotherhood of Rome. Indeed from time immemorial the clan of the Romilii, once the chief probably of all the Roman clans, was settled in this very quarter; the Janiculum formed a part of the city itself, and Ostia was a burgess colony or, in other words, a suburb.

The Tiber and Its Traffic

This cannot have been the result of mere accident. The Tiber was the natural highway for the traffic of Latium; and its mouth, on a coast scantily provided with harbours, became necessarily the anchorage of seafarers. Moreover, the Tiber formed from very ancient times the frontier defence of the Latin stock against their northern neighbours. There was no place better fitted for an emporium of the Latin river and sea traffic, and for a maritime frontier fortress of Latium, than Rome. It combined the advantages of a strong position and of immediate vicinity to the river; it commanded both banks of the stream down to its mouth; it was so situated as to be equally convenient for the river navigator descending the Tiber or the Anio, and for the seafarer with vessels of so moderate a size as those which were then used; and it afforded greater protection from pirates than places situated immediately on the coast. That Rome was indebted, if not for its origin, at any rate for its importance, to these commercial and strategical advantages of its position, there are accordingly numerous further indications, which are of very different weight from the statements of quasi-historical romances. Thence arose its very ancient relations with Caere, which was to Etruria what Rome was to Latium, and accordingly became Rome's most intimate neighbour and commercial ally. Thence arose the unusual importance of the bridge over the Tiber, and of bridge-building generally in the Roman commonwealth. Thence came the galley in the city arms; thence, too, the very ancient Roman port-duties on the exports and imports of Ostia, which were from the first levied only on what was to be exposed for sale (-promercale-), not on what was for the shipper's own use (-usuarium-), and which were therefore in reality a tax upon commerce. Thence, to anticipate, the comparatively early occurrence in Rome of coined money, and of commercial treaties with transmarine states. In this sense, then, certainly Rome may have been, as the legend assumes, a creation rather than a growth, and the youngest rather than the oldest among the Latin cities. Beyond doubt the country was already in some degree cultivated, and the Alban range as well as various other heights of the Campagna were occupied by strongholds, when the Latin frontier emporium arose on the Tiber. Whether it was a resolution of the Latin confederacy, or the clear-sighted genius of some unknown founder, or the natural development of traffic, that called the city of Rome into being, it is vain even to surmise.

Early Urban Character of Rome

But in connection with this view of the position of Rome as the emporium of Latium another observation suggests itself. At the time when history begins to dawn on us, Rome appears, in contradistinction to the league of the Latin communities, as a compact urban unity. The Latin habit of dwelling in open villages, and of using the common stronghold only for festivals and assemblies or in case of special need, was subjected to restriction at a far earlier period, probably, in the canton of Rome than anywhere else in Latium. The Roman did not cease to manage his farm in person, or to regard it as his proper home; but the unwholesome atmosphere of the Campagna could not but induce him to take up his abode as much as possible on the more airy and salubrious city hills; and by the side of the cultivators of the soil there must have been a numerous non-agricultural population, partly foreigners, partly native, settled there from very early times. This to some extent accounts for the dense population of the old Roman territory, which may be estimated at the utmost at 115 square miles, partly of marshy or sandy soil, and which, even under the earliest constitution of the city, furnished a force of 3300 freemen; so that it must have numbered at least 10,000 free inhabitants. But further, every one acquainted with the Romans and their history is aware that it is their urban and mercantile character which forms the basis of whatever is peculiar in their public and private life, and that the distinction between them and the other Latins and Italians in general is pre-eminently the distinction between citizen and rustic. Rome, indeed, was not a mercantile city like Corinth or Carthage; for Latium was an essentially agricultural region, and Rome was in the first instance, and continued to be, pre-eminently a Latin city. But the distinction between Rome and the mass of the other Latin towns must certainly be traced back to its commercial position, and to the type of character produced by that position in its citizens. If Rome was the emporium of the Latin districts, we can readily understand how, along with and in addition to Latin husbandry, an urban life should have attained vigorous and rapid development there and thus have laid the foundation for its distinctive career.

It is far more important and more practicable to follow out the course of this mercantile and strategical growth of the city of Rome, than to attempt the useless task of chemically analysing the insignificant and but little diversified communities of primitive times. This urban development may still be so far recognized in the traditions regarding the successive circumvallations and fortifications of Rome, the formation of which necessarily kept pace with the growth of the Roman commonwealth in importance as a city.

The Palatine City

The town, which in the course of centuries grew up as Rome, in its original form embraced according to trustworthy testimony only the Palatine, or "square Rome" (-Roma quadrata-), as it was called in later times from the irregularly quadrangular form of the Palatine hill. The gates and walls that enclosed this original city remained visible down to the period of the empire: the sites of two of the former, the Porta Romana near S. Giorgio in Velabro, and the Porta Mugionis at the Arch of Titus, are still known to us, and the Palatine ring-wall is described by Tacitus from his own observation at least on the sides looking towards the Aventine and Caelian. Many traces indicate that this was the centre and original seat of the urban settlement. On the Palatine was to be found the sacred symbol of that settlement, the "outfit-vault" (-mundus-) as it was called, in which the first settlers deposited a sufficiency of everything necessary for a household and added a clod of their dear native earth. There, too, was situated the building in which all the curies assembled for religious and other purposes, each at its own hearth (-curiae veteres-). There stood the meetinghouse of the "Leapers" (-curia Saliorum-) in which also the sacred shields of Mars were preserved, the sanctuary of the "Wolves" (-Lupercal-), and the dwelling of the priest of Jupiter. On and near this hill the legend of the founding of the city placed the scenes of its leading incidents, and the straw-covered house of Romulus, the shepherd's hut of his foster-father Faustulus, the sacred fig-tree towards which the cradle with the twins had floated, the cornelian cherry-tree that sprang from the shaft of the spear which the founder of the city had hurled from the Aventine over the valley of the Circus into this enclosure, and other such sacred relics were pointed out to the believer. Temples in the proper sense of the term were still at this time unknown, and accordingly the Palatine has nothing of that sort to show belonging to the primitive age. The public assemblies of the community were early transferred to another locality, so that their original site is unknown; only it may be conjectured that the free space round the -mundus-, afterwards called the -area Apollinis-, was the primitive place of assembly for the burgesses and the senate, and the stage erected over the -mundus- itself the primitive seat of justice of the Roman community.

The Seven Mounts

The "festival of the Seven Mounts" (-septimontium-), again, has preserved the memory of the more extended settlement which gradually formed round the Palatine. Suburbs grew up one after another, each protected by its own separate though weaker circumvallation and joined to the original ring-wall of the Palatine, as in fen districts the outer dikes are joined on to the main dike. The "Seven Rings" were, the Palatine itself; the Cermalus, the slope of the Palatine in the direction of the morass that extended between it and the Capitol towards the river (-velabrum-); the Velia, the ridge which connected the Palatine with the Esquiline, but in subsequent times was almost wholly obliterated by the buildings of the empire; the Fagutal, the Oppius, and the Cispius, the three summits of the Esquiline; lastly, the Sucusa, or Subura, a fortress constructed outside of the earthen rampart which protected the new town on the Carinae, in the depression between the Esquiline and the Quirinal beneath S. Pietro in Vincoli. These additions, manifestly the results of a gradual growth, clearly reveal to a certain extent the earliest history of the Palatine Rome, especially when we compare with them the Servian arrangement of districts which was afterwards formed on the basis of this earliest division.

Oldest Settlements in the Palatine and Suburan Regions

The Palatine was the original seat of the Roman community, the oldest and originally the only ring-wall. The urban settlement, however, began at Rome as well as elsewhere not within, but under the protection of, the stronghold; and the oldest settlements with which we are acquainted, and which afterwards formed the first and second regions in the Servian division of the city, lay in a circle round the Palatine. These included the settlement on the declivity of the Cermalus with the "street of the Tuscans"—a name in which there may have been preserved a reminiscence of the commercial intercourse between the Caerites and Romans already perhaps carried on with vigour in the Palatine city—and the settlement on the Velia; both of which subsequently along with the stronghold-hill itself constituted one region in the Servian city. Further, there were the component elements of the subsequent second region—the suburb on the Caelian, which probably embraced only its extreme point above the Colosseum; that on the Carinae, the spur which projects from the Esquiline towards the Palatine; and, lastly, the valley and outwork of the Subura, from which the whole region received its name. These two regions jointly constituted the incipient city; and the Suburan district of it, which extended at the base of the stronghold, nearly from the Arch of Constantine to S. Pietro in Vincoli, and over the valley beneath, appears to have been more considerable and perhaps older than the settlements incorporated by the Servian arrangement in the Palatine district, because in the order of the regions the former takes precedence of the latter. A remarkable memorial of the distinction between these two portions of the city was preserved in one of the oldest sacred customs of the later Rome, the sacrifice of the October horse yearly offered in the -Campus Martius-: down to a late period a struggle took place at this festival for the horse's head between the men of the Subura and those of the Via Sacra, and according as victory lay with the former or with the latter, the head was nailed either to the Mamilian Tower (site unknown) in the Subura, or to the king's palace under the Palatine. It was the two halves of the old city that thus competed with each other on equal terms. At that time, accordingly, the Esquiliae (which name strictly used is exclusive of the Carinae) were in reality what they were called, the "outer buildings" (-exquiliae-, like -inquilinus-, from -colere-) or suburb: this became the third region in the later city division, and it was always held in inferior consideration as compared with the Suburan and Palatine regions. Other neighbouring heights also, such as the Capitol and the Aventine, may probably have been occupied by the community of the Seven Mounts; the "bridge of piles" in particular (-pons sublicius-), thrown over the natural pier of the island in the Tiber, must have existed even then—the pontifical college alone is sufficient evidence of this—and the -tete de pont- on the Etruscan bank, the height of the Janiculum, would not be left unoccupied; but the community had not as yet brought either within the circuit of its fortifications. The regulation which was adhered to as a ritual rule down to the latest times, that the bridge should be composed simply of wood without iron, manifestly shows that in its original practical use it was to be merely a flying bridge, which must be capable of being easily at any time broken off or burnt. We recognize in this circumstance how insecure for a long time and liable to interruption was the command of the passage of the river on the part of the Roman community.

No relation is discoverable between the urban settlements thus gradually formed and the three communities into which from an immemorially early period the Roman commonwealth was in political law divided. As the Ramnes, Tities, and Luceres appear to have been communities originally independent, they must have had their settlements originally apart; but they certainly did not dwell in separate circumvallations on the Seven Hills, and all fictions to this effect in ancient or modern times must be consigned by the intelligent inquirer to the same fate with the charming tale of Tarpeia and the battle of the Palatine. On the contrary each of the three tribes of Ramnes, Tities, and Luceres must have been distributed throughout the two regions of the oldest city, the Subura and Palatine, and the suburban region as well: with this may be connected the fact, that afterwards not only in the Suburan and Palatine, but in each of the regions subsequently added to the city, there were three pairs of Argean chapels. The Palatine city of the Seven Mounts may have had a history of its own; no other tradition of it has survived than simply that of its having once existed. But as the leaves of the forest make room for the new growth of spring, although they fall unseen by human eyes, so has this unknown city of the Seven Mounts made room for the Rome of history.

The Hill-Romans on the Quirinal

But the Palatine city was not the only one that in ancient times existed within the circle afterwards enclosed by the Servian walls; opposite to it, in its immediate vicinity, there lay a second city on the Quirinal. The "old stronghold" (-Capitolium vetus-) with a sanctuary of Jupiter, Juno, and Minerva, and a temple of the goddess of Fidelity in which state treaties were publicly deposited, forms the evident counterpart of the later Capitol with its temple to Jupiter, Juno, and Minerva, and with its shrine of Fides Romana likewise destined as it were for a repository of international law, and furnishes a sure proof that the Quirinal also was once the centre of an independent commonwealth. The same fact may be inferred from the double worship of Mars on the Palatine and the Quirinal; for Mars was the type of the warrior and the oldest chief divinity of the burgess communities of Italy. With this is connected the further circumstance that his ministers, the two primitive colleges of the "Leapers" (-Salii-) and of the "Wolves" (-Luperci-) existed in the later Rome in duplicate: by the side of the Salii of the Palatine there were also Salii of the Quirinal; by the side of the Quinctian Luperci of the Palatine there was a Fabian guild of Luperci, which in all probability had their sanctuary on the Quirinal.(5)

All these indications, which even in themselves are of great weight, become more significant when we recollect that the accurately known circuit of the Palatine city of the Seven Mounts excluded the Quirinal, and that afterwards in the Servian Rome, while the first three regions corresponded to the former Palatine city, a fourth region was formed out of the Quirinal along with the neighbouring Viminal. Thus, too, we discover an explanation of the reason why the strong outwork of the Subura was constructed beyond the city wall in the valley between the Esquiline and Quirinal; it was at that point, in fact, that the two territories came into contact, and the Palatine Romans, after having taken possession of the low ground, were under the necessity of constructing a stronghold for protection against those of the Quirinal.

Lastly, even the name has not been lost by which the men of the Quirinal distinguished themselves from their Palatine neighbours. As the Palatine city took the name of "the Seven Mounts," its citizens called themselves the "mount-men" (-montani-), and the term "mount," while applied to the other heights belonging to the city, was above all associated with the Palatine; so the Quirinal height—although not lower, but on the contrary somewhat higher, than the former—as well as the adjacent Viminal never in the strict use of the language received any other name than "hill" (collis). In the ritual records, indeed, the Quirinal was not unfrequently designated as the "hill" without further addition. In like manner the gate leading out from this height was usually called the "hill-gate" (-porta collina-); the priests of Mars settled there were called those "of the hill" (-Salii collini-) in contrast to those of the Palatium (-Salii Palatini-) and the fourth Servian region formed out of this district was termed the hill-region (-tribus collina-)(6) The name of Romans primarily associated with the locality was probably appropriated by these "Hill-men" as well as by those of the "Mounts;" and the former perhaps designated themselves as "Romans of the Hill" (-Romani collini-). That a diversity of race may have lain at the foundation of this distinction between the two neighbouring cities is possible; but evidence sufficient to warrant our pronouncing a community established on Latin soil to be of alien lineage is, in the case of the Quirinal community, totally wanting.(7)

Relations between the Palatine and Quirinal Communities

Thus the site of the Roman commonwealth was still at this period occupied by the Mount-Romans of the Palatine and the Hill-Romans of the Quirinal as two separate communities confronting each other and doubtless in many respects at feud, in some degree resembling the Montigiani and the Trasteverini in modern Rome. That the community of the Seven Mounts early attained a great preponderance over that of the Quirinal may with certainty be inferred both from the greater extent of its newer portions and suburbs, and from the position of inferiority in which the former Hill-Romans were obliged to acquiesce under the later Servian arrangement. But even within the Palatine city there was hardly a true and complete amalgamation of the different constituent elements of the settlement. We have already mentioned how the Subura and the Palatine annually contended for the horse's head; the several Mounts also, and even the several curies (there was as yet no common hearth for the city, but the various hearths of the curies subsisted side by side, although in the same locality) probably felt themselves to be as yet more separated than united; and Rome as a whole was probably rather an aggregate of urban settlements than a single city. It appears from many indications that the houses of the old and powerful families were constructed somewhat after the manner of fortresses and were rendered capable of defence—a precaution, it may be presumed, not unnecessary. It was the magnificent structure ascribed to king Servius Tullius that first surrounded not merely those two cities of the Palatine and Quirinal, but also the heights of the Capitol and the Aventine which were not comprehended within their enclosure, with a single great ring-wall, and thereby created the new Rome—the Rome of history. But ere this mighty work was undertaken, the relations of Rome to the surrounding country had beyond doubt undergone a complete revolution. As the period, during which the husbandman guided his plough on the seven hills of Rome just as on the other hills of Latium, and the usually unoccupied places of refuge on particular summits alone presented the germs of a more permanent settlement, corresponds to the earliest epoch of the Latin stock without trace of traffic or achievement; as thereafter the flourishing settlement on the Palatine and in the "Seven Rings" was coincident with the occupation of the mouths of the Tiber by the Roman community, and with the progress of the Latins to a more stirring and freer intercourse, to an urban civilization in Rome more especially, and perhaps also to a more consolidated political union in the individual states as well as in the confederacy; so the Servian wall, which was the foundation of a single great city, was connected with the epoch at which the city of Rome was able to contend for, and at length to achieve, the sovereignty of the Latin league.

Notes for Book I Chapter IV

1. A similar change of sound is exhibited in the case of the following formations, all of them of a very ancient kind: -pars—portio-, -Mars- -Mors-, -farreum- ancient form for -horreum-, -Fabii- -Fovii-, -Valerius- -Volesus-, -vacuus- -vacivus-.

2. The —synoikismos— did not necessarily involve an actual settlement together at one spot; but while each resided as formerly on his own land, there was thenceforth only one council-hall and court-house for the whole (Thucyd. ii. 15; Herodot. i. 170).

3. We might even, looking to the Attic —trittus— and the Umbrian -trifo-, raise the question whether a triple division of the community was not a fundamental principle of the Graeco-ltalians: in that case the triple division of the Roman community would not be referable to the amalgamation of several once independent tribes. But, in order to the establishment of a hypothesis so much at variance with tradition, such a threefold division would require to present itself more generally throughout the Graeco-Italian field than seems to be the case, and to appear uniformly everywhere as the ground-scheme. The Umbrians may possibly have adopted the word -tribus- only when they came under the influence of Roman rule; it cannot with certainty be traced in Oscan.

4. Although the older opinion, that Latin is to be viewed as a mixed language made up of Greek and non-Greek elements, has been now abandoned on all sides, judicious inquirers even (e. g. Schwegler, R. G. i. 184, 193) still seek to discover in Latin a mixture of two nearly related Italian dialects. But we ask in vain for the linguistic or historical facts which render such an hypothesis necessary. When a language presents the appearance of being an intermediate link between two others, every philologist knows that the phenomenon may quite as probably depend, and more frequently does depend, on organic development than on external intermixture.

5. That the Quinctian Luperci had precedence in rank over the Fabian is evident from the circumstance that the fabulists attribute the Quinctii to Romulus, the Fabii to Remus (Ovid, Fast. ii. 373 seq.; Vict. De Orig. 22). That the Fabii belonged to the Hill-Romans is shown by the sacrifice of their -gens- on the Quirinal (Liv. v. 46, 52), whether that sacrifice may or may not have been connected with the Lupercalia.

Moreover, the Lupercus of the former college is called in inscriptions (Orelli, 2253) - Lupercus Quinctialis vetus-; and the -praenomen-Kaeso, which was most probably connected with the Lupercal worship (see Rom. Forschungen, i. 17), is found exclusively among the Quinctii and Fabii: the form commonly occurring in authors, -Lupercus Quinctilius- and -Quinctilianus-, is therefore a misnomer, and the college belonged not to the comparatively recent Quinctilii, but to the far older Quinctii. When, again, the Quinctii (Liv. i. 30), or Quinctilii (Dion. iii. 29), are named among the Alban clans, the latter reading is here to be preferred, and the Quinctii are to be regarded rather as an old Roman -gens-.

6. Although the name "Hill of Quirinus" was afterwards ordinarily used to designate the height where the Hill-Romans had their abode, we need not at all on that account regard the name "Quirites" as having been originally reserved for the burgesses on the Quirinal. For, as has been shown, all the earliest indications point, as regards these, to the name -Collini-; while it is indisputably certain that the name Quirites denoted from the first, as well as subsequently, simply the full burgess, and had no connection with the distinction between montani and collini (comp. chap. v. infra). The later designation of the Quirinal rests on the circumstance that, while the -Mars quirinus-, the spear-bearing god of Death, was originally worshipped as well on the Palatine as on the Quirinal—as indeed the oldest inscriptions found at what was afterwards called the Temple of Quirinus designate this divinity simply as Mars,—at a later period for the sake of distinction the god of the Mount-Romans more especially was called Mars, the god of the Hill Romans more especially Quirinus.

When the Quirinal is called -collis agonalis-, "hill of sacrifice," it is so designated merely as the centre of the religious rites of the Hill-Romans.

7. The evidence alleged for this (comp. e. g. Schwegler, S. G. i. 480) mainly rests on an etymologico-historical hypothesis started by Varro and as usual unanimously echoed by later writers, that the Latin -quiris- and -quirinus- are akin to the name of the Sabine town -Cures-, and that the Quirinal hill accordingly had been peopled from -Cures-. Even if the linguistic affinity of these words were more assured, there would be little warrant for deducing from it such a historical inference. That the old sanctuaries on this eminence (where, besides, there was also a "Collis Latiaris") were Sabine, has been asserted, but has not been proved. Mars quirinus, Sol, Salus, Flora, Semo Sancus or Deus fidius were doubtless Sabine, but they were also Latin, divinities, formed evidently during the epoch when Latins and Sabines still lived undivided. If a name like that of Semo Sancus (which moreover occurs in connection with the Tiber-island) is especially associated with the sacred places of the Quirinal which afterwards diminished in its importance (comp. the Porta Sanqualis deriving its name therefrom), every unbiassed inquirer will recognize in such a circumstance only a proof of the high antiquity of that worship, not a proof of its derivation from a neighbouring land. In so speaking we do not mean to deny that it is possible that old distinctions of race may have co-operated in producing this state of things; but if such was the case, they have, so far as we are concerned, totally disappeared, and the views current among our contemporaries as to the Sabine element in the constitution of Rome are only fitted seriously to warn us against such baseless speculations leading to no result.

CHAPTER V

The Original Constitution of Rome

The Roman House

Father and mother, sons and daughters, home and homestead, servants and chattels—such are the natural elements constituting the household in all cases, where polygamy has not obliterated the distinctive position of the mother. But the nations that have been most susceptible of culture have diverged widely from each other in their conception and treatment of the natural distinctions which the household thus presents. By some they have been apprehended and wrought out more profoundly, by others more superficially; by some more under their moral, by others more under their legal aspects. None has equalled the Roman in the simple but inexorable embodiment in law of the principles pointed out by nature herself.

The House-father and His Household

The family formed an unity. It consisted of the free man who upon his father's death had become his own master, and the spouse whom the priests by the ceremony of the sacred salted cake (-confarreatio-) had solemnly wedded to share with him water and fire, with their son and sons' sons and the lawful wives of these, and their unmarried daughters and sons' daughters, along with all goods and substance pertaining to any of its members. The children of daughters on the other hand were excluded, because, if born in wedlock, they belonged to the family of the husband; and if begotten out of wedlock, they had no place in a family at all. To the Roman citizen a house of his own and the blessing of children appeared the end and essence of life. The death of the individual was not an evil, for it was a matter of necessity; but the extinction of a household or of a clan was injurious to the community itself, which in the earliest times therefore opened up to the childless the means of avoiding such a fatality by their adopting the children of others as their own.

The Roman family from the first contained within it the conditions of a higher culture in the moral adjustment of the mutual relations of its members. Man alone could be head of a family. Woman did not indeed occupy a position inferior to man in the acquiring of property and money; on the contrary the daughter inherited an equal share with her brother, and the mother an equal share with her children. But woman always and necessarily belonged to the household, not to the community; and in the household itself she necessarily held a position of domestic subjection—the daughter to her father, the wife to her husband,(1) the fatherless unmarried woman to her nearest male relatives; it was by these, and not by the king, that in case of need woman was called to account. Within the house, however, woman was not servant but mistress. Exempted from the tasks of corn-grinding and cooking which according to Roman ideas belonged to the menials, the Roman housewife devoted herself in the main to the superintendence of her maid-servants, and to the accompanying labours of the distaff, which was to woman what the plough was to man.(2) In like manner, the moral obligations of parents towards their children were fully and deeply felt by the Roman nation; and it was reckoned a heinous offence if a father neglected or corrupted his child, or if he even squandered his property to his child's disadvantage.

In a legal point of view, however, the family was absolutely guided and governed by the single all-powerful will of the "father of the household" (-pater familias-). In relation to him all in the household were destitute of legal rights—the wife and the child no less than the bullock or the slave. As the virgin became by the free choice of her husband his wedded wife, so it rested with his own free will to rear or not to rear the child which she bore to him. This maxim was not suggested by indifference to the possession of a family; on the contrary, the conviction that the founding of a house and the begetting of children were a moral necessity and a public duty had a deep and earnest hold of the Roman mind. Perhaps the only instance of support accorded on the part of the community in Rome is the enactment that aid should be given to the father who had three children presented to him at a birth; while their ideas regarding exposure are indicated by the prohibition of it so far as concerned all the sons—deformed births excepted—and at least the first daughter. Injurious, however, to the public weal as exposure might appear, the prohibition of it soon changed its form from that of legal punishment into that of religious curse; for the father was, above all, thoroughly and absolutely master in his household. The father of the household not only maintained the strictest discipline over its members, but he had the right and duty of exercising judicial authority over them and of punishing them as he deemed fit in life and limb. The grown-up son might establish a separate household or, as the Romans expressed it, maintain his "own cattle" (-peculium-) assigned to him by his father; but in law all that the son acquired, whether by his own labour or by gift from a stranger, whether in his father's household or in his own, remained the father's property. So long as the father lived, the persons legally subject to him could never hold property of their own, and therefore could not alienate unless by him so empowered, or yet bequeath. In this respect wife and child stood quite on the same level with the slave, who was not unfrequently allowed to manage a household of his own, and who was likewise entitled to alienate when commissioned by his master. Indeed a father might convey his son as well as his slave in property to a third person: if the purchaser was a foreigner, the son became his slave; if he was a Roman, the son, while as a Roman he could not become a Roman's slave, stood at least to his purchaser in a slave's stead (-in mancipii causa-). The paternal and marital power was subject to a legal restriction, besides the one already mentioned on the right Of exposure, only in so far as some of the worst abuses were visited by legal punishment as well as by religious curse. Thus these penalties fell upon the man who sold his wife or married son; and it was a matter of family usage that in the exercise of domestic jurisdiction the father, and still more the husband, should not pronounce sentence on child or wife without having previously consulted the nearest blood-relatives, his wife's as well as his own. But the latter arrangement involved no legal diminution of power, for the blood-relatives called in to the domestic judgment had not to judge, but simply to advise the father of the household in judging.

But not only was the power of the master of the house substantially unlimited and responsible to no one on earth; it was also, as long as he lived, unchangeable and indestructible. According to the Greek as well as Germanic laws the grown-up son, who was practically independent of his father, was also independent legally; but the power of the Roman father could not be dissolved during his life either by age or by insanity, or even by his own free will, excepting only that the person of the holder of the power might change, for the child might certainly pass by way of adoption into the power of another father, and the daughter might pass by a lawful marriage out of the hand of her father into the hand of her husband and, leaving her own -gens- and the protection of her own god to enter into the -gens- of her husband and the protection of his god, became thenceforth subject to him as she had hitherto been to her father. According to Roman law it was made easier for the slave to obtain release from his master than for the son to obtain release from his father; the manumission of the former was permitted at an early period, and by simple forms; the release of the latter was only rendered possible at a much later date, and by very circuitous means. Indeed, if a master sold his slave and a father his son and the purchaser released both, the slave obtained his freedom, but the son by the release simply reverted into his father's power as before. Thus the inexorable consistency with which the Romans carried out their conception of the paternal and marital power converted it into a real right of property.

Closely, however, as the power of the master of the household over wife and child approximated to his proprietary power over slaves and cattle, the members of the family were nevertheless separated by a broad line of distinction, not merely in fact but in law, from the family property. The power of the house-master—even apart from the fact that it appeared in operation only within the house—was of a transient, and in some degree of a representative, character. Wife and child did not exist merely for the house-father's sake in the sense in which property exists only for the proprietor, or in which the subjects of an absolute state exist only for the king; they were the objects indeed of a legal right on his part, but they had at the same time capacities of right of their own; they were not things, but persons. Their rights were dormant in respect of exercise, simply because the unity of the household demanded that it should be governed by a single representative; but when the master of the household died, his sons at once came forward as its masters and now obtained on their own account over the women and children and property the rights hitherto exercised over these by the father. On the other hand the death of the master occasioned no change in the legal position of the slave.

Family and Clan (-Gens-)

So strongly was the unity of the family realized, that even the death of the master of the house did not entirely dissolve it. The descendants, who were rendered by that occurrence independent, regarded themselves as still in many respects an unity; a principle which was made use of in arranging the succession of heirs and in many other relations, but especially in regulating the position of the widow and unmarried daughters. As according to the older Roman view a woman was not capable of having power either over others or over herself, the power over her, or, as it was in this case more mildly expressed, the "guardianship" (-tutela-) remained with the house to which she belonged, and was now exercised in the room of the deceased house-master by the whole of the nearest male members of the family; ordinarily, therefore, by sons over their mother and by brothers over their sisters. In this sense the family, once founded, endured unchanged till the male stock of its founder died out; only the bond of connection must of course have become practically more lax from generation to generation, until at length it became impossible to prove the original unity. On this, and on this alone, rested the distinction between family and clan, or, according to the Roman expression, between -agnati- and -gentiles-. Both denoted the male stock; but the family embraced only those individuals who, mounting up from generation to generation, were able to set forth the successive steps of their descent from a common progenitor; the clan (-gens-) on the other hand comprehended also those who were merely able to lay claim to such descent from a common ancestor, but could no longer point out fully the intermediate links so as to establish the degree of their relationship. This is very clearly expressed in the Roman names: when they speak of "Quintus, son of Quintus, grandson of Quintus and so on, the Quintian," the family reaches as far as the ascendants are designated individually, and where the family terminates the clan is introduced supplementary, indicating derivation from the common ancestor who has bequeathed to all his descendants the name of the "children of Quintus."

Dependents of the Household

To these strictly closed unities—the family or household united under the control of a living master, and the clan which originated out of the breaking-up of such households—there further belonged the dependents or "listeners" (-clientes-, from -cluere-). This term denoted not the guests, that is, the members of other similar circles who were temporarily sojourning in another household than their own, and as little the slaves, who were looked upon in law as the property of the household and not as members of it, but those individuals who, while they were not free burgesses of any commonwealth, yet lived within one in a condition of protected freedom. These included refugees who had found a reception with a foreign protector, and those slaves in respect of whom their master had for the time being waived the exercise of his rights, and so conferred on them practical freedom. This relation had not the distinctive character of a strict relation -de jure-, like that of a man to his guest: the client remained a man non-free, in whose case good faith and use and wont alleviated the condition of non-freedom. Hence the "listeners" of the household (-clientes-) together with the slaves strictly so called formed the "body of servants" (-familia-) dependent on the will of the "burgess" (-patronus-, like -patricius-). Hence according to original right the burgess was entitled partially or wholly to resume the property of the client, to reduce him on emergency once more to the state of slavery, to inflict even capital punishment on him; and it was simply in virtue of a distinction -de facto-, that these patrimonial rights were not asserted with the same rigour against the client as against the actual slave, and that on the other hand the moral obligation of the master to provide for his own people and to protect them acquired a greater importance in the case of the client, who was practically in a more free position, than in the case of the slave. Especially must the -de facto-freedom of the client have approximated to freedom -de jure- in those cases where the relation had subsisted for several generations: when the releaser and the released had themselves died, the -dominium- over the descendants of the released person could not be without flagrant impiety claimed by the heirs at law of the releaser; and thus there was gradually formed within the household itself a class of persons in dependent freedom, who were different alike from the slaves and from the members of the -gens- entitled in the eye of the law to full and equal rights.

The Roman Community

On this Roman household was based the Roman state, as respected both its constituent elements and its form. The community of the Roman people arose out of the junction (in whatever way brought about) of such ancient clanships as the Romilii, Voltinii, Fabii, *etc.*; the Roman domain comprehended the united lands of those clans.(3) Whoever belonged to one of these clans was a burgess of Rome. Every marriage concluded in the usual forms within this circle was valid as a true Roman marriage, and conferred burgess-rights on the children begotten of it. Whoever was begotten in an illegal marriage, or out of marriage, was excluded from the membership of the community. On this account the Roman burgesses assumed the name of the "father's children" (-patricii-), inasmuch as they alone in the eye of the law had a father. The clans with all the families that they contained were incorporated with the state just as they stood. The spheres of the household and the clan continued to subsist within the state; but the position which a man held in these did not affect his relations towards the state. The son was subject to the father within the household, but in political duties and rights he stood on a footing of equality. The position of the protected dependents was naturally so far changed that the freedmen and clients of every patron received on his account toleration in the community at large; they continued indeed to be immediately dependent on the protection of the family to which they belonged, but the very nature of the case implied that the clients of members of the community could not be wholly excluded from its worship and its festivals, although, of course, they were not capable of the proper rights or liable to the proper duties of burgesses. This remark applies still more to the case of the protected dependents of the community at large. The state thus consisted, like the household, of persons properly belonging to it and of dependents—of "burgesses" and of "inmates" or —metoeci—.

The King

As the clans resting upon a family basis were the constituent elements of the state, so the form of the body-politic was modelled after the family both generally and in detail. The household was provided by nature herself with a head in the person of the father with whom it originated, and with whom it perished. But in the community of the people, which was designed to be imperishable, there was no natural master; not at least in that of Rome, which was composed of free and equal husbandmen and could not boast of a nobility by the grace of God. Accordingly one from its own ranks became its "leader" (-rex-) and lord in the household of the Roman community; as indeed at a later period there were to be found in or near to his dwelling the always blazing hearth and the well-barred store-chamber of the community, the Roman Vestas and the Roman Penates—indications of the visible unity of that supreme household which included all Rome. The regal office began at once and by right, when the position had become vacant and the successor had been designated; but the community did not owe full obedience to the king until he had convoked the assembly of freemen capable of bearing arms and had formally challenged its allegiance. Then he possessed in its entireness that power over the community which belonged to the house-father in his household; and, like him, he ruled for life. He held intercourse with the gods of the community, whom he consulted and appeased (-auspicia publica-), and he nominated all the priests and priestesses. The agreements which he concluded in name of the community with foreigners were binding upon the whole people; although in other instances no member of the community was bound by an agreement with a non-member. His "command" (-imperium-) was all-powerful in peace and in war, on which account "messengers" (-lictores-, from -licere-, to summon) preceded him with axes and rods on all occasions when he appeared officially. He alone had the right of publicly addressing the burgesses, and it was he who kept the keys of the public treasury. He had the same right as a father had to exercise discipline and jurisdiction. He inflicted penalties for breaches of order, and, in particular, flogging for military offences. He sat in judgment in all private and in all criminal processes, and decided absolutely regarding life and death as well as regarding freedom; he might hand over one burgess to fill the place of a slave to another; he might even order a burgess to be sold into actual slavery or, in other words, into banishment. When he had pronounced sentence of death, he was entitled, but not obliged, to allow an appeal to the people for pardon. He called out the people for service in war and commanded the army; but with these high functions he was no less bound, when an alarm of fire was raised, to appear in person at the scene of the burning.

As the house-master was not simply the greatest but the only power in the house, so the king was not merely the first but the only holder of power in the state. He might indeed form colleges of men of skill composed of those specially conversant with the rules of sacred or of public law, and call upon them for their advice; he might, to facilitate his exercise of power, entrust to others particular functions, such as the making communications to the burgesses, the command in war, the decision of processes of minor importance, the inquisition of crimes; he might in particular, if he was compelled to quit the bounds of the city, leave behind him a "city-warden" (-

praefectus urbi-) with the full powers of an -alter ego-; but all official power existing by the side of the king's was derived from the latter, and every official held his office by the king's appointment and during the king's pleasure. All the officials of the earliest period, the extraordinary city-warden as well as the "leaders of division" (-tribuni-, from -tribus-, part) of the infantry (-milites-) and of the cavalry (-celeres-) were merely commissioned by the king, and not magistrates in the subsequent sense of the term. The regal power had not and could not have any external check imposed upon it by law: the master of the community had no judge of his acts within the community, any more than the housefather had a judge within his household. Death alone terminated his power. The choice of the new king lay with the council of elders, to which in case of a vacancy the interim-kingship (-interregnum-) passed. A formal cooperation in the election of king pertained to the burgesses only after his nomination; -de jure- the kingly office was based on the permanent college of the Fathers (-patres-), which by means of the interim holder of the power installed the new king for life. Thus "the august blessing of the gods, under which renowned Rome was founded," was transmitted from its first regal recipient in constant succession to those that followed him, and the unity of the state was preserved unchanged notwithstanding the personal change of the holders of power.

This unity of the Roman people, represented in the field of religion by the Roman Diovis, was in the field of law represented by the prince, and therefore his costume was the same as that of the supreme god; the chariot even in the city, where every one else went on foot, the ivory sceptre with the eagle, the vermilion-painted face, the chaplet of oaken leaves in gold, belonged alike to the Roman god and to the Roman king. It would be a great error, however, to regard the Roman constitution on that account as a theocracy: among the Italians the ideas of god and king never faded away into each other, as they did in Egypt and the East. The king was not the god of the people; it were much more correct to designate him as the proprietor of the state. Accordingly the Romans knew nothing of special divine grace granted to a particular family, or of any other sort of mystical charm by which a king should be made of different stuff from other men: noble descent and relationship with earlier rulers were recommendations, but were not necessary conditions; the office might be lawfully filled by any Roman come to years of discretion and sound in body and mind.(4) The king was thus simply an ordinary burgess, whom merit or fortune, and the primary necessity of having one as master in every house, had placed as master over his equals—a husbandman set over husbandmen, a warrior set over warriors. As the son absolutely obeyed his father and yet did not esteem himself inferior, so the burgess submitted to his ruler without precisely accounting him his better. This constituted the moral and practical limitation of the regal power. The king might, it is true, do much that was inconsistent with equity without exactly breaking the law of the land: he might diminish his fellow-combatants' share of the spoil; he might impose exorbitant task-works or otherwise by his imposts unreasonably encroach upon the property of the burgess; but if he did so, he forgot that his plenary power came not from God, but under God's consent from the people, whose representative he was; and who was there to protect him, if the people should in return forget the oath of allegiance which they had sworn? The legal limitation, again, of the king's power lay in the principle that he was entitled only to execute the law, not to alterit. Every deviation from the law had to receive the previous approval of the assembly of the people and the council of elders; if it was not so approved, it was a null and tyrannical act carrying no legal effect. Thus the power of the king in Rome was, both morally and legally, at bottom altogether different from the sovereignty of the present day; and there is no counterpart at all in modern life either to the Roman household or to the Roman state.

The Community

The division of the body of burgesses was based on the "wardship," -curia-
(probably related to -curare- = -coerare-, —koiranos—); ten wardships formed the
community; every wardship furnished a hundred men to the infantry (hence -mil-es-,
like -equ-es-, the thousand-walker), ten horsemen and ten councillors. When
communities combined, each of course appeared as a part (-tribus-) of the whole
community (-tota-in Umbrian and Oscan), and the original unit became multiplied by
the number of such parts. This division had reference primarily to the personal
composition of the burgess-body, but it was applied also to the domain so far as the
latter was apportioned at all. That the curies had their lands as well as the tribes,
admits of the less doubt, since among the few names of the Roman curies that have
been handed down to us we find along with some apparently derived from -gentes-,
e. g. -Faucia-, others certainly of local origin, e. g. -Veliensis-; each one of them
embraced, in this primitive period of joint possession of land, a number of clan-
lands, of which we have already spoken.(5)

We find this constitution under its simplest form(6) in the scheme of the Latin or
burgess communities that subsequently sprang up under the influence of Rome; these
had uniformly the number of a hundred councillors (-centumviri-). But the same
normal numbers make their appearance throughout in the earliest tradition regarding
the tripartite Rome, which assigns to it thirty curies, three hundred horsemen, three
hundred senators, three thousand foot-soldiers.

Nothing is more certain than that this earliest constitutional scheme did not originate
in Rome; it was a primitive institution common to all the Latins, and perhaps reached
back to a period anterior to the separation of the stocks. The Roman constitutional
tradition quite deserving of credit in such matters, while it accounts historically for
the other divisions of the burgesses, makes the division into curies alone originate
with the origin of the city; and in entire harmony with that view not only does the
curial constitution present itself in Rome, but in the recently discovered scheme of
the organization of the Latin communities it appears as an essential part of the Latin
municipal system.

The essence of this scheme was, and remained, the distribution into curies. The
tribes ("parts") cannot have been an element of essential importance for the simple
reason that their occurrence at all was, not less than their number, the result of
accident; where there were tribes, they certainly had no other significance than that
of preserving the remembrance of an epoch when such "parts" had themselves been
wholes.(7) There is no tradition that the individual tribes had special presiding
magistrates or special assemblies of their own; and it is highly probable that in the
interest of the unity of the commonwealth the tribes which had joined together to
form it were never in reality allowed to have such institutions. Even in the army, it is
true, the infantry had as many pairs of leaders as there were tribes; but each of these
pairs of military tribunes did not command the contingent of a tribe; on the contrary
each individual war-tribune, as well as all in conjunction, exercised command over
the whole infantry. The clans were distributed among the several curies; their limits

and those of the household were furnished by nature. That the legislative power interfered in these groups by way of modification, that it subdivided the large clan and counted it as two, or joined several weak ones together, there is no indication at all in Roman tradition; at any rate this took place only in a way so limited that the fundamental character of affinity belonging to the clan was not thereby altered. We may not therefore conceive the number of the clans, and still less that of the households, as a legally fixed one; if the -curia- had to furnish a hundred men on foot and ten horsemen, it is not affirmed by tradition, nor is it credible, that one horseman was taken from each clan and one foot-soldier from each house. The only member that discharged functions in the oldest constitutional organization was the -curia-. Of these there were ten, or, where there were several tribes, ten to each tribe. Such a "wardship" was a real corporate unity, the members of which assembled at least for holding common festivals. Each wardship was under the charge of a special warden (-curio-), and had a priest of its own (-flamen curialis-); beyond doubt also levies and valuations took place according to curies, and in judicial matters the burgesses met by curies and voted by curies. This organization, however, cannot have been introduced primarily with a view to voting, for in that case they would certainly have made the number of subdivisions uneven.

Equality of the Burgesses

Sternly defined as was the contrast between burgess and non-burgess, the equality of rights within the burgess-body was complete. No people has ever perhaps equalled that of Rome in the inexorable rigour with which it has carried out these principles, the one as fully as the other. The strictness of the Roman distinction between burgesses and non-burgesses is nowhere perhaps brought out with such clearness as in the treatment of the primitive institution of honorary citizenship, which was originally designed to mediate between the two. When a stranger was, by resolution of the community, adopted into the circle of the burgesses, he might surrender his previous citizenship, in which case he passed over wholly into the new community; but he might also combine his former citizenship with that which had just been granted to him. Such was the primitive custom, and such it always remained in Hellas, where in later ages the same person not unfrequently held the freedom of several communities at the same time. But the greater vividness with which the conception of the community as such was realized in Latium could not tolerate the idea that a man might simultaneously belong in the character of a burgess to two communities; and accordingly, when the newly-chosen burgess did not intend to surrender his previous franchise, it attached to the nominal honorary citizenship no further meaning than that of an obligation to befriend and protect the guest (-jus hospitii-), such as had always been recognized as incumbent in reference to foreigners. But this rigorous retention of barriers against those that were without was accompanied by an absolute banishment of all difference of rights among the members included in the burgess community of Rome. We have already mentioned that the distinctions existing in the household, which of course could not be set aside, were at least ignored in the community; the son who as such was subject in property to his father might thus, in the character of a burgess, come to have command over his father as master. There were no class-privileges: the fact that the Tities took precedence of the Ramnes, and both ranked before the Luceres, did not affect their equality in all legal rights. The burgess cavalry, which at this period was used for single combat in front of the line on horseback or even on foot, and was rather a select or reserve corps than a special arm of the service, and which accordingly contained by far the wealthiest, best-armed, and best-trained men, was naturally held in higher estimation than the burgess infantry; but this was a distinction purely -de facto-, and admittance to the cavalry was doubtless conceded to any patrician. It was simply and solely the constitutional subdivision of the burgess-body that gave rise to distinctions recognized by the law; otherwise the legal equality of all the members of the community was carried out even in their external appearance. Dress indeed served to distinguish the president of the community from its members, the grown-up man under obligation of military service from the boy not yet capable of enrolment; but otherwise the rich and the noble as well as the poor and low-born were only allowed to appear in public in the like simple wrapper (-toga-) of white woollen stuff. This complete equality of rights among the burgesses had beyond doubt its original basis in the Indo-Germanic type of constitution; but in the precision with which it was thus apprehended and embodied it formed one of the most characteristic and influential peculiarities of the Latin nation. And in connection with this we may recall the fact that in Italy we do not meet with any race of earlier settlers less capable of culture, that had become subject to the Latin immigrants.(8) They had no conquered race to deal with, and therefore no such condition of things as that which gave rise to the Indian system of caste, to the nobility of Thessaly and Sparta and perhaps of Hellas generally, and probably also to the Germanic distinction of ranks.

Burdens of the Burgesses

The maintenance of the state economy devolved, of course, upon the burgesses. The most important function of the burgess was his service in the army; for the burgesses had the right and duty of bearing arms. The burgesses were at the same time the "body of warriors" (-populus-, related to -populari-, to lay waste): in the old litanies it is upon the "spear-armed body of warriors" (-pilumnus poplus-) that the blessing of Mars is invoked; and even the designation with which the king addresses them, that of Quirites,(9) is taken as signifying "warrior." We have already stated how the army of aggression, the "gathering" (-legio-), was formed. In the tripartite Roman community it consisted of three "hundreds" (-centuriae-) of horsemen (-celeres-, "the swift," or -flexuntes-, "the wheelers") under the three leaders-of-division of the horsemen (-tribuni celerum-)(10) and three "thousands" of footmen (-milties-) under the three leaders-of-division of the infantry (-tribuni militum-), the latter were probably from the first the flower of the general levy. To these there may perhaps have been added a number of light-armed men, archers especially, fighting outside of the ranks.(11) The general was regularly the king himself. Besides service in war, other personal burdens might devolve upon the burgesses; such as the obligation of undertaking the king's commissions in peace and in war,(12) and the task-work of tilling the king's lands or of constructing public buildings. How heavily in particular the burden of building the walls of the city pressed upon the community, is evidenced by the fact that the ring-walls retained the name of "tasks" (-moenia-). There was no regular direct taxation, nor was there any direct regular expenditure on the part of the state. Taxation was not needed for defraying the burdens of the community, since the state gave no recompense for serving in the army, for task-work, or for public service generally; so far as there was any such recompense at all, it was given to the person who performed the service either by the district primarily concerned in it, or by the person who could not or would not himself serve. The victims needed for the public service of the gods were procured by a tax on actions at law; the defeated party in an ordinary process paid down to the state a cattle-fine (-sacramentum-) proportioned to the value of the object in dispute. There is no mention of any regular presents to the king on the part of the burgesses. On the other hand there flowed into the royal coffers the port-duties,(13) as well as the income from the domains—in particular, the pasture tribute (-scriptura-) from the cattle driven out upon the common pasture, and the quotas of produce (-vectigalia-) which those enjoying the use of the lands of the state had to pay instead of rent. To this was added the produce of cattle-fines and confiscations and the gains of war. In cases of need a contribution (-tributum-) was imposed, which was looked upon, however, as a forced loan and was repaid when the times improved; whether it fell upon the burgesses generally, or only upon the —metoeci—, cannot be determined; the latter supposition is, however, the more probable.

The king managed the finances. The property of the state, however, was not identified with the private property of the king; which, judging from the statements regarding the extensive landed possessions of the last Roman royal house, the Tarquins, must have been considerable. The ground won by arms, in particular, appears to have been constantly regarded as property of the state. Whether and how far the king was restricted by use and wont in the administration of the public property, can no longer be ascertained; only the subsequent course of things shows that the burgesses can never have been consulted regarding it, whereas it was probably the custom to consult the senate in the imposition of the -tributum- and in the distribution of the lands won in war.

Rights of the Burgesses

The Roman burgesses, however, do not merely come into view as furnishing contributions and rendering service; they also bore a part in the public government. For this purpose all the members of the community (with the exception of the women, and the children still incapable of bearing arms)—in other words, the "spearmen" (-quirites-) as in addressing them they were designated—assembled at the seat of justice, when the king convoked them for the purpose of making a communication (-conventio-, -contio-) or formally bade them meet (-comitia-) for the third week (-in trinum noundinum-), to consult them by curies. He appointed such formal assemblies of the community to be held regularly twice a year, on the 24th of March and the 24th of May, and as often besides as seemed to him necessary. The burgesses, however, were always summoned not to speak, but to hear; not to ask questions, but to answer. No one spoke in the assembly but the king, or he to whom the king saw fit to grant liberty of speech; and the speaking of the burgesses consisted of a simple answer to the question of the king, without discussion, without reasons, without conditions, without breaking up the question even into parts. Nevertheless the Roman burgess-community, like the Germanic and not improbably the primitive Indo-Germanic communities in general, was the real and ultimate basis of the political idea of sovereignty. But in the ordinary course of things this sovereignty was dormant, or only had its expression in the fact that the burgess-body voluntarily bound itself to render allegiance to its president. For that purpose the king, after he had entered on his office, addressed to the assembled curies the question whether they would be true and loyal to him and would according to use and wont acknowledge himself as well as his messengers (-lictores-); a question, which undoubtedly might no more be answered in the negative than the parallel homage in the case of a hereditary monarchy might be refused.

It was in thorough consistency with constitutional principles that the burgesses, just as being the sovereign power, should not on ordinary occasions take part in the course of public business. So long as public action was confined to the carrying into execution of the existing legal arrangements, the power which was, properly speaking, sovereign in the state could not and might not interfere: the laws governed, not the lawgiver. But it was different where a change of the existing legal arrangements or even a mere deviation from them in a particular case was necessary; and here accordingly, under the Roman constitution, the burgesses emerge without exception as actors; so that each act of the sovereign authority is accomplished by the co-operation of the burgesses and the king or -interrex-. As the legal relation between ruler and ruled was itself sanctioned after the manner of a contract by oral question and answer, so every sovereign act of the community was accomplished by means of a question (-rogatio-), which the king addressed to the burgesses, and to which the majority of the curies gave an affirmative answer. In this case their consent might undoubtedly be refused. Among the Romans, therefore, law was not primarily, as we conceive it, a command addressed by the sovereign to the whole members of the community, but primarily a contract concluded between the constitutive powers of the state by address and counter-address.(14) Such a legislative contract was -de jure- requisite in all cases which involved a deviation from the ordinary consistency of the legal system. In the ordinary course of law any one might without restriction give away his property to whom he would, but only upon condition of its immediate transfer: that the property should continue for the time being with the owner, and at his death pass over to another, was a legal impossibility—unless the community should allow it; a permission which in this case the burgesses could grant not only when assembled in their curies, but also when drawn up for battle. This was the origin of testaments. In the ordinary course of law the freeman could not lose or surrender the inalienable blessing of freedom, and therefore one who was subject to no housemaster could not subject himself to another in the place of a son—unless the community should grant him leave to do so. This was the -abrogatio-. In the ordinary course of law burgess-rights could only be acquired by birth and could never be lost—unless the community should confer the patriciate or allow its surrender; neither of which acts, doubtless, could be validly done originally without a decree of the curies. In the ordinary course of law the criminal whose crime deserved death, when once the king or his deputy had pronounced sentence according to judgment and justice, was inexorably executed; for the king could only judge, not pardon—unless the condemned burgess appealed to the mercy of the community and the judge allowed him the opportunity of pleading for pardon. This was the beginning of the -provocatio-, which for that reason was especially permitted not to the transgressor who had refused to plead guilty and had been convicted, but to him who confessed his crime and urged reasons in palliation of it. In the ordinary course of law the perpetual treaty concluded with a neighbouring state might not be broken—unless the burgesses deemed themselves released from it on account of injuries inflicted on them. Hence it was necessary that they should be consulted when an aggressive war was contemplated, but not on occasion of a defensive war, where the other state had broken the treaty, nor on the conclusion of peace; it appears, however, that the question was in such a case addressed not to the usual assembly of the burgesses, but to the army. Thus, in general, it was necessary to consult the burgesses whenever the king meditated any innovation, any change of the existing public law; and in so far the right of legislation was from antiquity not a right of the king, but a right of the king and the community. In these and all similar cases the king could not act with legal effect without the cooperation of the community; the man whom the king alone declared a patrician remained as before a non-burgess, and the invalid act could only carry consequences possibly -de facto-, not -de jure-. Thus far the assembly of the community, however restricted and bound at its emergence, was yet from antiquity a constituent element of the Roman commonwealth, and was in law superior to, rather than co-ordinate with, the king.

The Senate

But by the side of the king and of the burgess-assembly there appears in the earliest constitution of the community a third original power, not destined for acting like the former or for resolving like the latter, and yet co-ordinate with both and within its own rightful sphere placed over both. This was the council of elders or -senatus-. Beyond doubt it had its origin in the clan-constitution: the old tradition that in the original Rome the senate was composed of all the heads of households is correct in state-law to this extent, that each of the clans of the later Rome which had not merely migrated thither at a more recent date referred its origin to one of those household-fathers of the primitive city as its ancestor and patriarch. If, as is probable, there was once in Rome or at any rate in Latium a time when, like the state itself, each of its ultimate constituents, that is to say each clan, had virtually a monarchical organization and was under the rule of an elder—whether raised to that position by the choice of the clansmen or of his predecessor, or in virtue of hereditary succession—the senate of that time was nothing but the collective body of these clan-elders, and accordingly an institution independent of the king and of the burgess-assembly; in contradistinction to the latter, which was directly composed of the whole body of the burgesses, it was in some measure a representative assembly of persons acting for the people. Certainly that stage of independence when each clan was virtually a state was surmounted in the Latin stock at an immemorially early period, and the first and perhaps most difficult step towards developing the community out of the clan-organization—the setting aside of the clan-elders—had possibly been taken in Latium long before the foundation of Rome; the Roman clan, as we know it, is without any visible head, and no one of the living clansmen is especially called to represent the common patriarch from whom all the clansmen descend or profess to descend so that even inheritance and guardianship, when they fall by death to the clan, devolve on the clan-members as a whole. Nevertheless the original character of the council of elders bequeathed many and important legal consequences to the Roman senate. To express the matter briefly, the position of the senate as something other and more than a mere state-council—than an assemblage of a number of trusty men whose advice the king found it fitting to obtain—hinged entirely on the fact that it was once an assembly, like that described by Homer, of the princes and rulers of the people sitting for deliberation in a circle round the king. So long as the senate was formed by the aggregate of the heads of clans, the number of the members cannot have been a fixed one, since that of the clans was not so; but in the earliest, perhaps even in pre-Roman, times the number of the members of the council of elders for the community had been fixed without respect to the number of the then existing clans at a hundred, so that the amalgamation of the three primitive communities had in state-law the necessary consequence of an increase of the seats in the senate to what was thenceforth the fixed normal number of three hundred. Moreover the senators were at all times called to sit for life; and if at a later period the lifelong tenure subsisted more -de facto-than -de jure-, and the revisions of the senatorial list that took place from time to time afforded an opportunity to remove the unworthy or the unacceptable senator, it can be shown that this arrangement only arose in the course of time. The selection of the senators certainly, after there were no longer heads of clans, lay with the king; but in this selection during the earlier epoch, so long as the people retained a vivid sense of the individuality of the clans, it was probably the rule that, when a senator died, the king should call another experienced and aged man of the same clanship to fill his place. It was only, we may surmise, when the community became more thoroughly amalgamated and inwardly united, that this usage was departed from and the selection of the senators was left entirely to the free judgment of the king, so that he was only regarded as failing in his duty when he omitted to fill up vacancies.

Prerogatives of the Senate. The -Interregnum-

The prerogatives of this council of elders were based on the view that the rule over the community composed of clans rightfully belonged to the collective clan-elders, although in accordance with the monarchical principle of the Romans, which already found so stern an expression in the household, that rule could only be exercised for the time being by one of these elders, namely the king. Every member of the senate accordingly was as such, not in practice but in prerogative, likewise king of the community; and therefore his insignia, though inferior to those of the king, were of a similar character: he wore the red shoe like the king; only that of the king was higher and more handsome than that of the senator. On this ground, moreover, as was already mentioned, the royal power in the Roman community could never be left vacant When the king died, the elders at once took his place and exercised the prerogatives of regal power. According to the immutable principle however that only one can be master at a time, even now it was only one of them that ruled, and such an "interim king" (-interrex-) was distinguished from the king nominated for life simply in respect to the duration, not in respect to the plenitude, of his authority. The duration of the office of -interrex- was fixed for the individual holders at not more than five days; it circulated accordingly among the senators on the footing that, until the royal office was again permanently filled up, the temporary holder at the expiry of that term nominated a successor to himself, likewise for five days, agreeably to the order of succession fixed by lot. There was not, as may readily be conceived, any declaration of allegiance to the -interrex- on the part of the community. Nevertheless the -interrex-was entitled and bound not merely to perform all the official acts otherwise pertaining to the king, but even to nominate a king for life— with the single exception, that this latter right was not vested in the first who held the office, presumably because the first was regarded as defectively appointed inasmuch as he was not nominated by his predecessor. Thus this assembly of elders was the ultimate holder of the ruling power (-imperium-) and the divine protection (-auspicia-) of the Roman commonwealth, and furnished the guarantee for the uninterrupted continuance of that commonwealth and of its monarchical—though not hereditarily monarchical—organization. If therefore this senate subsequently seemed to the Greeks to be an assembly of kings, this was only what was to be expected; it had in fact been such originally.

The Senate and the Resolutions of the Community: -Patrum Auctoritas-

But it was not merely in so far as the idea of a perpetual kingdom found its living expression in this assembly, that it was an essential member of the Roman constitution. The council of elders, indeed, had no title to interfere with the official functions of the king. The latter doubtless, in the event of his being unable personally to lead the army or to decide a legal dispute, took his deputies at all times from the senate; for which reason subsequently the highest posts of command were regularly bestowed on senators alone, and senators were likewise employed by preference as jurymen. But the senate, in its collective capacity, was never consulted in the leading of the army or in the administration of justice; and therefore there was no right of military command and no jurisdiction vested in the senate of the later Rome. On the other hand the council of elders was held as called to the guardianship of the existing constitution against encroachments by the king and the burgesses. On the senate devolved the duty of examining every resolution adopted by the burgesses at the suggestion of the king, and of refusing to confirm it if it seemed to violate existing rights; or, which was the same thing, in all cases where a resolution of the community was constitutionally requisite—as on every alteration of the constitution, on the reception of new burgesses, on the declaration of an aggressive war—the council of elders had a right of veto. This may not indeed be regarded in the light of legislation pertaining jointly to the burgesses and the senate, somewhat in the same way as to the two chambers in the constitutional state of the present day; the senate was not so much law-maker as law-guardian, and could only cancel a decree when the community seemed to have exceeded its competence—to have violated by its decree existing obligations towards the gods or towards foreign states or organic institutions of the community. But still it was a matter of the greatest importance that—to take an example—when the Roman king had proposed a declaration of war and the burgesses had converted it into a decree, and when the satisfaction which the foreign community seemed bound to furnish had been demanded in vain, the Roman envoy invoked the gods as witnesses of the wrong and concluded with the words, "But on these matters we shall consult the elders at home how we may obtain our rights;" it was only when the council of elders had declared its consent, that the war now decreed by the burgesses and approved by the senate was formally declared. Certainly it was neither the design nor the effect of this rule to occasion a constant interference of the senate with the resolutions of the burgesses, and by such guardianship to divest them of their sovereign power; but, as in the event of a vacancy in the supreme office the senate secured the continuance of the constitution, we find it here also as the shield of legal order in opposition even to the supreme power—the community.

The Senate As State-Council

With this arrangement was probably connected the apparently very ancient usage, in virtue of which the king previously submitted to the senate the proposals that were to be brought before the burgesses, and caused all its members one after another to give their opinion on the subject. As the senate had the right of cancelling the resolution adopted, it was natural for the king to assure himself beforehand that no opposition was to be apprehended from that quarter; as indeed in general, on the one hand, it was in accordance with Roman habits not to decide matters of importance without having taken counsel with other men, and on the other hand the senate was called, in virtue of its very composition, to act as a state-council to the ruler of the community. It was from this usage of giving counsel, far more than from the prerogatives which we have previously described, that the subsequent extensive powers of the senate were developed; but it was in its origin insignificant and really amounted only to the prerogative of the senators to answer, when they were asked a question. It may have been usual to ask the previous opinion of the senate in affairs of importance which were neither judicial nor military, as, for instance—apart from the proposals to be submitted to the assembly of the people—in the imposition of task-works and taxes, in the summoning of the burgesses to war-service, and in the disposal of the conquered territory; but such a previous consultation, though usual, was not legally necessary. The king convoked the senate when he pleased, and laid before it his questions; no senator might declare his opinion unasked, still less might the senate meet without being summoned, except in the single case of its meeting on occasion of a vacancy to settle the order of succession in the office of -interrex-. That the king was moreover at liberty to call in and consult other men whom he trusted alongside of, and at the same time with, the senators, is in a high degree probable. The advice, accordingly, was not a command; the king might omit to comply with it, while the senate had no other means for giving practical effect to its views except the already-mentioned right of cassation, which was far from being universally applicable. "I have chosen you, not that ye may be my guides, but that ye may do my bidding:" these words, which a later author puts into the mouth of king Romulus, certainly express with substantial correctness the position of the senate in this respect.

The Original Constitution of Rome

Let us now sum up the results. Sovereignty, as conceived by the Romans, was inherent in the community of burgesses; but the burgess-body was never entitled to act alone, and was only entitled to co-operate in action, when there was to be a departure from existing rules. By its side stood the assembly of the elders of the community appointed for life, virtually a college of magistrates with regal power, called in the event of a vacancy in the royal office to administer it by means of their own members until it should be once more definitively filled, and entitled to overturn the illegal decrees of the community. The royal power itself was, as Sallust says, at once absolute and limited by the laws (-imperium legitimum-); absolute, in so far as the king's command, whether righteous or not, must in the first instance be unconditionally obeyed; limited, in so far as a command contravening established usage and not sanctioned by the true sovereign—the people—carried no permanent legal consequences. The oldest constitution of Rome was thus in some measure constitutional monarchy inverted. In that form of government the king is regarded as the possessor and vehicle of the plenary power of the state, and accordingly acts of grace, for example, proceed solely from him, while the administration of the state belongs to the representatives of the people and to the executive responsible to them. In the Roman constitution the community of the people exercised very much the same functions as belong to the king in England: the right of pardon, which in England is a prerogative of the crown, was in Rome a prerogative of the community; while all government was vested in the president of the state.

If, in conclusion, we inquire as to the relation of the state itself to its individual members, we find the Roman polity equally remote from the laxity of a mere defensive combination and from the modern idea of an absolute omnipotence of the state. The community doubtless exercised power over the person of the burgess in the imposition of public burdens, and in the punishment of offences and crimes; but any special law inflicting, or threatening to inflict, punishment on an individual on account of acts not universally recognized as penal always appeared to the Romans, even when there was no flaw in point of form, an arbitrary and unjust proceeding. Far more restricted still was the power of the community in respect of the rights of property and the rights of family which were coincident, rather than merely connected, with these; in Rome the household was not absolutely annihilated and the community aggrandized at its expense, as was the case in the police organization of Lycurgus. It was one of the most undeniable as well as one of the most remarkable principles of the primitive constitution of Rome, that the state might imprison or hang the burgess, but might not take away from him his son or his field or even lay permanent taxation on him. In these and similar things the community itself was restricted from encroaching on the burgess, nor was this restriction merely ideal; it found its expression and its practical application in the constitutional veto of the senate, which was certainly entitled and bound to annul any resolution of the community contravening such an original right. No community was so all-powerful within its own sphere as the Roman; but in no community did the burgess who conducted himself un-blameably live in an equally absolute security from the risk of encroachment on the part either of his fellow-burgesses or of the state itself.

These were the principles on which the community of Rome governed itself—a free people, understanding the duty of obedience, clearly disowning all mystical priestly delusion, absolutely equal in the eye of the law and one with another, bearing the sharply-defined impress of a nationality of their own, while at the same time (as will be afterwards shown) they wisely as well as magnanimously opened their gates wide for intercourse with other lands. This constitution was neither manufactured nor borrowed; it grew up amidst and along with the Roman people. It was based, of course, upon the earlier constitutions—the Italian, the Graeco-Italian, and the Indo-Germanic; but a long succession of phases of political development must have intervened between such constitutions as the poems of Homer and the Germania of Tacitus delineate and the oldest organization of the Roman community. In the acclamation of the Hellenic and in the shield-striking of the Germanic assemblies there was involved an expression of the sovereign power of the community; but a wide interval separated forms such as these from the organized jurisdiction and the regulated declaration of opinion of the Latin assembly of curies. It is possible, moreover, that as the Roman kings certainly borrowed the purple mantle and the ivory sceptre from the Greeks (not from the Etruscans), the twelve lictors also and various other external arrangements were introduced from abroad. But that the development of the Roman constitutional law belonged decidedly to Rome or, at any rate, to Latium, and that the borrowed elements in it are but small and unimportant, is clearly demonstrated by the fact that all its ideas are uniformly expressed by words of Latin coinage. This constitution practically established for all time the fundamental conceptions of the Roman state; for, as long as there existed a Roman community, in spite of changes of form it was always held that the magistrate had absolute command, that the council of elders was the highest authority in the state, and that every exceptional resolution required the sanction of the sovereign or, in other words, of the community of the people.

Notes for Book I Chapter V

1. This was not merely the case under the old religious marriage (-matrimonium confarreatione-); the civil marriage also (-matrimonium consensu-), although not in itself giving to the husband proprietary power over his wife, opened up the way for his acquiring this proprietary power, inasmuch as the legal ideas of "formal delivery" (-coemptio-), and "prescription" (-usus-), were applied without ceremony to such a marriage. Till he acquired it, and in particular therefore during the period which elapsed before the completion of the prescription, the wife was (just as in the later marriage by -causae probatio-, until that took place), not -uxor-, but -pro uxore-. Down to the period when Roman jurisprudence became a completed system the principle maintained its ground, that the wife who was not in her husband's power was not a married wife, but only passed as such (-uxor tantummodo habetur-. Cicero, Top. 3, 14).

2. The following epitaph, although belonging to a much later period, is not unworthy to have a place here. It is the stone that speaks:—

-Hospes, quod deico, paullum est. Asta ac pellige. Heic est sepulcrum haud pulcrum pulcrai feminae, Nomen parentes nominarunt Claudiam, Suom mareitum corde dilexit sovo, Gnatos duos creavit, horunc alterum In terra linquit, alium sub terra locat; Sermone lepido, tum autem incessu commodo, Domum servavit, lanam fecit. Dixi. Abei.-

(Corp. Inscr. Lat. 1007.)

Still more characteristic, perhaps, is the introduction of wool-spinning among purely moral qualities; which is no very unusual occurrence in Roman epitaphs. Orelli, 4639: -optima et pulcherrima, lanifica pia pudica frugi casta domiseda-. Orelli, 4861: -modestia probitate pudicitia obsequio lanificio diligentia fide par similisque cetereis probeis femina fuit-. Epitaph of Turia, i. 30: domestica bona pudicitiae, opsequi, comitatis, facilitatis, lanificiis [tuis adsiduitatis, religionis] sine superstitione, ornatus non conspiciendi, cultus modici.

3. I. III. Clan-villages

4. Dionysius affirms (v. 25) that lameness excluded from the supreme magistracy. That Roman citizenship was a condition for the regal office as well as for the consulate, is so very self-evident as to make it scarcely worth while to repudiate expressly the fictions respecting the burgess of Cures.

5. I. III. Clan-villages

6. Even in Rome, where the simple constitution of ten curies otherwise early disappeared, we still discover one practical application of it, and that singularly enough in the very same formality which we have other reasons for regarding as the

100

oldest of all those that are mentioned in our legal traditions, the -confarreatio-. It seems scarcely doubtful that the ten witnesses in that ceremony had the same relation to the constitution of ten curies the thirty lictors had to the constitution of thirty curies.

7. This is implied in their very name. The "part" (-tribus-) is, as jurists know, simply that which has once been or may hereafter come to be a whole, and so has no real standing of its own in the present.

8. I. II. Primitive Races of Italy

9. -Quiris-, -quiritis-, or -quirinus- is interpreted by the ancients as "lance-bearer," from -quiris- or -curis- = lance and -ire-, and so far in their view agrees with -samnis- , -samnitis-and -sabinus-, which also among the ancients was derived from — saunion—, spear. This etymology, which associates the word with -arquites-, -milites-, -pedites-, -equites-, -velites- —those respectively who go with the bow, in bodies of a thousand, on foot, on horseback, without armour in their mere over-garment—may be incorrect, but it is bound up with the Roman conception of a burgess. So too Juno quiritis, (Mars) quirinus, Janus quirinus, are conceived as divinities that hurl the spear; and, employed in reference to men, -quiris- is the warrior, that is, the full burgess. With this view the -usus loquendi- coincides. Where the locality was to be referred to, "Quirites" was never used, but always "Rome" and "Romans" (-urbs Roma-, -populus-, -civis-, -ager Romanus-), because the term -quiris- had as little of a local meaning as -civis- or -miles-. For the same reason these designations could not be combined; they did not say -civis quiris-, because both denoted, though from different points of view, the same legal conception. On the other hand the solemn announcement of the funeral of a burgess ran in the words "this warrior has departed in death" (-ollus quiris leto datus-); and in like manner the king addressed the assembled community by this name, and, when he sat in judgment, gave sentence according to the law of the warrior-freemen (-ex iure quiritium-, quite similar to the later -ex iure civili-). The phrase -populus Romanus-, -quirites- (-populus Romanus quiritium-is not sufficiently attested), thus means "the community and the individual burgesses," and therefore in an old formula (Liv. i. 32) to the -populus Romanus- are opposed the -prisci Latini-, to the -quirites- the -homines prisci Latini- (Becker, Handb. ii. 20 seq.)

In the face of these facts nothing but ignorance of language and of history can still adhere to the idea that the Roman community was once confronted by a Quirite community of a similar kind, and that after their incorporation the name of the newly received community supplanted in ritual and legal phraseology that of the receiver.—Comp. iv. The Hill-Romans On The Quirinal, note.

10. Among the eight ritual institutions of Numa, Dionysius (ii. 64) after naming the Curiones and Flamines, specifies as the third the leaders of the horsemen (—oi eigemones ton Kelerion—). According to the Praenestine calendar a festival was celebrated at the Comitium on the 19th March [adstantibus pon]tificibus et trib(unis) celer(um). Valerius Antias (in Dionys. i. 13, comp. iii. 41) assigns to the earliest

Roman cavalry a leader, Celer, and three centurions; whereas in the treatise De viris ill. i, Celer himself is termed -centurio-. Moreover Brutus is affirmed to have been -tribunus celerum- at the expulsion of the kings (Liv. i. 59), and according to Dionysius (iv. 71) to have even by virtue of this office made the proposal to banish the Tarquins. And, lastly, Pomponius (Dig. i. 2, 2, 15, 19) and Lydus in a similar way, partly perhaps borrowing from him (De Mag. i. 14, 37), identify the -tribunus celerum- with the Celer of Antias, the -magister equitum- of the dictator under the republic, and the -Praefectus praetorio- of the empire.

Of these-the only statements which are extant regarding the -tribuni celerum- —the last mentioned not only proceeds from late and quite untrustworthy authorities, but is inconsistent with the meaning of the term, which can only signify "divisional leaders of horsemen," and above all the master of the horse of the republican period, who was nominated only on extraordinary occasions and was in later times no longer nominated at all, cannot possibly have been identical with the magistracy that was required for the annual festival of the 19th March and was consequently a standing office. Laying aside, as we necessarily must, the account of Pomponius, which has evidently arisen solely out of the anecdote of Brutus dressed up with ever-increasing ignorance as history, we reach the simple result that the -tribuni celerum- entirely correspond in number and character to the -tribuni militum-, and that they were the leaders-of-division of the horsemen, consequently quite distinct from the -magister equitum-.

11. This is indicated by the evidently very old forms -velites-and -arquites-and by the subsequent organization of the legion.

12. I. V. The King

13. I. IV. The Tibur and Its Traffic

14. -Lex- ("that which binds," related to -legare-, "to bind to something") denotes, as is well known, a contract in general, along, however, with the connotation of a contract whose terms the proposer dictates and the other party simply accepts or declines; as was usually the case, e. g. with public -licitationes-. In the -lex publica populi Romani- the proposer was the king, the acceptor the people; the limited co-operation of the latter was thus significantly indicated in the very language.

CHAPTER VI

The Non-Burgesses and the Reformed Constitution

Amalgamation of the Palatine and Quirinal Cities

The history of every nation, and of Italy more especially, is a —synoikismos— on a great scale. Rome, in the earliest form in which we have any knowledge of it, was already triune, and similar incorporations only ceased when the spirit of Roman vigour had wholly died away. Apart from that primitive process of amalgamation of the Ramnes, Titles, and Luceres, of which hardly anything beyond the bare fact is known, the earliest act of incorporation of this sort was that by which the Hill-burgesses became merged in the Palatine Rome. The organization of the two communities, when they were about to be amalgamated, may be conceived to have been substantially similar; and in solving the problem of union they would have to choose between the alternatives of retaining duplicate institutions or of abolishing one set of these and extending the other to the whole united community. They adopted the former course with respect to all sanctuaries and priesthoods. Thenceforth the Roman community had its two guilds of Salii and two of Luperci, and as it had two forms of Mars, it had also two priests for that divinity—the Palatine priest, who afterwards usually took the designation of priest of Mars, and the Colline, who was termed priest of Quirinus. It is likely, although it can no longer be proved, that all the old Latin priesthoods of Rome—the Augurs, Pontifices, Vestals, and Fetials—originated in the same way from a combination of the priestly colleges of the Palatine and Quirinal communities. In the division into local regions the town on the Quirinal hill was added as a fourth region to the three belonging to the Palatine city, *viz.* the Suburan, Palatine, and suburban (-Esquiliae-). In the case of the original —synoikismos— the annexed community was recognized after the union as at least a tribe (part) of the new burgess-body, and thus had in some sense a continued political existence; but this course was not followed in the case of the Hill-Romans or in any of the later processes of annexation. After the union the Roman community continued to be divided as formerly into three tribes, each containing ten wardships (-curiae-); and the Hill-Romans—whether they were or were not previously distributed into tribes of their own—must have been inserted into the existing tribes and wardships. This insertion was probably so arranged that, while each tribe and wardship received its assigned proportion of the new burgesses, the new burgesses in these divisions were not amalgamated completely with the old; the tribes henceforth presented two ranks: the Tities, Ramnes, and Luceres being respectively subdivided into first and second (-priores-, -posteriores-). With this division was connected in all probability that arrangement of the organic institutions of the community in pairs, which meets us everywhere. The three pairs of Sacred Virgins are expressly described as representatives of the three tribes with their first and second ranks; and it may be conjectured that the pair of Lares worshipped in each street had a similar origin. This arrangement is especially apparent in the army: after the union each half-tribe of the tripartite community furnished a hundred horsemen, and the Roman burgess cavalry was thus raised to six "hundreds," and the number of its captains probably from three to six. There is no tradition of any corresponding increase to the infantry; but to this origin we may refer the subsequent custom of calling out the legions regularly two by two, and this doubling of the levy probably led to the rule of having not three, as was perhaps originally the case, but six leaders-of-division to command the legion. It is certain that no corresponding increase of seats in the senate took place: on the contrary, the primitive number of three hundred senators remained the normal number down to the seventh century; with which it is quite compatible that a number of the more prominent men of the newly annexed community may have been received into the senate of the Palatine city. The same course was followed with the magistracies: a single king presided over the united community, and there was no change as to his principal deputies, particularly the warden of the city. It thus appears that the ritual institutions of the Hill-city were continued, and that the doubled burgess-body was required to furnish a military force of double the numerical strength; but in other respects the incorporation of the Quirinal city into the Palatine was really a subordination of the former to the latter. If we have rightly assumed that the contrast between the Palatine old and the Quirinal new burgesses was identical with the contrast between the first and second Tities, Ramnes, and Luceres, it was thus the -gentes-of the Quirinal city that formed the "second" or the "lesser." The distinction, however, was certainly more an honorary than a legal precedence. At the taking of the vote in the senate the senators taken from the old clans were asked before those of the "lesser." In like manner the Colline region ranked as inferior even to the suburban (Esquiline) region of the Palatine city; the priest of the Quirinal Mars as inferior to the priest of the Palatine Mars; the Quirinal Salii and Luperci as inferior to those of the Palatine. It thus appears that the —synoikismos—, by which the Palatine community incorporated that of the Quirinal, marked an intermediate stage between the earliest —synoikismos— by which the Tities, Ramnes, and Luceres became blended, and all those that took place afterwards. The annexed community was no longer allowed to form a separate tribe in the new whole, but it was permitted to furnish at least a distinct portion of each tribe; and its ritual institutions were not only allowed to subsist—as was afterwards done in other cases, after the capture of Alba for example—but were elevated into institutions of the united community, a course which was not pursued in any subsequent instance.

Dependents and Guests

This amalgamation of two substantially similar commonwealths produced rather an increase in the size than a change in the intrinsic character of the existing community. A second process of incorporation, which was carried out far more gradually and had far deeper effects, may be traced back, so far as the first steps in it are concerned, to this epoch; we refer to the amalgamation of the burgesses and the —metoeci—. At all times there existed side by side with the burgesses in the Roman community persons who were protected, the "listeners" (-clientes-), as they were called from their being dependents on the several burgess-households, or the "multitude" (-plebes-, from -pleo-, -plenus-), as they were termed negatively with reference to their want of political rights.(1) The elements of this intermediate stage between the freeman and the slave were, as has been shown(2) already in existence in the Roman household: but in the community this class necessarily acquired greater importance -de facto- and -de jure-, and that from two reasons. In the first place the community might itself possess half-free clients as well as slaves; especially after the conquest of a town and the breaking up of its commonwealth it might often appear to the conquering community advisable not to sell the mass of the burgesses formally as slaves, but to allow them the continued possession of freedom -de facto-, so that in the capacity as it were of freedmen of the community they entered into relations of clientship whether to the clans, or to the king. In the second place by means of the community and its power over the individual burgesses, there was given the possibility of protecting the clients against an abusive exercise of the -dominium- still subsisting in law. At an immemorially early period there was introduced into Roman law the principle on which rested the whole legal position of the —metoeci—, that, when a master on occasion of a public legal act—such as in the making of a testament, in an action at law, or in the census—expressly or tacitly surrendered his -dominium-, neither he himself nor his lawful successors should ever have power arbitrarily to recall that resignation or reassert a claim to the person of the freedman himself or of his descendants. The clients and their posterity did not by virtue of their position possess either the rights of burgesses or those of guests: for to constitute a burgess a formal bestowal of the privilege was requisite on the part of the community, while the relation of guest presumed the holding of burgess-rights in a community which had a treaty with Rome. What they did obtain was a legally protected possession of freedom, while they continued to be -de jure- non-free. Accordingly for a lengthened period their relations in all matters of property seem to have been, like those of slaves, regarded in law as relations of the patron, so that it was necessary that the latter should represent them in processes at law; in connection with which the patron might levy contributions from them in case of need, and call them to account before him criminally. By degrees, however, the body of —metoeci— outgrew these fetters; they began to acquire and to alienate in their own name, and to claim and obtain legal redress from the Roman burgess-tribunals without the formal intervention of their patron.

In matters of marriage and inheritance, equality of rights with the burgesses was far sooner conceded to foreigners(3) than to those who were strictly non-free and belonged to no community; but the latter could not well be prohibited from contracting marriages in their own circle and from forming the legal relations arising out of marriage—those of marital and paternal power, of -agnatio- and -gentilitas- of heritage and of tutelage—after the model of the corresponding relations among the burgesses.

Similar consequences to some extent were produced by the exercise of the -ius hospitii-, in so far as by virtue of it foreigners settled permanently in Rome and established a domestic position there. In this respect the most liberal principles must have prevailed in Rome from primitive times. The Roman law knew no distinctions of quality in inheritance and no locking up of estates. It allowed on the one hand to every man capable of making a disposition the entirely unlimited disposal of his property during his lifetime; and on the other hand, so far as we know, to every one who was at all entitled to have dealings with Roman burgesses, even to the foreigner and the client, the unlimited right of acquiring moveable, and (from the time when immoveables could be held as private property at all) within certain limits also immoveable, estate in Rome. Rome was in fact a commercial city, which was indebted for the commencement of its importance to international commerce, and which with a noble liberality granted the privilege of settlement to every child of an unequal marriage, to every manumitted slave, and to every stranger who surrendering his rights in his native land emigrated to Rome.

Class of —Metoeci— Subsisting by the Side of the Community

At first, therefore, the burgesses were in reality the protectors, the non-burgesses were the protected; but in Rome as in all communities which freely admit settlement but do not throw open the rights of citizenship, it soon became a matter of increasing difficulty to harmonize this relation -de jure- with the actual state of things. The flourishing of commerce, the full equality of private rights guaranteed to all Latins by the Latin league (including even the acquisition of landed property), the greater frequency of manumissions as prosperity increased, necessarily occasioned even in peace a disproportionate increase of the number of —metoeci—. That number was further augmented by the greater part of the population of the neighbouring towns subdued by force of arms and incorporated with Rome; which, whether it removed to the city or remained in its old home now reduced to the rank of a village, ordinarily exchanged its native burgess-rights for those of a Roman —metoikos—. Moreover the burdens of war fell exclusively on the old burgesses and were constantly thinning the ranks of their patrician descendants, while the —metoeci— shared in the results of victory without having to pay for it with their blood.

Under such circumstances the only wonder is that the Roman patriciate did not disappear much more rapidly than it actually did. The fact of its still continuing for a prolonged period a numerous community can scarcely be accounted for by the bestowal of Roman burgess-rights on several distinguished foreign clans, which after emigrating from their homes or after the conquest of their cities received the Roman franchise—for such grants appear to have occurred but sparingly from the first, and to have become always the more rare as the franchise increased in value. A cause of greater influence, in all likelihood, was the introduction of the civil marriage, by which a child begotten of patrician parents living together as married persons, although without -confarreatio-, acquired full burgess-rights equally with the child of a -confarreatio- marriage. It is at least probable that the civil marriage, which already existed in Rome before the Twelve Tables but was certainly not an original institution, was introduced for the purpose of preventing the disappearance of the patriciate.(4) To this connection belong also the measures which were already in the earliest times adopted with a view to maintain a numerous posterity in the several households.(5)

Nevertheless the number of the —metoeci— was of necessity constantly on the increase and liable to no diminution, while that of the burgesses was at the utmost perhaps not decreasing; and in consequence the —metoeci— necessarily acquired by imperceptible degrees another and a freer position. The non-burgesses were no longer merely emancipated slaves or strangers needing protection; their ranks included the former burgesses of the Latin communities vanquished in war, and more especially the Latin settlers who lived in Rome not by the favour of the king or of any other burgess, but by federal right. Legally unrestricted in the acquiring of property, they gained money and estate in their new home, and bequeathed, like the burgesses, their homesteads to their children and children's children. The vexatious relation of dependence on particular burgess-households became gradually relaxed. If the liberated slave or the immigrant stranger still held an entirely isolated position in the state, such was no longer the case with his children, still less with his grandchildren, and this very circumstance of itself rendered their relations to the patron of less moment. While in earlier times the client was exclusively left dependent for legal protection on the intervention of the patron, the more the state became consolidated and the importance of the clanships and households in consequence diminished, the more frequently must the individual client have obtained justice and redress of injury, even without the intervention of his patron, from the king. A great number of the non-burgesses, particularly the members of the dissolved Latin communities, had, as we have already said, probably from the outset not any place as clients of the royal or other great clans, and obeyed the king nearly in the same manner as did the burgesses. The king, whose sovereignty over the burgesses was in truth ultimately dependent on the good-will of those obeying, must have welcomed the means of forming out of his own -proteges- essentially dependent on him a body bound to him by closer ties.

Plebs

Thus there grew up by the side of the burgesses a second community in Rome: out of the clients arose the Plebs. This change of name is significant. In law there was no difference between the client and the plebeian, the "dependent" and the "man of the multitude;" but in fact there was a very important one, for the former term brought into prominence the relation of dependence on a member of the politically privileged class; the latter suggested merely the want of political rights. As the feeling of special dependence diminished, that of political inferiority forced itself on the thoughts of the free —metoeci—; and it was only the sovereignty of the king ruling equally over all that prevented the outbreak of political conflict between the privileged and the non-privileged classes.

The Servian Constitution

The first step, however, towards the amalgamation of the two portions of the people scarcely took place in the revolutionary way which their antagonism appeared to foreshadow. The reform of the constitution, which bears the name of king Servius Tullius, is indeed, as to its historical origin, involved in the same darkness with all the events of a period respecting which we learn whatever we know not by means of historical tradition, but solely by means of inference from the institutions of later times. But its character testifies that it cannot have been a change demanded by the plebeians, for the new constitution assigned to them duties alone, and not rights. It must rather have owed its origin either to the wisdom of one of the Roman kings, or to the urgency of the burgesses that they should be delivered from exclusive liability to burdens, and that the non-burgesses should be made to share on the one hand in taxation—that is, in the obligation to make advances to the state (the -tributum-)—-and rendering task-work, and on the other hand in the levy. Both were comprehended in the Servian constitution, but they hardly took place at the same time. The bringing in of the non-burgesses presumably arose out of the economic burdens; these were early extended to such as were "possessed of means" (-locupletes-) or "settled people" (-adsidui-, freeholders), and only those wholly without means, the "children-producers" (-proletarii-, -capite censi-) remained free from them. Thereupon followed the politically more important step of bringing in the non-burgesses to military duty. This was thenceforth laid not upon the burgesses as such, but upon the possessors of land, the -tribules-, whether they might be burgesses or mere —metoeci—; service in the army was changed from a personal burden into a burden on property. The details of the arrangement were as follow.

The Five Classes

Every freeholder from the eighteenth to the sixtieth year of his age, including children in the household of freeholder fathers, without distinction of birth, was under obligation of service, so that even the manumitted slave had to serve, if in an exceptional case he had come into possession of landed property. The Latins also possessing land—others from without were not allowed to acquire Roman soil—-were called in to service, so far as they had, as was beyond doubt the case with most of them, taken up their abode on Roman territory. The body of men liable to serve was distributed, according to the size of their portions of land, into those bound to full service or the possessors of a full hide,(6) who were obliged to appear in complete armour and in so far formed pre-eminently the war army (-classis-), and the four following ranks of smaller landholders—the possessors respectively of three fourths, of a half, of a quarter, or of an eighth of a whole farm—from whom was required fulfilment of service, but not equipment in complete armour, and they thus had a position below the full rate (-infra classem-). As the land happened to be at that time apportioned, almost the half of the farms were full hides, while each of the classes possessing respectively three-fourths, the half, and the quarter of a hide, amounted to scarcely an eighth of the freeholders, and those again holding an eighth of a hide amounted to fully an eighth. It was accordingly laid down as a rule that in the case of the infantry the levy should be in the proportion of eighty holders of a full hide, twenty from each of the three next ranks, and twenty-eight from the last.

Cavalry

The cavalry was similarly dealt with. The number of divisions in it was tripled, and the only difference in this case was that the six divisions already existing with the old names (-Tities-, -Ramnes-, -Luceres- -primi- and -secundi-) were left to the patricians, while the twelve new divisions were formed chiefly from the non-burgesses. The reason for this difference is probably to be sought in the fact that at that period the infantry were formed anew for each campaign and discharged on their return home, whereas the cavalry with their horses were on military grounds kept together also in time of peace, and held their regular drills, which continued to subsist as festivals of the Roman equites down to the latest times.(7) Accordingly the squadrons once constituted were allowed, even under this reform, to keep their ancient names. In order to make the cavalry accessible to every burgess, the unmarried women and orphans under age, so far as they had possession of land, were bound instead of personal service to provide the horses for particular troopers (each trooper had two of them), and to furnish them with fodder. On the whole there was one horseman to nine foot-soldiers; but in actual service the horsemen were used more sparingly.

The non-freeholders (-adcensi-, people standing at the side of the list of those owing military service) had to supply the army with workmen and musicians as well as with a number of substitutes who marched with the army unarmed (-velati-), and, when vacancies occurred in the field, took their places in the ranks equipped with the weapons of the sick or of the fallen.

Levy-Districts

To facilitate the levying of the infantry, the city was distributed into four "parts" (-tribus-); by which the old triple division was superseded, at least so far as concerned its local significance. These were the Palatine, which comprehended the height of that name along with the Velia; the Suburan, to which the street so named, the Carinae, and the Caelian belonged; the Esquiline; and the Colline, formed by the Quirinal and Viminal, the "hills" as contrasted with the "mounts" of the Capitol and Palatine. We have already spoken of the formation of these regions(8) and shown how they originated out of the ancient double city of the Palatine and the Quirinal. By what process it came to pass that every freeholder burgess belonged to one of those city-districts, we cannot tell; but this was now the case; and that the four regions were nearly on an equality in point of numbers, is evident from their being equally drawn upon in the levy. This division, which had primary reference to the soil alone and applied only inferentially to those who possessed it, was merely for administrative purposes, and in particular never had any religious significance attached to it; for the fact that in each of the city-districts there were six chapels of the enigmatical Argei no more confers upon them the character of ritual districts than the erection of an altar to the Lares in each street implies such a character in the streets.

Each of these four levy-districts had to furnish approximately the fourth part not only of the force as a whole, but of each of its military subdivisions, so that each legion and each century numbered an equal proportion of conscripts from each region, in order to merge all distinctions of a gentile and local nature in the one common levy of the community and, especially through the powerful levelling influence of the military spirit, to blend the —metoeci— and the burgesses into one people.

Organization of the Army

In a military point of view, the male population capable of bearing arms was divided into a first and second levy, the former of which, the "juniors" from the commencement of the eighteenth to the completion of the forty-sixth year, were especially employed for service in the field, while the "seniors" guarded the walls at home. The military unit came to be in the infantry the now doubled legion(9)—a phalanx, arranged and armed completely in the old Doric style, of 6000 men who, six file deep, formed a front of 1000 heavy-armed soldiers; to which were attached 2400 "unarmed".(10) The four first ranks of the phalanx, the -classis-, were formed by the fully-armed hoplites of those possessing a full hide; in the fifth and sixth were placed the less completely equipped farmers of the second and third division; the two last divisions were annexed as rear ranks to the phalanx or fought by its side as light-armed troops. Provision was made for readily supplying the accidental gaps which were so injurious to the phalanx. Thus there served in it 84 centuries or 8400 men, of whom 6000 were hoplites, 4000 of the first division, 1000 from each of the two following, and 2400 light-armed, of whom 1000 belonged to the fourth, and 1200 to the fifth division; approximately each levy-district furnished to the phalanx 2100, and to each century 25 men. This phalanx was the army destined for the field, while a like force of troops was reckoned for the seniors who remained behind to defend the city. In this way the normal amount of the infantry came to 16,800 men, 80 centuries of the first division, 20 from each of the three following, and 28 from the last division—not taking into account the two centuries of substitutes or those of the workmen or the musicians. To all these fell to be added the cavalry, which consisted of 1800 horse; often when the army took the field, however, only the third part of the whole number was attached to it. The normal amount of the Roman army of the first and second levy rose accordingly to close upon 20,000 men: which number must beyond doubt have corresponded on the whole to the effective strength of the Roman population capable of arms, as it stood at the time when this new organization was introduced. As the population increased the number of centuries was not augmented, but the several divisions were strengthened by persons added, without altogether losing sight, however, of the fundamental number. Indeed the Roman corporations in general, closed as to numbers, very frequently evaded the limit imposed upon them by admitting supernumerary members.

Census

This new organization of the army was accompanied by a more careful supervision of landed property on the part of the state. It was now either ordained for the first time or, if not, at any rate defined more carefully, that a land-register should be established, in which the several proprietors of land should have their fields with all their appurtenances, servitudes, slaves, beasts of draught and of burden, duly recorded. Every act of alienation, which did not take place publicly and before witnesses, was declared null; and a revision of the register of landed property, which was at the same time the levy-roll, was directed to be made every fourth year. The -mancipatio- and the -census- thus arose out of the Servian military organization.

Political Effects of the Servian Military Organization

It is evident at a glance that this whole institution was from the outset of a military nature. In the whole detailed scheme we do not encounter a single feature suggestive of any destination of the centuries to other than purely military purposes; and this alone must, with every one accustomed to consider such matters, form a sufficient reason for pronouncing its application to political objects a later innovation. If, as is probable, in the earliest period every one who had passed his sixtieth year was excluded from the centuries, this has no meaning, so far as they were intended from the first to form a representation of the burgess-community similar to and parallel with the curies. Although, however, the organization of the centuries was introduced merely to enlarge the military resources of the burgesses by the inclusion of the — metoeci— and, in so far, there is no greater error than to exhibit the Servian organization as the introduction of a timocracy in Rome—yet the new obligation imposed upon the inhabitants to bear arms exercised in its consequences a material influence on their political position. He who is obliged to become a soldier must also, so long as the state is not rotten, have it in his power to become an officer; beyond question plebeians also could now be nominated in Rome as centurions and as military tribunes. Although, moreover, the institution of the centuries was not intended to curtail the political privileges exclusively possessed by the burgesses as hitherto represented in the curies, yet it was inevitable that those rights, which the burgesses hitherto had exercised not as the assembly of curies, but as the burgess-levy, should pass over to the new centuries of burgesses and —metoeci—. Henceforward, accordingly, it was the centuries whose consent the king had to ask before beginning an aggressive war.(11) It is important, on account of the subsequent course of development, to note these first steps towards the centuries taking part in public affairs; but the centuries came to acquire such rights at first more in the way of natural sequence than of direct design, and subsequently to the Servian reform, as before, the assembly of the curies was regarded as the proper burgess-community, whose homage bound the whole people in allegiance to the king. By the side of these new landowning full-burgesses stood the domiciled foreigners from the allied Latium, as participating in the public burdens, tribute and task-works (hence -municipes-); while the burgesses not domiciled, who were beyond the pale of the tribes, and had not the right to serve in war and vote, came into view only as "owing tribute" (-aerarii-).

In this way, while hitherto there had been distinguished only two classes of members of the community, burgesses and clients, there were now established those three political classes, which exercised a dominant influence over the constitutional law of Rome for many centuries.

Time and Occasion of the Reform

When and how this new military organization of the Roman community came into existence, can only be conjectured. It presupposes the existence of the four regions; in other words, the Servian wall must have been erected before the reform took place. But the territory of the city must also have considerably exceeded its original limits, when it could furnish 8000 holders of full hides and as many who held lesser portions, or sons of such holders. We are not acquainted with the superficial extent of the normal Roman farm; but it is not possible to estimate it as under twenty - jugera-.(12) If we reckon as a minimum 10,000 full hides, this would imply a superficies of 190 square miles of arable land; and on this calculation, if we make a very moderate allowance for pasture, the space occupied by houses, and ground not capable of culture, the territory, at the period when this reform was carried out, must have had at least an extent of 420 square miles, probably an extent still more considerable. If we follow tradition, we must assume a number of 84,000 burgesses who were freeholders and capable of bearing arms; for such, we are told, were the numbers ascertained by Servius at the first census. A glance at the map, however, shows that this number must be fabulous; it is not even a genuine tradition, but a conjectural calculation, by which the 16,800 capable of bearing arms who constituted the normal strength of the infantry appeared to yield, on an average of five persons to each family, the number of 84,000 burgesses, and this number was confounded with that of those capable of bearing arms. But even according to the more moderate estimates laid down above, with a territory of some 16,000 hides containing a population of nearly 20,000 capable of bearing arms and at least three times that number of women, children, and old men, persons who had no land, and slaves, it is necessary to assume not merely that the region between the Tiber and Anio had been acquired, but that the Alban territory had also been conquered, before the Servian constitution was established; a result with which tradition agrees. What were the numerical proportions of patricians and plebeians originally in the army, cannot be ascertained.

Upon the whole it is plain that this Servian institution did not originate in a conflict between the orders. On the contrary, it bears the stamp of a reforming legislator like the constitutions of Lycurgus, Solon, and Zaleucus; and it has evidently been produced under Greek influence. Particular analogies may be deceptive, such as the coincidence noticed by the ancients that in Corinth also widows and orphans were charged with the provision of horses for the cavalry; but the adoption of the armour and arrangements of the Greek hoplite system was certainly no accidental coincidence. Now if we consider the fact that it was in the second century of the city that the Greek states in Lower Italy advanced from the pure clan-constitution to a modified one, which placed the preponderance in the hands of the landholders, we shall recognize in that movement the impulse which called forth in Rome the Servian reform—a change of constitution resting in the main on the same fundamental idea, and only directed into a somewhat different course by the strictly monarchical form of the Roman state.(13)

118

Notes for Book I Chapter VI

1. I. V. Dependents of the Household

2. -Habuit plebem in clientelas principium descriptam-. Cicero, de Rep. ii. 9.

3. I. III. The Latin League

4. The enactments of the Twelve Tables respecting -usus- show clearly that they found the civil marriage already in existence. In like manner the high antiquity of the civil marriage is clearly evident from the fact that it, equally with the religious marriage, necessarily involved the marital power (v. The House-father and His Household), and only differed from the religious marriage as respected the manner in which that power was acquired. The religious marriage itself was held as the proprietary and legally necessary form of acquiring a wife; whereas, in the case of civil marriage, one of the general forms of acquiring property used on other occasions—delivery on the part of a person entitled to give away, or prescription—-was requisite in order to lay the foundation of a valid marital power.

5. I. V. The House-father and His Household.

6. -Hufe-, hide, as much as can be properly tilled with one plough, called in Scotland a plough-gate.

7. For the same reason, when the levy was enlarged after the admission of the Hill-Romans, the equites were doubled, while in the infantry force instead of the single "gathering" (-legio-) two legions were called out (vi. Amalgamation of the Palatine and Quirinal Cities).

8. I. IV. Oldest Settlements In the Palatine and Suburan Regions

9. I. V. Burdens of the Burgesses

10. -velites-, see v. Burdens of the Burgesses, note

11. I. V. Rights of the Burgesses

12. Even about 480, allotments of land of seven -jugera- appeared to those that received them small (Val. Max. iii. 3, 5; Colum. i, praef. 14; i. 3, ii; Plin. H. N. xviii. 3, 18: fourteen -jugera-, Victor, 33; Plutarch, Apophth. Reg. et Imp. p. 235 Dubner, in accordance with which Plutarch, Crass. 2, is to be corrected).

A comparison of the Germanic proportions gives the same result. The -jugerum- and the -morgen- [nearly 5/8 of an English acre], both originally measures rather of labour than of surface, may be looked upon as originally identical. As the German hide consisted ordinarily of 30, but not unfrequently of 20 or 40 -morgen-, and the homestead frequently, at least among the Anglo-Saxons, amounted to a tenth of the hide, it will appear, taking into account the diversity of climate and the size of the Roman -heredium- of 2 -jugera-, that the hypothesis of a Roman hide of 20 -jugera- is not unsuitable to the circumstances of the case. It is to be regretted certainly that on this very point tradition leaves us without precise information.

13. The analogy also between the so-called Servian constitution and the treatment of the Attic —metoeci— deserves to be particularly noticed. Athens, like Rome, opened her gates at a comparatively early period to the —metoeci—, and afterwards summoned them also to share the burdens of the state. We cannot suppose that any direct connection existed in this instance between Athens and Rome; but the coincidence serves all the more distinctly to show how the same causes—urban centralization and urban development—everywhere and of necessity produce similar effects.

CHAPTER VII

The Hegemony of Rome in Latium

Extension of the Roman Territory

The brave and impassioned Italian race doubtless never lacked feuds among themselves and with their neighbours: as the country flourished and civilization advanced, feuds must have become gradually changed into war and raids for pillage into conquest, and political powers must have begun to assume shape. No Italian Homer, however, has preserved for us a picture of these earliest frays and plundering excursions, in which the character of nations is moulded and expressed like the mind of the man in the sports and enterprises of the boy; nor does historical tradition enable us to form a judgment, with even approximate accuracy, as to the outward development of power and the comparative resources of the several Latin cantons. It is only in the case of Rome, at the utmost, that we can trace in some degree the extension of its power and of its territory. The earliest demonstrable boundaries of the united Roman community have been already stated;(1) in the landward direction they were on an average just about five miles distant from the capital of the canton, and it was only toward the coast that they extended as far as the mouth of the Tiber (-Ostia-), at a distance of somewhat more than fourteen miles from Rome. "The new city," says Strabo, in his description of the primitive Rome, "was surrounded by larger and smaller tribes, some of whom dwelt in independent villages and were not subordinate to any national union." It seems to have been at the expense of these neighbours of kindred lineage in the first instance that the earliest extensions of the Roman territory took place.

Territory on the Anio—Alba

The Latin communities situated on the upper Tiber and between the Tiber and the Anio-Antemnae, Crustumerium, Ficulnea, Medullia, Caenina, Corniculum, Cameria, Collatia,—were those which pressed most closely and sorely on Rome, and they appear to have forfeited their independence in very early times to the arms of the Romans. The only community that subsequently appears as independent in this district was Nomentum; which perhaps saved its freedom by alliance with Rome. The possession of Fidenae, the -tete de pont- of the Etruscans on the left bank of the Tiber, was contested between the Latins and the Etruscans—in other words, between the Romans and Veientes—with varying results. The struggle with Gabii, which held the plain between the Anio and the Alban hills, was for a long period equally balanced: down to late times the Gabine dress was deemed synonymous with that of war, and Gabine ground the prototype of hostile soil.(2) By these conquests the Roman territory was probably extended to about 190 square miles. Another very early achievement of the Roman arms was preserved, although in a legendary dress, in the memory of posterity with greater vividness than those obsolete struggles: Alba, the ancient sacred metropolis of Latium, was conquered and destroyed by Roman troops. How the collision arose, and how it was decided, tradition does not tell: the battle of the three Roman with the three Alban brothers born at one birth is nothing but a personification of the struggle between two powerful and closely related cantons, of which the Roman at least was triune. We know nothing at all beyond the naked fact of the subjugation and destruction of Alba by Rome.(3)

It is not improbable, although wholly a matter of conjecture, that, at the same period when Rome was establishing herself on the Anio and on the Alban hills, Praeneste, which appears at a later date as mistress of eight neighbouring townships, Tibur, and others of the Latin communities were similarly occupied in enlarging their territory and laying the foundations of their subsequent far from inconsiderable power.

Treatment of the Earliest Acquisitons

We feel the want of accurate information as to the legal character and legal effects of these early Latin conquests, still more than we miss the records of the wars in which they were won. Upon the whole it is not to be doubted that they were treated in accordance with the system of incorporation, out of which the tripartite community of Rome had arisen; excepting that the cantons who were compelled by arms to enter the combination did not, like the primitive three, preserve some sort of relative independence as separate regions in the new united community, but became so entirely merged in the general whole as to be no longer traced.(4) However far the power of a Latin canton might extend, in the earliest times it tolerated no political centre except the proper capital; and still less founded independent settlements, such as the Phoenicians and the Greeks established, thereby creating in their colonies clients for the time being and future rivals to the mother city. In this respect, the treatment which Ostia experienced from Rome deserves special notice: the Romans could not and did not wish to prevent the rise -de facto- of a town at that spot, but they allowed the place no political independence, and accordingly they did not bestow on those who settled there any local burgess-rights, but merely allowed them to retain, if they already possessed, the general burgess-rights of Rome.(5) This principle also determined the fate of the weaker cantons, which by force of arms or by voluntary submission became subject to a stronger. The stronghold of the canton was razed, its domain was added to the domain of the conquerors, and a new home was instituted for the inhabitants as well as for their gods in the capital of the victorious canton. This must not be understood absolutely to imply a formal transportation of the conquered inhabitants to the new capital, such as was the rule at the founding of cities in the East. The towns of Latium at this time can have been little more than the strongholds and weekly markets of the husbandmen: it was sufficient in general that the market and the seat of justice should be transferred to the new capital. That even the temples often remained at the old spot is shown in the instances of Alba and of Caenina, towns which must still after their destruction have retained some semblance of existence in connection with religion. Even where the strength of the place that was razed rendered it really necessary to remove the inhabitants, they would be frequently settled, with a view to the cultivation of the soil, in the open hamlets of their old domain. That the conquered, however, were not unfrequently compelled either as a whole or in part to settle in their new capital, is proved, more satisfactorily than all the several stories from the legendary period of Latium could prove it, by the maxim of Roman state-law, that only he who had extended the boundaries of the territory was entitled to advance the wall of the city (the -pomerium-). Of course the conquered, whether transferred or not, were ordinarily compelled to occupy the legal position of clients;(6) but particular individuals or clans occasionally had burgess-rights or, in other words, the patriciate conferred upon them. In the time of the empire there were still recognized Alban clans which were introduced among the burgesses of Rome after the fall of their native seat; amongst these were the Julii, Servilii, Quinctilii, Cloelii, Geganii, Curiatii, Metilii: the memory of their descent was preserved by their Alban family shrines, among which the sanctuary of the -gens- of the Julii at Bovillae again rose under the empire into great repute.

This centralizing process, by which several small communities became absorbed in a larger one, of course was far from being an idea specially Roman. Not only did the development of Latium and of the Sabellian stocks hinge upon the distinction between national centralization and cantonal independence; the case was the same with the development of the Hellenes. Rome in Latium and Athens in Attica arose out of a like amalgamation of many cantons into one state; and the wise Thales suggested a similar fusion to the hard-pressed league of the Ionic cities as the only means of saving their nationality. But Rome adhered to this principle of unity with more consistency, earnestness, and success than any other Italian canton; and just as the prominent position of Athens in Hellas was the effect of her early centralization, so Rome was indebted for her greatness solely to the same system, in her case far more energetically applied,

The Hegemony of Rome over Latium—Alba

While the conquests of Rome in Latium may be mainly regarded as direct extensions of her territory and people presenting the same general features, a further and special significance attached to the conquest of Alba. It was not merely the problematical size and presumed riches of Alba that led tradition to assign a prominence so peculiar to its capture. Alba was regarded as the metropolis of the Latin confederacy, and had the right of presiding among the thirty communities that belonged to it. The destruction of Alba, of course, no more dissolved the league itself than the destruction of Thebes dissolved the Boeotian confederacy;(7) but, in entire consistency with the strict application of the -ius privatum- which was characteristic of the Latin laws of war, Rome now claimed the presidency of the league as the heir-at-law of Alba. What sort of crises, if any, preceded or followed the acknowledgment of this claim, we cannot tell. Upon the whole the hegemony of Rome over Latium appears to have been speedily and generally recognized, although particular communities, such as Labici and above all Gabii, may for a time have declined to own it. Even at that time Rome was probably a maritime power in contrast to the Latin "land," a city in contrast to the Latin villages, and a single state in contrast to the Latin confederacy; even at that time it was only in conjunction with and by means of Rome that the Latins could defend their coasts against Carthaginians, Hellenes, and Etruscans, and maintain and extend their landward frontier in opposition to their restless neighbours of the Sabellian stock. Whether the accession to her material resources which Rome obtained by the subjugation of Alba was greater than the increase of her power obtained by the capture of Antemnae or Collatia, cannot be ascertained: it is quite possible that it was not by the conquest of Alba that Rome was first constituted the most powerful community in Latium; she may have been so long before; but she did gain in consequence of that event the presidency at the Latin festival, which became the basis of the future hegemony of the Roman community over the whole Latin confederacy. It is important to indicate as definitely as possible the nature of a relation so influential.

Relation of Rome to Latium

The form of the Roman hegemony over Latium was, in general, that of an alliance on equal terms between the Roman community on the one hand and the Latin confederacy on the other, establishing a perpetual peace throughout the whole domain and a perpetual league for offence and defence. "There shall be peace between the Romans and all communities of the Latins, as long as heaven and earth endure; they shall not wage war with each other, nor call enemies into the land, nor grant passage to enemies: help shall be rendered by all in concert to any community assailed, and whatever is won in joint warfare shall be equally distributed." The stipulated equality of rights in trade and exchange, in commercial credit and in inheritance, tended, by the manifold relations of business intercourse to which it led, still further to interweave the interests of communities already connected by the ties of similar language and manners, and in this way produced an effect somewhat similar to that of the abolition of customs-restrictions in our own day. Each community certainly retained in form its own law: down to the time of the Social war Latin law was not necessarily identical with Roman: we find, for example, that the enforcing of betrothal by action at law, which was abolished at an early period in Rome, continued to subsist in the Latin communities. But the simple and purely national development of Latin law, and the endeavour to maintain as far as possible uniformity of rights, led at length to the result, that the law of private relations was in matter and form substantially the same throughout all Latium. This uniformity of rights comes most distinctly into view in the rules laid down regarding the loss and recovery of freedom on the part of the individual burgess. According to an ancient and venerable maxim of law among the Latin stock no burgess could become a slave in the state wherein he had been free, or suffer the loss of his burgess-rights while he remained within it: if he was to be punished with the loss of freedom and of burgess-rights (which was the same thing), it was necessary that he should be expelled from the state and should enter on the condition of slavery among strangers. This maxim of law was now extended to the whole territory of the league; no member of any of the federal states might live as a slave within the bounds of the league. Applications of this principle are seen in the enactment embodied in the Twelve Tables, that the insolvent debtor, in the event of his creditor wishing to sell him, must be sold beyond the boundary of the Tiber, in other words, beyond the territory of the league; and in the clause of the second treaty between Rome and Carthage, that an ally of Rome who might be taken prisoner by the Carthaginians should be free so soon as he entered a Roman seaport. Although there did not probably subsist a general intercommunion of marriage within the league, yet, as has been already remarked(8) intermarriage between the different communities frequently occurred. Each Latin could primarily exercise political rights only where he was enrolled as a burgess; but on the other hand it was implied in an equality of private rights, that any Latin could take up his abode in any place within the Latin bounds; or, to use the phraseology of the present day, there existed, side by side with the special burgess-rights of the individual communities, a general right of settlement co-extensive with the confederacy; and, after the plebeian was acknowledged in Rome as a burgess, this right became converted as regards Rome into full freedom of settlement. It is easy to understand how this should have turned materially to the advantage of the capital, which alone in Latium offered the means of urban intercourse, urban acquisition, and urban enjoyments; and how the number of —metoeci— in Rome should have increased with remarkable rapidity, after the Latin land came to live in perpetual peace with Rome.

In constitution and administration the several communities not only remained independent and sovereign, so far as the federal obligations did not interfere, but, what was of more importance, the league of the thirty communities as such retained its autonomy in contradistinction to Rome. When we are assured that the position of Alba towards the federal communities was a position superior to that of Rome, and that on the fall of Alba these communities attained autonomy, this may well have been the case, in so far as Alba was essentially a member of the league, while Rome from the first had rather the position of a separate state confronting the league than of a member included in it; but, just as the states of the confederation of the Rhine were formally sovereign, while those of the German empire had a master, the presidency of Alba may have been in reality an honorary right(9) like that of the German emperors, and the protectorate of Rome from the first a supremacy like that of Napoleon. In fact Alba appears to have exercised the right of presiding in the federal council, while Rome allowed the Latin deputies to hold their consultations by themselves under the guidance, as it appears, of a president selected from their own number, and contented herself with the honorary presidency at the federal festival where sacrifice was offered for Rome and Latium, and with the erection of a second federal sanctuary in Rome—the temple of Diana on the Aventine—so that thenceforth sacrifice was offered both on Roman soil for Rome and Latium, and on Latin soil for Latium and Rome. With equal deference to the interests of the league the Romans in the treaty with Latium bound themselves not to enter into a separate alliance with any Latin community—a stipulation which very clearly reveals the apprehensions entertained, doubtless not without reason, by the confederacy with reference to the powerful community taking the lead. The position of Rome not within, but alongside of Latium, is most clearly apparent in the arrangements for warfare. The fighting force of the league was composed, as the later mode of making the levy incontrovertibly shows, of two masses of equal strength, a Roman and a Latin. The supreme command lay once for all with the Roman generals; year by year the Latin contingent had to appear before the gates of Rome, and there saluted the elected commander by acclamation as its general, after the Romans commissioned by the Latin federal council to take the auspices had thereby assured themselves of the contentment of the gods with the choice that had been made. Whatever land or property was acquired in the wars of the league was apportioned among its members according to the judgment of the Romans. That the Romano-Latin federation was represented as regards its external relations solely by Rome, cannot with certainty be maintained. The federal agreement did not prohibit either Rome or Latium from undertaking an aggressive war on their own behoof; and if a war was waged by the league, whether pursuant to a resolution of its own or in consequence of a hostile attack, the Latin federal council may have been legally entitled to take part in the conduct as well as in the termination of the war. Practically indeed Rome must have possessed the hegemony even then, for, wherever a single state and a federation enter into a permanent connection with each other, the preponderance usually falls to the side of the former.

Extension of the Roman Territory after the Fall of Alba—-Hernici—Rutulli and Volscii

The steps by which after the fall of Alba Rome—now mistress of a territory comparatively considerable, and presumably the leading power in the Latin confederacy—extended still further her direct and indirect dominion, can no longer be traced. There was no lack of feuds with the Etruscans and with the Veientes in particular, chiefly respecting the possession of Fidenae; but it does not appear that the Romans were successful in acquiring permanent mastery over that Etruscan outpost, which was situated on the Latin bank of the river not much more than five miles from Rome, or in dislodging the Veientes from that formidable basis of offensive operations. On the other hand they maintained apparently undisputed possession of the Janiculum and of both banks of the mouth of the Tiber. As regards the Sabines and Aequi Rome appears in a more advantageous position; the connection which afterwards became so intimate with the more distant Hernici must have had at least its beginning under the monarchy, and the united Latins and Hernici enclosed on two sides and held in check their eastern neighbours. But on the south frontier the territory of the Rutuli and still more that of the Volsci were scenes of perpetual war. The earliest extension of the Latin land took place in this direction, and it is here that we first encounter those communities founded by Rome and Latium on the enemy's soil and constituted as autonomous members of the Latin confederacy—the Latin colonies, as they were called—the oldest of which appear to reach back to the regal period. How far, however, the territory reduced under the power of the Romans extended at the close of the monarchy, can by no means be determined. Of feuds with the neighbouring Latin and Volscian communities the Roman annals of the regal period recount more than enough; but only a few detached notices, such as that perhaps of the capture of Suessa in the Pomptine plain, can be held to contain a nucleus of historical fact. That the regal period laid not only the political foundations of Rome, but the foundations also of her external power, cannot be doubted; the position of the city of Rome as contradistinguished from, rather than forming part of, the league of Latin states is already decidedly marked at the beginning of the republic, and enables us to perceive that an energetic development of external power must have taken place in Rome during the time of the kings. Certainly great deeds, uncommon achievements have in this case passed into oblivion; but the splendour of them lingers over the regal period of Rome, especially over the royal house of the Tarquins, like a distant evening twilight in which outlines disappear.

Enlargement of the City of Rome—Servian Wall

While the Latin stock was thus tending towards union under the leadership of Rome and was at the same time extending its territory on the east and south, Rome itself, by the favour of fortune and the energy of its citizens, had been converted from a stirring commercial and rural town into the powerful capital of a flourishing country. The remodelling of the Roman military system and the political reform of which it contained the germ, known to us by the name of the Servian constitution, stand in intimate connection with this internal change in the character of the Roman community. But externally also the character of the city cannot but have changed with the influx of ampler resources, with the rising requirements of its position, and with the extension of its political horizon. The amalgamation of the adjoining community on the Quirinal with that on the Palatine must have been already accomplished when the Servian reform, as it is called, took place; and after this reform had united and consolidated the military strength of the community, the burgesses could no longer rest content with entrenching the several hills, as one after another they were filled with buildings, and with possibly also keeping the island in the Tiber and the height on the opposite bank occupied so that they might command the course of the river. The capital of Latium required another and more complete system of defence; they proceeded to construct the Servian wall. The new continuous city-wall began at the river below the Aventine, and included that hill, on which there have been brought to light recently (1855) at two different places, the one on the western slope towards the river, the other on the opposite eastern slope, colossal remains of those primitive fortifications—portions of wall as high as the walls of Alatri and Ferentino, built of large square hewn blocks of tufo in courses of unequal height—emerging as it were from the tomb to testify to the might of an epoch, whose buildings subsist imperishably in these walls of rock, and whose intellectual achievements will continue to exercise an influence more lasting even than these. The ring-wall further embraced the Caelian and the whole space of the Esquiline, Viminal, and Quirinal, where a structure likewise but recently brought to light on a great scale (1862)—on the outside composed of blocks of peperino and protected by a moat in front, on the inside forming a huge earthen rampart sloped towards the city and imposing even at the present day—supplied the want of natural means of defence. From thence it ran to the Capitoline, the steep declivity of which towards the Campus Martius served as part of the city-wall, and it again abutted on the river above the island in the Tiber. The Tiber island with the bridge of piles and the Janiculum did not belong strictly to the city, but the latter height was probably a fortified outwork. Hitherto the Palatine had been the stronghold, but now this hill was left open to be built upon by the growing city; and on the other hand upon the Tarpeian Hill, standing free on every side, and from its moderate extent easily defensible, there was constructed the new "stronghold" (-arx-, -capitolium-(10)), containing the stronghold-spring, the carefully enclosed "well-house" (-tullianum-), the treasury (-aerarium-), the prison, and the most ancient place of assemblage for the burgesses (-area Capitolina-), where still in after times the regular announcements of the changes of the moon continued to be made. Private dwellings of a permanent kind, on the other hand, were not tolerated in earlier times on the stronghold-hill;(11) and the space between the two summits of the hill, the sanctuary of the evil god (-Ve-diovis-), or as it was termed in the later Hellenizing epoch, the

Asylum, was covered with wood and presumably intended for the reception of the husbandmen and their herds, when inundation or war drove them from the plain. The Capitol was in reality as well as in name the Acropolis of Rome, an independent castle capable of being defended even after the city had fallen: its gate lay probably towards what was afterwards the Forum.(12) The Aventine seems to have been fortified in a similar style, although less strongly, and to have been preserved free from permanent occupation. With this is connected the fact, that for purposes strictly urban, such as the distribution of the introduced water, the inhabitants of Rome were divided into the inhabitants of the city proper (-montani-), and those of the districts situated within the general ring-wall, but yet not reckoned as strictly belonging to the city (-pagani Aventinensis-, -Ianiculenses-, -collegia Capitolinorum et Mercurialium-).(13) The space enclosed by the new city wall thus embraced, in addition to the former Palatine and Quirinal cities, the two federal strongholds of the Capitol and the Aventine, and also the Janiculum;(14) the Palatine, as the oldest and proper city, was enclosed by the other heights along which the wall was carried, as if encircled with a wreath, and the two castles occupied the middle.

The work, however, was not complete so long as the ground, protected by so laborious exertions from outward foes, was not also reclaimed from the dominion of the water, which permanently occupied the valley between the Palatine and the Capitol, so that there was perhaps even a ferry there, and which converted the valleys between the Capitol and the Velia and between the Palatine and the Aventine into marshes. The subterranean drains still existing at the present day, composed of magnificent square blocks, which excited the astonishment of posterity as a marvellous work of regal Rome, must rather be reckoned to belong to the following epoch, for travertine is the material employed and we have many accounts of new structures of the kind in the times of the republic; but the scheme itself belongs beyond doubt to the regal period, although presumably to a later epoch than the designing of the Servian wall and the Capitoline stronghold. The spots thus drained or dried supplied large open spaces such as were needed by the new enlarged city. The assembling-place of the community, which had hitherto been the Area Capitolina at the stronghold itself, was now transferred to the flat space, where the ground fell from the stronghold towards the city (-comitium-), and which stretched thence between the Palatine and the Carinae, in the direction of the Velia. At that side of the -comitium- which adjoined the stronghold, and upon the stronghold-wall which arose above the -comitium- in the fashion of a balcony, the members of the senate and the guests of the city had the place of honour assigned to them on occasion of festivals and assemblies of the people; and at the place of assembly itself was erected the senate-house, which afterwards bore the name of the Curia Hostilia. The platform for the judgment-seat (-tribunal-), and the stage whence the burgesses were addressed (the later rostra), were likewise erected on the -comitium- itself. Its prolongation in the direction of the Velia became the new market (-forum Romanum-). At the end of the latter, beneath the Palatine, rose the community-house, which included the official dwelling of the king (-regia-) and the common hearth of the city, the rotunda forming the temple of Vesta; at no great distance, on the south side of the Forum, there was erected a second round building connected with the former, the store-room of the community or temple of the Penates, which still stands at the present day as the porch of the church Santi Cosma e Damiano. It is a feature significant of the new city now united in a way very different from the settlement of the "seven mounts," that, over and above the hearths of the thirty curies which the Palatine Rome had been content with associating in one building, the Servian Rome presented this general and single hearth for the city at large.(15) Along the two longer sides of the Forum butchers' shops and other traders' stalls were arranged. In the valley between the Palatine and Aventine a "ring" was staked off for races; this became the Circus. The cattle-market was laid out immediately adjoining the river, and this soon became one of the most densely peopled quarters of Rome. Temples and sanctuaries arose on all the summits, above all the federal sanctuary of Diana on the Aventine,(16) and on the summit of the stronghold the far-seen temple of Father Diovis, who had given to his people all this glory, and who now, when the Romans were triumphing over the surrounding nations, triumphed along with them over the subject gods of the vanquished.

The names of the men, at whose bidding these great buildings of the city arose, are almost as completely lost in oblivion as those of the leaders in the earliest battles and victories of Rome. Tradition indeed assigns the different works to different kings—-the senate-house to Tullus Hostilius, the Janiculum and the wooden bridge to Ancus Marcius, the great Cloaca, the Circus, and the temple of Jupiter to the elder Tarquinius, the temple of Diana and the ring-wall to Servius Tullius. Some of these statements may perhaps be correct; and it is apparently not the result of accident that the building of the new ring-wall is associated both as to date and author with the new organization of the army, which in fact bore special reference to the regular defence of the city walls. But upon the whole we must be content to learn from this tradition—what is indeed evident of itself—that this second creation of Rome stood in intimate connection with the commencement of her hegemony over Latium and with the remodelling of her burgess-army, and that, while it originated in one and the same great conception, its execution was not the work either of a single man or of a single generation. It is impossible to doubt that Hellenic influences exercised a powerful effect on this remodelling of the Roman community, but it is equally impossible to demonstrate the mode or the degree of their operation. It has already been observed that the Servian military constitution is essentially of an Hellenic type;(17) and it will be afterwards shown that the games of the Circus were organized on an Hellenic model. The new -regia-with the city hearth was quite a Greek —prytaneion—, and the round temple of Vesta, looking towards the east and not so much as consecrated by the augurs, was constructed in no respect according to Italian, but wholly in accordance with Hellenic, ritual. With these facts before us, the statement of tradition appears not at all incredible that the Ionian confederacy in Asia Minor to some extent served as a model for the Romano-Latin league, and that the new federal sanctuary on the Aventine was for that reason constructed in imitation of the Artemision at Ephesus.

Notes for Book I Chapter VII

1. I. IV. Earliest Limits of the Roman Territory

2. The formulae of accursing for Gabii and Fidenae are quite as characteristic (Macrob. Sat. iii. 9). It cannot, however, be proved and is extremely improbable that, as respects these towns, there was an actual historical accursing of the ground on which they were built, such as really took place at Veii, Carthage, and Fregellae. It may be conjectured that old accursing formularies were applied to those two hated towns, and were considered by later antiquaries as historical documents.

3. But there seems to be no good ground for the doubt recently expressed in a quarter deserving of respect as to the destruction of Alba having really been the act of Rome. It is true, indeed, that the account of the destruction of Alba is in its details a series of improbabilities and impossibilities; but that is true of every historical fact inwoven into legend. To the question as to the attitude of the rest of Latium towards the struggle between Rome and Alba, we are unable to give an answer; but the question itself rests on a false assumption, for it is not proved that the constitution of the Latin league absolutely prohibited a separate war between two Latin communities (I. III. The Latin League). Still less is the fact that a number of Alban families were received into the burgess-union of Rome inconsistent with the destruction of Alba by the Romans. Why may there not have been a Roman party in Alba just as there was in Capua? The circumstance, however, of Rome claiming to be in a religious and political point of view the heir-at-law of Alba may be regarded as decisive of the matter; for such a claim could not be based on the migration of individual clans to Rome, but could only be based, as it actually was, on the conquest of the town.

4. I. VI. Amalgamation of the Palatine and Quirinal Cities

5. Hence was developed the conception, in political law, of the maritime colony or colony of burgesses (-colonia civium Romanorum-), that is, of a community separate in fact, but not independent or possessing a will of its own in law; a community which merged in the capital as the -peculium- of the son merged in the property of the father, and which as a standing garrison was exempt from serving in the legion.

6. To this the enactment of the Twelve Tables undoubtedly has reference: -Nex[i mancipiique] forti sanatique idem ius esto-, that is, in dealings of private law the "sound" and the "recovered" shall be on a footing of equality. The Latin allies cannot be here referred to, because their legal position was defined by federal treaties, and the law of the Twelve Tables treated only of the law of Rome. The -sanates- were the -Latini prisci cives Romani-, or in other words, the communities of Latium compelled by the Romans to enter the plebeiate.

7. The community of Bovillae appears even to have been formed out of part of the Alban domain, and to have been admitted in room of Alba among the autonomous

Latin towns. Its Alban origin is attested by its having been the seat of worship for the Julian gens and by the name -Albani Longani Bovillenses- (Orelli-Henzen, 119, 2252, 6019); its autonomy by Dionysius, v. 61, and Cicero, pro Plancio, 9, 23.

8. I. III. The Latin League

9. I. III. The Latin League

10. Both names, although afterwards employed as local names (-capitolium- being applied to the summit of the stronghold-hill that lay next to the river, -arx- to that next to the Quirinal), were originally appellatives, corresponding exactly to the Greek —akra— and —koruphei— every Latin town had its -capitolium-as well as Rome. The local name of the Roman stronghold-hill was -mons Tarpeius-.

11. The enactment -ne quis patricius in arce aut capitolio habitaret-probably prohibited only the conversion of the ground into private property, not the construction of dwelling-houses. Comp. Becker, Top. p. 386.

12. For the chief thoroughfare, the -Via Sacra-, led from that quarter to the stronghold; and the bending in towards the gate may still be clearly recognized in the turn which this makes to the left at the arch of Severus. The gate itself must have disappeared under the huge structures which were raised in after ages on the Clivus. The so-called gate at the steepest part of the Capitoline Mount, which is known by the name of Janualis or Saturnia, or the "open," and which had to stand always open in times of war, evidently had merely a religious significance, and never was a real gate.

13. Four such guilds are mentioned (1) the -Capitolini- (Cicero, ad Q. fr. ii. 5, 2), with -magistri- of their own (Henzen, 6010, 6011), and annual games (Liv. v. 50; comp. Corp. Inscr. Lat. i. n. 805); (2) the -Mercuriales- (Liv. ii. 27; Cicero, l. c.; Preller, Myth. p. 597) likewise with -magistri- (Henzen, 6010), the guild from the valley of the Circus, where the temple of Mercury stood; (3) the -pagani Aventinenses- likewise with -magistri- (Henzen, 6010); and (4) the -pagani pagi Ianiculensis- likewise with -magistri-(C. I. L. i. n. 801, 802). It is certainly not accidental that these four guilds, the only ones of the sort that occur in Rome, belong to the very two hills excluded from the four local tribes but enclosed by the Servian wall, the Capitol and the Aventine, and the Janiculum belonging to the same fortification; and connected with this is the further fact that the expression -montani paganive-is employed as a designation of the whole inhabitants in connection with the city (comp. besides the well-known passage, Cic. de Domo, 28, 74, especially the law as to the city aqueducts in Festus, v. sifus, p. 340; [-mon]tani paganive si[fis aquam dividunto-]). The -montani-, properly the inhabitants of the three regions of the Palatine town (iv. The Hill-Romans On the Quirinal), appear to be here put -a potiori- for the whole population of the four regions of the city proper. The -pagani-are, undoubtedly, the residents of the Aventine and Janiculum not included in the tribes, and the analogous -collegia- of the Capitol and the Circus valley.

14. The "Seven-hill-city" in the proper and religious sense was and continued to be the narrower Old-Rome of the Palatine (iv. The Palatine City). Certainly the Servian Rome also regarded itself, at least as early as the time of Cicero (comp. e. g. Cic. ad Att. vi. 5, 2; Plutarch, Q. Rom. 69), as "Seven-hill-city," probably because the festival of the Septimontium, which was celebrated with great zeal even under the Empire, began to be regarded as a festival for the city generally; but there was hardly any definite agreement reached as to which of the heights embraced by the Servian ring-wall belonged to the "seven." The enumeration of the Seven Mounts familiar to us, *viz.* Palatine, Aventine, Caelian, Esquiline, Viminal, Quirinal, Capitoline, is not given by any ancient author. It is put together from the traditional narrative of the gradual rise of the city (Jordan, Topographie, ii. 206 seq.), and the Janiculum is passed over in it, simply because otherwise the number would come out as eight. The earliest authority that enumerates the Seven Mounts (-montes-) of Rome is the description of the city from the age of Constantine the Great. It names as such the Palatine, Aventine, Caelian, Esquiline, Tarpeian, Vatican, and Janiculum,—where the Quirinal and Viminal are, evidently as -colles-, omitted, and in their stead two "-montes-" are introduced from the right bank of the Tiber, including even the Vatican which lay outside of the Servian wall. Other still later lists are given by Servius (ad Aen. vi. 783), the Berne Scholia to Virgil's Georgics (ii. 535), and Lydus (de Mens. p. 118, Bekker).

15. Both the situation of the two temples, and the express testimony of Dionysius, ii. 65, that the temple of Vesta lay outside of the Roma quadrata, prove that these structures were connected with the foundation not of the Palatine, but of the second (Servian) city. Posterity reckoned this -regia- with the temple of Vesta as a scheme of Numa; but the cause which gave rise to that hypothesis is too manifest to allow of our attaching any weight to it.

16. I. VII. Relation of Rome to Latium

17. I. VI. Time and Occasion of the Reform

CHAPTER VIII

The Umbro-Sabellian Stocks—Beginnings of the Samnites

Umbro-Sabellian Migration

The migration of the Umbrian stocks appears to have begun at a period later than that of the Latins. Like the Latin, it moved in a southerly direction, but it kept more in the centre of the peninsula and towards the east coast. It is painful to speak of it; for our information regarding it comes to us like the sound of bells from a town that has been sunk in the sea. The Umbrian people extended according to Herodotus as far as the Alps, and it is not improbable that in very ancient times they occupied the whole of Northern Italy, to the point where the settlements of the Illyrian stocks began on the east, and those of the Ligurians on the west. As to the latter, there are traditions of their conflicts with the Umbrians, and we may perhaps draw an inference regarding their extension in very early times towards the south from isolated names, such as that of the island of Ilva (Elba) compared with the Ligurian Ilvates. To this period of Umbrian greatness the evidently Italian names of the most ancient settlements in the valley of the Po, Atria (black-town), and Spina (thorn-town), probably owe their origin, as well as the numerous traces of Umbrians in southern Etruria (such as the river Umbro, Camars the old name of Clusium, Castrum Amerinum). Such indications of an Italian population having preceded the Etruscan especially occur in the most southern portion of Etruria, the district between the Ciminian Forest (below Viterbo) and the Tiber. In Falerii, the town of Etruria nearest to the frontier of Umbria and the Sabine country, according to the testimony of Strabo a language was spoken different from the Etruscan, and inscriptions bearing out that statement have recently been brought to light there, the alphabet and language of which, while presenting points of contact with the Etruscan, exhibit a general resemblance to the Latin.(1) The local worship also presents traces of a Sabellian character; and a similar inference is suggested by the primitive relations subsisting in sacred as well as other matters between Caere and Rome. It is probable that the Etruscans wrested those southern districts from the Umbrians at a period considerably subsequent to their occupation of the country on the north of the Ciminian Forest, and that an Umbrian population maintained itself there even after the Tuscan conquest. In this fact we may presumably find the ultimate explanation of the surprising rapidity with which the southern portion of Etruria became Latinized, as compared with the tenacious retention of the Etruscan language and manners in northern Etruria, after the Roman conquest. That the Umbrians were after obstinate struggles driven back from the north and west into the narrow mountainous country between the two arms of the Apennines which they subsequently held, is clearly indicated by the very fact of their geographical position, just as the position of the inhabitants of the Grisons and that of the Basques at the present day indicates the similar fate that has befallen them. Tradition also has to report that the Tuscans wrested from the Umbrians three hundred towns; and, what is of more importance as evidence, in the national prayers of the Umbrian Iguvini, which we still possess, along with other stocks the Tuscans especially are cursed as public foes.

In consequence, as may be presumed, of this pressure exerted upon them from the north, the Umbrians advanced towards the south, keeping in general upon the heights, because they found the plains already occupied by Latin stocks, but beyond doubt frequently making inroads and encroachments on the territory of the kindred race, and intermingling with them the more readily, that the distinction in language and habits could not have been at all so marked then as we find it afterwards. To the class of such inroads belongs the tradition of the irruption of the Reatini and Sabines into Latium and their conflicts with the Romans; similar phenomena were probably repeated all along the west coast. Upon the whole the Sabines maintained their footing in the mountains, as in the district bordering on Latium which has since been called by their name, and so too in the Volscian land, presumably because the Latin population did not extend thither or was there less dense; while on the other hand the well-peopled plains were better able to offer resistance to the invaders, although they were not in all cases able or desirous to prevent isolated bands from gaining a footing, such as the Tities and afterwards the Claudii in Rome.(2) In this way the stocks here became variously mingled, a state of things which serves to explain the numerous relations that subsisted between the Volscians and Latins, and how it happened that their district, as well as Sabina, afterwards became so early and speedily Latinized.

Samnites

The chief branch, however, of the Umbrian stock threw itself eastward from Sabina into the mountains of the Abruzzi, and the adjacent hill-country to the south of them. Here, as on the west coast, they occupied the mountainous districts, whose thinly scattered population gave way before the immigrants or submitted to their yoke; while in the plain along the Apulian coast the ancient native population, the Iapygians, upon the whole maintained their ground, although involved in constant feuds, especially on the northern frontier about Luceria and Arpi. When these migrations took place, cannot of course be determined; but it was presumably about the time when kings ruled in Rome. Tradition reports that the Sabines, pressed by the Umbrians, vowed a -ver sacrum-, that is, swore that they would give up and send beyond their bounds the sons and daughters born in the year of war, so soon as these should reach maturity, that the gods might at their pleasure destroy them or bestow upon them new abodes in other lands. One band was led by the ox of Mars; these were the Safini or Samnites, who in the first instance established themselves on the mountains adjoining the river Sagrus, and at a later period proceeded to occupy the beautiful plain on the east of the Matese chain, near the sources of the Tifernus. Both in their old and in their new territory they named their place of public assembly—which in the one case was situated near Agnone, in the other near Bojano—from the ox which led them Bovianum. A second band was led by the woodpecker of Mars; these were the Picentes, "the woodpecker-people," who took possession of what is now the March of Ancona. A third band was led by the wolf (-hirpus-) into the region of Beneventum; these were the Hirpini. In a similar manner the other small tribes branched off from the common stock—the Praetuttii near Teramo; the Vestini on the Gran Sasso; the Marrucini near Chieti; the Frentani on the frontier of Apulia; the Paeligni on the Majella mountains; and lastly the Marsi on the Fucine lake, coming in contact with the Volscians and Latins. All of these tribes retained, as these legends clearly show, a vivid sense of their relationship and of their having come forth from the Sabine land. While the Umbrians succumbed in the unequal struggle and the western offshoots of the same stock became amalgamated with the Latin or Hellenic population, the Sabellian tribes prospered in the seclusion of their distant mountain land, equally remote from collision with the Etruscans, the Latins, and the Greeks. There was little or no development of an urban life amongst them; their geographical position almost wholly precluded them from engaging in commercial intercourse, and the mountain-tops and strongholds sufficed for the necessities of defence, while the husbandmen continued to dwell in open hamlets or wherever each found the well-spring and the forest or pasture that he desired. In such circumstances their constitution remained stationary; like the similarly situated Arcadians in Greece, their communities never became incorporated into a single state; at the utmost they only formed confederacies more or less loosely connected. In the Abruzzi especially, the strict seclusion of the mountain valleys seems to have debarred the several cantons from intercourse either with each other or with the outer world. They maintained but little connection with each other and continued to live in complete isolation from the rest of Italy; and in consequence, notwithstanding the bravery of their inhabitants, they exercised less influence than any other portion of the Italian nation on the development of the history of the peninsula.

Their Political Development

On the other hand the Samnite people decidedly exhibited the highest political development among the eastern Italian stock, as the Latin nation did among the western. From an early period, perhaps from its first immigration, a comparatively strong political bond held together the Samnite nation, and gave to it the strength which subsequently enabled it to contend with Rome on equal terms for the first place in Italy. We are as ignorant of the time and manner of the formation of the bond, as we are of its federal constitution; but it is clear that in Samnium no single community was preponderant, and still less was there any town to serve as a central rallying point and bond of union for the Samnite stock, such as Rome was for the Latins. The strength of the land lay in its -communes-of husbandmen, and authority was vested in the assembly formed of their representatives; it was this assembly which in case of need nominated a federal commander-in-chief. In consequence of its constitution the policy of this confederacy was not aggressive like the Roman, but was limited to the defence of its own bounds; only where the state forms a unity is power so concentrated and passion so strong, that the extension of territory can be systematically pursued. Accordingly the whole history of the two nations is prefigured in their diametrically opposite systems of colonization. Whatever the Romans gained, was a gain to the state: the conquests of the Samnites were achieved by bands of volunteers who went forth in search of plunder and, whether they prospered or were unfortunate, were left to their own resources by their native home. The conquests, however, which the Samnites made on the coasts of the Tyrrhenian and Ionic seas, belong to a later age; during the regal period in Rome they seem to have been only gaining possession of the settlements in which we afterwards find them. As a single incident in the series of movements among the neighbouring peoples caused by this Samnite settlement may be mentioned the surprise of Cumae by Tyrrhenians from the Upper Sea, Umbrians, and Daunians in the year 230. If we may give credit to the accounts of the matter which present certainly a considerable colouring of romance, it would appear that in this instance, as was often the case in such expeditions, the intruders and those whom they supplanted combined to form one army, the Etruscans joining with their Umbrian enemies, and these again joined by the Iapygians whom the Umbrian settlers had driven towards the south. Nevertheless the undertaking proved a failure: on this occasion at least the Hellenic superiority in the art of war, and the bravery of the tyrant Aristodemus, succeeded in repelling the barbarian assault on the beautiful seaport.

Notes for Book I Chapter VIII

1. In the alphabet the -"id:r" especially deserves notice, being of the Latin (-"id:R")
and not of the Etruscan form (-"id:D"), and also the -"id:z" (—"id:XI"); it can only
be derived from the primitive Latin, and must very faithfully represent it. The
language likewise has close affinity with the oldest Latin; -Marci Acarcelini he cupa-
, that is, -Marcius Acarcelinius heic cubat-: -Menerva A. Cotena La. f...zenatuo
sentem..dedet cuando..cuncaptum-, that is, -Minervae A(ulus?) Cotena La(rtis)
f(ilius) de senatus sententia dedit quando (perhaps=olim) conceptum-. At the same
time with these and similar inscriptions there have been found some others in a
different character and language, undoubtedly Etruscan.

2. I. IV. Tities, Luceres

CHAPTER IX

The Etruscans

Etruscan Nationality

The Etruscan people, or Ras,(1) as they called themselves, present a most striking contrast to the Latin and Sabellian Italians as well as to the Greeks. They were distinguished from these nations by their very bodily structure: instead of the slender and symmetrical proportions of the Greeks and Italians, the sculptures of the Etruscans exhibit only short sturdy figures with large head and thick arms. Their manners and customs also, so far as we are acquainted with them, point to a deep and original diversity from the Graeco-Italian stocks. The religion of the Tuscans in particular, presenting a gloomy fantastic character and delighting in the mystical handling of numbers and in wild and horrible speculations and practices, is equally remote from the clear rationalism of the Romans and the genial image-worship of the Hellenes. The conclusion which these facts suggest is confirmed by the most important and authoritative evidence of nationality, the evidence of language. The remains of the Etruscan tongue which have reached us, numerous as they are and presenting as they do various data to aid in deciphering it, occupy a position of isolation so complete, that not only has no one hitherto succeeded in interpreting these remains, but no one has been able even to determine precisely the place of Etruscan in the classification of languages. Two periods in the development of the language may be clearly distinguished. In the older period the vocalization of the language was completely carried out, and the collision of two consonants was almost without exception avoided.(2) By throwing off the vocal and consonantal terminations, and by the weakening or rejection of the vowels, this soft and melodious language was gradually changed in character, and became intolerably harsh and rugged.(3) They changed for example -ramu*af-into -ram*a-, Tarquinius into -Tarchnaf-, Minerva into -Menrva-, Menelaos, Polydeukes, Alexandros, into -Menle-, -Pultuke-, -Elchsentre-. The indistinct and rugged nature of their pronunciation is shown most clearly by the fact that at a very early period the Etruscans made no distinction of -o from -u, -b from -p, -c from -g, -d from -t. At the same time the accent was, as in Latin and in the more rugged Greek dialects, uniformly thrown back upon the initial syllable. The aspirate consonants were treated in a similar fashion; while the Italians rejected them with the exception of the aspirated -b or the -f, and the Greeks, reversing the case, rejected this sound and retained the others —theta, —phi, —chi, the Etruscans allowed the softest and most pleasing of them, the —phi, to drop entirely except in words borrowed from other languages, but made use of the other three to an extraordinary extent, even where they had no proper place; Thetis for example became -Thethis-, Telephus -Thelaphe-, Odysseus -Utuze- or -Uthuze-. Of the few terminations and words, whose meaning has been ascertained, the greater part are far remote from all Graeco-Italian analogies; such as, all the numerals; the termination -al employed as a designation of descent, frequently of descent from the mother, e. g. -Cania-, which on a bilingual inscription of Chiusi is translated by -Cainnia natus-; and the termination -sa in the names of women, used to indicate the clan into which they have married, e. g. -Lecnesa-denoting the spouse of a -Licinius-. So -cela- or -clan- with the inflection -clensi- means son; -se(—chi)- daughter; -ril- year; the god Hermes becomes -Turms-, Aphrodite -Turan-, Hephaestos -Sethlans-, Bakchos -Fufluns-. Alongside of these strange forms and sounds there certainly occur isolated analogies between the Etruscan and the Italian languages. Proper names are formed, substantially, after the general Italian system. The frequent gentile termination -enas or -ena(4) recurs in the termination -enus which is likewise of frequent occurrence in Italian, especially in Sabellian clan-names; thus the Etruscan names -Maecenas- and -Spurinna-correspond closely to the Roman -Maecius-and -Spurius-. A number of names of divinities, which occur as Etruscan on Etruscan monuments or in authors, have in their roots, and to some extent even in their terminations, a form so thoroughly Latin, that, if these names were really originally Etruscan, the two languages must have been closely related; such as -Usil- (sun and dawn, connected with -ausum-, -aurum-, -aurora-, -sol-), -Minerva-(-menervare-) -Lasa-(-lascivus-), -Neptunus-, -Voltumna-. As these analogies, however, may have had their origin only in the subsequent political and religious relations between the Etruscans and Latins, and in the accommodations and borrowings to which these relations gave rise, they do not invalidate the conclusion to which we are led by the other observed phenomena, that the Tuscan language differed at least as widely from all the Graeco-Italian dialects as did the language of the Celts or of the Slavonians. So at least it sounded to the Roman ear; "Tuscan and Gallic" were the languages of barbarians, "Oscan and Volscian" were but rustic dialects.

But, while the Etruscans differed thus widely from the Graeco-Italian family of languages, no one has yet succeeded in connecting them with any other known race. All sorts of dialects have been examined with a view to discover affinity with the Etruscan, sometimes by simple interrogation, sometimes by torture, but all without exception in vain. The geographical position of the Basque nation would naturally suggest it for comparison; but even in the Basque language no analogies of a decisive character have been brought forward. As little do the scanty remains of the Ligurian language which have reached our time, consisting of local and personal names, indicate any connection with the Tuscans. Even the extinct nation which has constructed those enigmatical sepulchral towers, called -Nuraghe-, by thousands in the islands of the Tuscan Sea, especially in Sardinia, cannot well be connected with the Etruscans, for not a single structure of the same character is to be met with in Etruscan territory. The utmost we can say is that several traces, that seem tolerably trustworthy, point to the conclusion that the Etruscans may be on the whole numbered with the Indo-Germans. Thus -mi- in the beginning of many of the older inscriptions is certainly —emi—, —eimi—, and the genitive form of consonantal stems veneruf -rafuvuf-is exactly reproduced in old Latin, corresponding to the old Sanscrit termination -as. In like manner the name of the Etruscan Zeus, -Tina-or -Tinia-, is probably connected with the Sanscrit -dina-, meaning day, as —Zan— is connected with the synonymous -diwan-. But, even granting this, the Etruscan people appears withal scarcely less isolated "The Etruscans," Dionysius said long ago, "are like no other nation in language and manners;" and we have nothing to add to his statement.

Home of the Etruscans

It is equally difficult to determine from what quarter the Etruscans migrated into Italy; nor is much lost through our inability to answer the question, for this migration belonged at any rate to the infancy of the people, and their historical development began and ended in Italy. No question, however, has been handled with greater zeal than this, in accordance with the principle which induces antiquaries especially to inquire into what is neither capable of being known nor worth the knowing—to inquire "who was Hecuba's mother," as the emperor Tiberius professed to do. As the oldest and most important Etruscan towns lay far inland—in fact we find not a single Etruscan town of any note immediately on the coast except Populonia, which we know for certain was not one of the old twelve cities— and the movement of the Etruscans in historical times was from north to south, it seems probable that they migrated into the peninsula by land. Indeed the low stage of civilization, in which we find them at first, would ill accord with the hypothesis of immigration by sea. Nations even in the earliest times crossed a strait as they would a stream; but to land on the west coast of Italy was a very different matter. We must therefore seek for the earlier home of the Etruscans to the west or north of Italy. It is not wholly improbable that the Etruscans may have come into Italy over the Raetian Alps; for the oldest traceable settlers in the Grisons and Tyrol, the Raeti, spoke Etruscan down to historical times, and their name sounds similar to that of the Ras. These may no doubt have been a remnant of the Etruscan settlements on the Po; but it is at least quite as likely that they may have been a portion of the people which remained behind in its earlier abode.

Story of Their Lydian Origin

In glaring contradiction to this simple and natural view stands the story that the Etruscans were Lydians who had emigrated from Asia. It is very ancient: it occurs even in Herodotus; and it reappears in later writers with innumerable changes and additions, although several intelligent inquirers, such as Dionysius, emphatically declared their disbelief in it, and pointed to the fact that there was not the slightest apparent similarity between the Lydians and Etruscans in religion, laws, manners, or language. It is possible that an isolated band of pirates from Asia Minor may have reached Etruria, and that their adventure may have given rise to such tales; but more probably the whole story rests on a mere verbal mistake. The Italian Etruscans or the -Turs-ennae- (for this appears to be the original form and the basis of the Greek —-Turs-einnoi—, —Turreinoi—, of the Umbrian -Turs-ci-, and of the two Roman forms -Tusci-, -Etrusci-) nearly coincide in name with the Lydian people of the —-Torreiboi— or perhaps also —Turr-einoi—, so named from the town —Turra—, This manifestly accidental resemblance in name seems to be in reality the only foundation for that hypothesis—not rendered more trustworthy by its great antiquity—and for all the pile of crude historical speculations that has been reared upon it. By connecting the ancient maritime commerce of the Etruscans with the piracy of the Lydians, and then by confounding (Thucydides is the first who has demonstrably done so) the Torrhebian pirates, whether rightly or wrongly, with the bucaneering Pelasgians who roamed and plundered on every sea, there has been produced one of the most mischievous complications of historical tradition. The term Tyrrhenians denotes sometimes the Lydian Torrhebi—as is the case in the earliest sources, such as the Homeric hymns; sometimes under the form Tyrrheno-Pelasgians or simply that of Tyrrhenians, the Pelasgian nation; sometimes, in fine, the Italian Etruscans, although the latter never came into lasting contact with the Pelasgians or Torrhebians, or were at all connected with them by common descent.

Settlements of the Etruscans in Italy

It is, on the other hand, a matter of historical interest to determine what were the oldest traceable abodes of the Etruscans, and what were their further movements when they issued thence. Various circumstances attest that before the great Celtic invasion they dwelt in the district to the north of the Po, being conterminous on the east along the Adige with the Veneti of Illyrian (Albanian?) descent, on the west with the Ligurians. This is proved in particular by the already-mentioned rugged Etruscan dialect, which was still spoken in the time of Livy by the inhabitants of the Raetian Alps, and by the fact that Mantua remained Tuscan down to a late period. To the south of the Po and at the mouths of that river Etruscans and Umbrians were mingled, the former as the dominant, the latter as the older race, which had founded the old commercial towns of Atria and Spina, while the Tuscans appear to have been the founders of Felsina (Bologna) and Ravenna. A long time elapsed ere the Celts crossed the Po; hence the Etruscans and Umbrians left deeper traces of their existence on the right bank of the river than they had done on the left, which they had to abandon at an early period. All the regions, however, to the north of the Apennines passed too rapidly out of the hands of one nation into those of another to permit the formation of any continuous national development there.

147

Etruria

Far more important in an historical point of view was the great settlement of the Tuscans in the land which still bears their name. Although Ligurians or Umbrians were probably at one time(5) settled there, the traces of them have been almost wholly effaced by the Etruscan occupation and civilization. In this region, which extends along the coast from Pisae to Tarquinii and is shut in on the east by the Apennines, the Etruscan nationality found its permanent abode and maintained itself with great tenacity down to the time of the empire. The northern boundary of the proper Tuscan territory was formed by the Arnus; the region north from the Arnus as far as the mouth of the Macra and the Apennines was a debateable border land in the possession sometimes of Ligurians, sometimes of Etruscans, and for this reason larger settlements were not successful there. The southern boundary was probably formed at first by the Ciminian Forest, a chain of hills south of Viterbo, and at a later period by the Tiber. We have already(6) noticed the fact that the territory between the Ciminian range and the Tiber with the towns of Sutrium, Nepete, Falerii, Veii, and Caere appears not to have been taken possession of by the Etruscans till a period considerably later than the more northern districts, possibly not earlier than in the second century of Rome, and that the original Italian population must have maintained its ground in this region, especially in Falerii, although in a relation of dependence.

Relations of the Etruscans to Latium

From the time at which the river Tiber became the line of demarcation between Etruria on the one side and Umbria and Latium on the other, peaceful relations probably upon the whole prevailed in that quarter, and no essential change seems to have taken place in the boundary line, at least so far as concerned the Latin frontier. Vividly as the Romans were impressed by the feeling that the Etruscan was a foreigner, while the Latin was their countryman, they yet seem to have stood in much less fear of attack or of danger from the right bank of the river than, for example, from their kinsmen in Gabii and Alba; and this was natural, for they were protected in that direction not merely by the broad stream which formed a natural boundary, but also by the circumstance, so momentous in its bearing on the mercantile and political development of Rome, that none of the more powerful Etruscan towns lay immediately on the river, as did Rome on the Latin bank. The Veientes were the nearest to the Tiber, and it was with them that Rome and Latium came most frequently into serious conflict, especially for the possession of Fidenae, which served the Veientes as a sort of -tete de pont- on the left bank just as the Janiculum served the Romans on the right, and which was sometimes in the hands of the Latins, sometimes in those of the Etruscans. The relations of Rome with the somewhat more distant Caere were on the whole far more peaceful and friendly than those which we usually find subsisting between neighbours in early times. There are doubtless vague legends, reaching back to times of distant antiquity, about conflicts between Latium and Caere; Mezentius the king of Caere, for instance, is asserted to have obtained great victories over the Latins, and to have imposed upon them a wine-tax; but evidence much more definite than that which attests a former state of feud is supplied by tradition as to an especially close connection between the two ancient centres of commercial and maritime intercourse in Latium and Etruria. Sure traces of any advance of the Etruscans beyond the Tiber, by land, are altogether wanting. It is true that Etruscans are named in the first ranks of the great barbarian host, which Aristodemus annihilated in 230 under the walls of Cumae;(7) but, even if we regard this account as deserving credit in all its details, it only shows that the Etruscans had taken part in a great plundering expedition. It is far more important to observe that south of the Tiber no Etruscan settlement can be pointed out as having owed its origin to founders who came by land; and that no indication whatever is discernible of any serious pressure by the Etruscans upon the Latin nation. The possession of the Janiculum and of both banks of the mouth of the Tiber remained, so far as we can see, undisputed in the hands of the Romans. As to the migrations of bodies of Etruscans to Rome, we find an isolated statement drawn from Tuscan annals, that a Tuscan band, led by Caelius Vivenna of Volsinii and after his death by his faithful companion Mastarna, was conducted by the latter to Rome. This may be trustworthy, although the derivation of the name of the Caelian Mount from this Caelius is evidently a philological invention, and even the addition that this Mastarna became king in Rome under the name of Servius Tullius is certainly nothing but an improbable conjecture of the archaeologists who busied themselves with legendary parallels. The name of the "Tuscan quarter" at the foot of the Palatine(8) points further to Etruscan settlements in Rome.

The Tarquins

It can hardly, moreover, be doubted that the last regal family which ruled over Rome, that of the Tarquins, was of Etruscan origin, whether it belonged to Tarquinii, as the legend asserts, or to Caere, where the family tomb of the Tarchnas has recently been discovered. The female name Tanaquil or Tanchvil interwoven with the legend, while it is not Latin, is common in Etruria. But the traditional story—according to which Tarquin was the son of a Greek who had migrated from Corinth to Tarquinii, and came to settle in Rome as a —metoikos— is neither history nor legend, and the historical chain of events is manifestly in this instance not confused merely, but completely torn asunder. If anything more can be deduced from this tradition beyond the bare and at bottom indifferent fact that at last a family of Tuscan descent swayed the regal sceptre in Rome, it can only be held as implying that this dominion of a man of Tuscan origin ought not to be viewed either as a dominion of the Tuscans or of any one Tuscan community over Rome, or conversely as the dominion of Rome over southern Etruria. There is, in fact, no sufficient ground either for the one hypothesis or for the other. The history of the Tarquins had its arena in Latium, not in Etruria; and Etruria, so far as we can see, during the whole regal period exercised no influence of any essential moment on either the language or customs of Rome, and did not at all interrupt the regular development of the Roman state or of the Latin league.

The cause of this comparatively passive attitude of Etruria towards the neighbouring land of Latium is probably to be sought partly in the struggles of the Etruscans with the Celts on the Po, which presumably the Celts did not cross until after the expulsion of the kings from Rome, and partly in the tendency of the Etruscan people towards seafaring and the acquisition of supremacy on the sea and seaboard—a tendency decidedly exhibited in their settlements in Campania, and of which we shall speak more fully in the next chapter.

150

The Etruscan Constitution

The Tuscan constitution, like the Greek and Latin, was based on the gradual transition of the community to an urban life. The early direction of the national energies towards navigation, trade, and manufactures appears to have called into existence urban commonwealths, in the strict sense of the term, earlier in Etruria than elsewhere in Italy. Caere is the first of all the Italian towns that is mentioned in Greek records. On the other hand we find that the Etruscans had on the whole less of the ability and the disposition for war than the Romans and Sabellians: the un-Italian custom of employing mercenaries for fighting occurs among the Etruscans at a very early period. The oldest constitution of the communities must in its general outlines have resembled that of Rome. Kings or Lucumones ruled, possessing similar insignia and probably therefore a similar plenitude of power with the Roman kings. A strict line of demarcation separated the nobles from the common people. The resemblance in the clan-organization is attested by the analogy of the system of names; only, among the Etruscans, descent on the mother's side received much more consideration than in Roman law. The constitution of their league appears to have been very lax. It did not embrace the whole nation; the northern and the Campanian Etruscans were associated in confederacies of their own, just in the same way as the communities of Etruria proper. Each of these leagues consisted of twelve communities, which recognized a metropolis, especially for purposes of worship, and a federal head or rather a high priest, but appear to have been substantially equal in respect of rights; while some of them at least were so powerful that neither could a hegemony establish itself, nor could the central authority attain consolidation. In Etruria proper Volsinii was the metropolis; of the rest of its twelve towns we know by trustworthy tradition only Perusia, Vetulonium, Volci, and Tarquinii. It was, however, quite as unusual for the Etruscans really to act in concert, as it was for the Latin confederacy to do otherwise. Wars were ordinarily carried on by a single community, which endeavoured to interest in its cause such of its neighbours as it could; and when an exceptional case occurred in which war was resolved on by the league, individual towns very frequently kept aloof from it. The Etruscan confederations appear to have been from the first—still more than the other Italian leagues formed on a similar basis of national affinity—deficient in a firm and paramount central authority.

Notes for Book I Chapter IX

1. -Ras-ennac-, with the gentile termination mentioned below.

2. To this period belong e. g. inscriptions on the clay vases of

umaramlisia(—"id:theta")ipurenaie(—"id:theta")eeraisieepanamine   (—-
"id:theta")unastavhelefu- or -mi ramu(—"id:theta")af kaiufinaia-.

3. We may form some idea of the sound which the language now had from the commencement of the great inscription of Perusia; -eulat tanna laresul ameva(—-"id:chi")r lautn vel(—"id:theta")inase stlaafunas slele(—"id:theta")caru-.

4. Such as Maecenas, Porsena, Vivenna, Caecina, Spurinna. The vowel in the penult is originally long, but in consequence of the throwing back of the accent upon the initial syllable is frequently shortened and even rejected. Thus we find Porse(n)na as well as Porsena, and Ceicne as well as Caecina.

5. I. VIII. Umbro-Sabellian Migration

6. I. VIII. Their Political Development

7. I. VIII. Their Political Development

8. I. IV. Oldest Settlements in the Palatine and Suburan Regions

CHAPTER X

The Hellenes in Italy—Maritime Supremacy of the Tuscans and Carthaginians

Relations of Italy with Other Lands

In the history of the nations of antiquity a gradual dawn ushered in the day; and in their case too the dawn was in the east. While the Italian peninsula still lay enveloped in the dim twilight of morning, the regions of the eastern basin of the Mediterranean had already emerged into the full light of a varied and richly developed civilization. It falls to the lot of most nations in the early stages of their development to be taught and trained by some rival sister-nation; and such was destined to be in an eminent degree the lot of the peoples of Italy. The circumstances of its geographical position, however, prevented this influence from being brought to bear upon the peninsula by land. No trace is to be found of any resort in early times to the difficult route by land between Italy and Greece. There were in all probability from time immemorial tracks for purposes of traffic, leading from Italy to the lands beyond the Alps; the oldest route of the amber trade from the Baltic joined the Mediterranean at the mouth of the Po—on which account the delta of the Po appears in Greek legend as the home of amber—and this route was joined by another leading across the peninsula over the Apennines to Pisae; but from these regions no elements of civilization could come to the Italians. It was the seafaring nations of the east that brought to Italy whatever foreign culture reached it in early times.

Phoenicians in Italy

The oldest civilized nation on the shores of the Mediterranean, the Egyptians, were not a seafaring people, and therefore exercised no influence on Italy. But the same may be with almost equal truth affirmed of the Phoenicians. It is true that, issuing from their narrow home on the extreme eastern verge of the Mediterranean, they were the first of all known races to venture forth in floating houses on the bosom of the deep, at first for the purpose of fishing and dredging, but soon also for the prosecution of trade. They were the first to open up maritime commerce; and at an incredibly early period they traversed the Mediterranean even to its furthest extremity in the west. Maritime stations of the Phoenicians appear on almost all its coasts earlier than those of the Hellenes: in Hellas itself, in Crete and Cyprus, in Egypt, Libya, and Spain, and likewise on the western Italian main. Thucydides tells us that all around Sicily, before the Greeks came thither or at least before they had established themselves there in any considerable numbers, the Phoenicians had set up their factories on the headlands and islets, not with a view to gain territory, but for the sake of trading with the natives. But it was otherwise in the case of continental Italy. No sure proof has hitherto been given of the existence of any Phoenician settlement there excepting one, a Punic factory at Caere, the memory of which has been preserved partly by the appellation -Punicum- given to a little village on the Caerite coast, partly by the other name of the town of Caere itself, -Agylla-, which is not, as idle fiction asserts, of Pelasgic origin, but is a Phoenician word signifying the "round town"—precisely the appearance which Caere presents when seen from the sea. That this station and any similar establishments which may have elsewhere existed on the coasts of Italy were neither of much importance nor of long standing, is evident from their having disappeared almost without leaving a trace. We have not the smallest reason to think them older than the Hellenic settlements of a similar kind on the same coasts. An evidence of no slight weight that Latium at least first became acquainted with the men of Canaan through the medium of the Hellenes is furnished by the Latin appellation "Poeni," which is borrowed from the Greek. All the oldest relations, indeed, of the Italians to the civilization of the east point decidedly towards Greece; and the rise of the Phoenician factory at Caere may be very well explained, without resorting to the pre-Hellenic period, by the subsequent well-known relations between the commercial state of Caere and Carthage. In fact, when we recall the circumstance that the earliest navigation was and continued to be essentially of a coasting character, it is plain that scarcely any country on the Mediterranean lay so remote from the Phoenicians as the Italian mainland. They could only reach it either from the west coast of Greece or from Sicily; and it may well be believed that the seamanship of the Hellenes became developed early enough to anticipate the Phoenicians in braving the dangers of the Adriatic and of the Tyrrhene seas. There is no ground therefore for the assumption that any direct influence was originally exercised by the Phoenicians over the Italians. To the subsequent relations between the Phoenicians holding the supremacy of the western Mediterranean and the Italians inhabiting the shores of the Tyrrhene sea our narrative will return in the sequel.

Greeks in Italy—Home of the Greek Immigrants

To all appearance, therefore, the Hellenic mariners were the first among the inhabitants of the eastern basin of the Mediterranean to navigate the coasts of Italy. Of the important questions however as to the region from which, and as to the period at which, the Greek seafarers came thither, only the former admits of being answered with some degree of precision and fulness. The Aeolian and Ionian coast of Asia Minor was the region where Hellenic maritime traffic first became developed on a large scale, and whence issued the Greeks who explored the interior of the Black Sea on the one hand and the coasts of Italy on the other. The name of the Ionian Sea, which was retained by the waters intervening between Epirus and Sicily, and that of the Ionian gulf, the term by which the Greeks in earlier times designated the Adriatic Sea, are memorials of the fact that the southern and eastern coasts of Italy were once discovered by seafarers from Ionia. The oldest Greek settlement in Italy, Kyme, was, as its name and legend tell, founded by the town of the same name on the Anatolian coast. According to trustworthy Hellenic tradition, the Phocaeans of Asia Minor were the first of the Hellenes to traverse the more remote western sea. Other Greeks soon followed in the paths which those of Asia Minor had opened up; Ionians from Naxos and from Chalcis in Euboea, Achaeans, Locrians, Rhodians, Corinthians, Megarians, Messenians, Spartans. After the discovery of America the civilized nations of Europe vied with one another in sending out expeditions and forming settlements there; and the new settlers when located amidst barbarians recognized their common character and common interests as civilized Europeans more strongly than they had done in their former home. So it was with the new discovery of the Greeks. The privilege of navigating the western waters and settling on the western land was not the exclusive property of a single Greek province or of a single Greek stock, but a common good for the whole Hellenic nation; and, just as in the formation of the new North American world, English and French, Dutch and German settlements became mingled and blended, Greek Sicily and "Great Greece" became peopled by a mixture of all sorts of Hellenic races often so amalgamated as to be no longer distinguishable. Leaving out of account some settlements occupying a more isolated position—such as that of the Locrians with its offsets Hipponium and Medama, and the settlement of the Phocaeans which was not founded till towards the close of this period, Hyele (Velia, Elea)—we may distinguish in a general view three leading groups. The original Ionian group, comprehended under the name of the Chalcidian towns, included in Italy Cumae with the other Greek settlements at Vesuvius and Rhegium, and in Sicily Zankle (afterwards Messana), Naxos, Catana, Leontini, and Himera. The Achaean group embraced Sybaris and the greater part of the cities of Magna Graecia. The Dorian group comprehended Syracuse, Gela, Agrigentum, and the majority of the Sicilian colonies, while in Italy nothing belonged to it but Taras (Tarentum) and its offset Heraclea. On the whole the preponderance lay with the immigrants who belonged to the more ancient Hellenic influx, that of the Ionians and the stocks settled in the Peloponnesus before the Doric immigration. Among the Dorians only the communities with a mixed population, such as Corinth and Megara, took a special part, whereas the purely Doric provinces had but a subordinate share in the movement. This result was naturally to be expected, for the Ionians were from ancient times a trading and sea-faring people, while it was only at a comparatively late period that the Dorian stocks descended from their inland mountains to the seaboard, and they always kept aloof from maritime commerce. The different groups of immigrants are very clearly distinguishable, especially by their monetary standards. The Phocaean settlers coined according to the Babylonian standard which prevailed in Asia. The Chalcidian towns followed in the earliest times the Aeginetan, in other words, that which originally prevailed throughout all European Greece, and more especially the modification of it which is found occurring in Euboea. The Achaean communities coined by the Corinthian standard; and lastly the Doric colonies followed that which Solon introduced in Attica in the year of Rome 160, with the exception of Tarentum and Heraclea, which in their principal pieces adopted rather the standard of their Achaean neighbours than that of the Dorians in Sicily.

Time of the Greek Immigration

The dates of the earlier voyages and settlements will probably always remain enveloped in darkness. We may still, however, distinctly recognize a certain order of sequence. In the oldest Greek document, which belongs, like the earliest intercourse with the west, to the Ionians of Asia Minor—the Homeric poems—the horizon scarcely extends beyond the eastern basin of the Mediterranean. Sailors driven by storms into the western sea might have brought to Asia Minor accounts of the existence of a western land and possibly also of its whirlpools and island-mountains vomiting fire: but in the age of the Homeric poetry there was an utter want of trustworthy information respecting Sicily and Italy, even in that Greek land which was the earliest to enter into intercourse with the west; and the story-tellers and poets of the east could without fear of contradiction fill the vacant realms of the west, as those of the west in their turn filled the fabulous east, with their castles in the air. In the poems of Hesiod the outlines of Italy and Sicily appear better defined; there is some acquaintance with the native names of tribes, mountains, and cities in both countries; but Italy is still regarded as a group of islands. On the other hand, in all the literature subsequent to Hesiod, Sicily and even the whole coast of Italy appear as known, at least in a general sense, to the Hellenes. The order of succession of the Greek settlements may in like manner be ascertained with some degree of precision. Thucydides evidently regarded Cumae as the earliest settlement of note in the west; and certainly he was not mistaken. It is true that many a landing-place lay nearer at hand for the Greek mariner, but none were so well protected from storms and from barbarians as the island of Ischia, upon which the town was originally situated; and that such were the prevailing considerations that led to this settlement, is evident from the very position which was subsequently selected for it on the mainland—the steep but well-protected cliff, which still bears to the present day the venerable name of the Anatolian mother-city. Nowhere in Italy, accordingly, were the scenes of the legends of Asia Minor so vividly and tenaciously localized as in the district of Cumae, where the earliest voyagers to the west, full of those legends of western wonders, first stepped upon the fabled land and left the traces of that world of story, which they believed that they were treading, in the rocks of the Sirens and the lake of Avernus leading to the lower world. On the supposition, moreover, that it was in Cumae that the Greeks first became the neighbours of the Italians, it is easy to explain why the name of that Italian stock which was settled immediately around Cumae, the name of Opicans, came to be employed by them for centuries afterwards to designate the Italians collectively. There is a further credible tradition, that a considerable interval elapsed between the settlement at Cumae and the main Hellenic immigration into Lower Italy and Sicily, and that in this immigration Ionians from Chalcis and from Naxos took the lead. Naxos in Sicily is said to have been the oldest of all the Greek towns founded by strict colonization in Italy or Sicily; the Achaean and Dorian colonizations followed, but not until a later period.

It appears, however, to be quite impossible to fix the dates of this series of events with even approximate accuracy. The founding of the Achaean city of Sybaris in 33, and that of the Dorian city Tarentum in 46, are probably the most ancient dates in Italian history, the correctness, or at least approximation to correctness, of which may be looked upon as established. But how far beyond that epoch the sending forth of the earlier Ionian colonies reached back, is quite as uncertain as is the age which gave birth to the poems of Hesiod or even of Homer. If Herodotus is correct in the period which he assigns to Homer, the Greeks were still unacquainted with Italy a century before the foundation of Rome. The date thus assigned however, like all other statements respecting the Homeric age, is matter not of testimony, but of inference; and any one who carefully weighs the history of the Italian alphabets as well as the remarkable fact that the Italians had become acquainted with the Greek people before the name "Hellenes" had emerged for the race, and the Italians borrowed their designation for the Hellenes from the stock of the -Grai- or -Graeci- that early fell into abeyance in Hellas,(1) will be inclined to carry back the earliest intercourse of the Italians with the Greeks to an age considerably mere remote.

Character of the Greek Immigration

The history of the Italian and Sicilian Greeks forms no part of the history of Italy; the Hellenic colonists of the west always retained the closest connection with their original home and participated in the national festivals and privileges of Hellenes. But it is of importance even as bearing on Italy, that we should indicate the diversities of character that prevailed in the Greek settlements there, and at least exhibit some of the leading features which enabled the Greek colonization to exercise so varied an influence on Italy.

The League of the Achaen Cities

Of all the Greek settlements, that which retained most thoroughly its distinctive character and was least affected by influences from without was the settlement which gave birth to the league of the Achaean cities, composed of the towns of Siris, Pandosia, Metabus or Metapontum, Sybaris with its offsets Posidonia and Laus, Croton, Caulonia, Temesa, Terina, and Pyxus. These colonists, taken as a whole, belonged to a Greek stock which steadfastly adhered to its own peculiar dialect, having closest affinity with the Doric, and for long retained no less steadfastly the old national Hellenic mode of writing, instead of adopting the more recent alphabet which had elsewhere come into general use; and which preserved its own nationality, as distinguished alike from the barbarians and from other Greeks, by the firm bond of a federal constitution. The language of Polybius regarding the Achaean symmachy in the Peloponnesus may be applied also to these Italian Achaeans; "Not only did they live in federal and friendly communion, but they made use of like laws, like weights, measures, and coins, as well as of the same magistrates, councillors, and judges."

This league of the Achaean cities was strictly a colonization. The cities had no harbours—Croton alone had a paltry roadstead—and they had no commerce of their own; the Sybarite prided himself on growing gray between the bridges of his lagoon-city, and Milesians and Etruscans bought and sold for him. These Achaean Greeks, however, were not merely in possession of a narrow belt along the coast, but ruled from sea to sea in the "land of wine" and "of oxen" (—Oinotria—, —Italia—) or the "great Hellas;" the native agricultural population was compelled to farm their lands and to pay to them tribute in the character of clients or even of serfs. Sybaris—in its time the largest city in Italy—exercised dominion over four barbarian tribes and five-and-twenty townships, and was able to found Laus and Posidonia on the other sea. The exceedingly fertile low grounds of the Crathis and Bradanus yielded a superabundant produce to the Sybarites and Metapontines—it was there perhaps that grain was first cultivated for exportation. The height of prosperity which these states in an incredibly short time attained is strikingly attested by the only surviving works of art of these Italian Achaeans, their coins of chaste antiquely beautiful workmanship—the earliest monuments of art and writing in Italy which we possess, as it can be shown that they had already begun to be coined in 174. These coins show that the Achaeans of the west did not simply participate in the noble development of plastic art that was at this very time taking place in the motherland, but were even superior in technical skill. For, while the silver pieces which were in use about that time in Greece proper and among the Dorians in Italy were thick, often stamped only on one side, and in general without inscription, the Italian Achaeans with great and independent skill struck from two similar dies partly cut in relief, partly sunk, large thin silver coins always furnished with inscriptions, and displaying the advanced organization of a civilized state in the mode of impression, by which they were carefully protected from the process of counterfeiting usual in that age—the plating of inferior metal with thin silver-foil.

Nevertheless this rapid bloom bore no fruit. Even Greeks speedily lost all elasticity of body and of mind in a life of indolence, in which their energies were never tried either by vigorous resistance on the part of the natives or by hard labour of their own. None of the brilliant names in Greek art or literature shed glory on the Italian Achaeans, while Sicily could claim ever so many of them, and even in Italy the Chalcidian Rhegium could produce its Ibycus and the Doric Tarentum its Archytas. With this people, among whom the spit was for ever turning on the hearth, nothing flourished from the outset but boxing. The rigid aristocracy which early gained the helm in the several communities, and which found in case of need a sure reserve of support in the federal power, prevented the rise of tyrants; but the danger to be apprehended was that the government of the best might be converted into a government of the few, especially if the privileged families in the different communities should combine to assist each other in carrying out their designs. Such was the predominant aim in the combination of mutually pledged "friends" which bore the name of Pythagoras. It enjoined the principle that the ruling class should be "honoured like gods," and that the subject class should be "held in subservience like beasts," and by such theory and practice provoked a formidable reaction, which terminated in the annihilation of the Pythagorean "friends" and the renewal of the ancient federal constitution. But frantic party feuds, insurrections en masse of the slaves, social abuses of all sorts, attempts to supply in practice an impracticable state-philosophy, in short, all the evils of demoralized civilization never ceased to rage in the Achaean communities, till under the accumulated pressure their political power utterly broke down.

It is no matter of wonder therefore that the Achaeans settled in Italy exercised less influence on its civilization than the other Greek settlements. An agricultural people, they had less occasion than those engaged in commerce to extend their influence beyond their political bounds. Within their own dominions they enslaved the native population and crushed the germs of their national development as Italians, while they refused to open up to them by means of complete Hellenization a new career. In this way the Greek characteristics, which were able elsewhere to retain a vigorous vitality notwithstanding all political misfortunes, disappeared more rapidly, more completely, and more ingloriously in Sybaris and Metapontum, in Croton and Posidonia, than in any other region; and the bilingual mongrel peoples, that arose in subsequent times out of the remains of the native Italians and Achaeans and the more recent immigrants of Sabellian descent, never attained any real prosperity. This catastrophe, however, belongs in point of time to the succeeding period.

Iono-Dorian Towns

The settlements of the other Greeks were of a different character, and exercised a very different effect upon Italy. They by no means despised agriculture and the acquisition of territory; it was not the wont of the Hellenes, at least when they had reached their full vigour, to rest content after the manner of the Phoenicians with a fortified factory in the midst of a barbarian land. But all their cities were founded primarily and especially for the sake of trade, and accordingly, altogether differing from those of the Achaeans, they were uniformly established beside the best harbours and lading-places. These cities were very various in their origin and in the occasion and period of their respective foundations; but there subsisted between them a certain fellowship, as in the common use by all of these towns of certain modern forms of the alphabet,(2) and in the very Dorism of their language, which made its way at an early date even into those towns that, like Cumae for example,(3) originally spoke the soft Ionic dialect. These settlements were of very various degrees of importance in their bearing on the development of Italy: it is sufficient at present to mention those which exercised a decided influence over the destinies of the Italian races, the Doric Tarentum and the Ionic Cumae.

Tarentum

Of all the Hellenic settlements in Italy, Tarentum was destined to play the most brilliant part. The excellent harbour, the only good one on the whole southern coast, rendered the city the natural emporium for the traffic of the south of Italy, and for some portion even of the commerce of the Adriatic. The rich fisheries of its gulf, the production and manufacture of its excellent wool, and the dyeing of it with the purple juice of the Tarentine -murex-, which rivalled that of Tyre—both branches of industry introduced there from Miletus in Asia Minor—employed thousands of hands, and added to the carrying trade a traffic of export. The coins struck at Tarentum in greater quantity than anywhere else in Grecian Italy, and struck pretty numerously even in gold, furnish to us a significant attestation of the lively and widely extended commerce of the Tarentines. At this epoch, when Tarentum was still contending with Sybaris for the first place among the Greek cities of Lower Italy, its extensive commercial connections must have been already forming; but the Tarentines seem never to have steadily and successfully directed their efforts to a substantial extension of their territory after the manner of the Achaean cities.

Greek Cities Near Vesuvius

While the most easterly of the Greek settlements in Italy thus rapidly rose into splendour, those which lay furthest to the north, in the neighbourhood of Vesuvius, attained a more moderate prosperity. There the Cumaeans had crossed from the fertile island of Aenaria (Ischia) to the mainland, and had built a second home on a hill close by the sea, from whence they founded the seaport of Dicaearchia (afterwards Puteoli) and, moreover, the "new city" Neapolis. They lived, like the Chalcidian cities generally in Italy and Sicily, in conformity with the laws which Charondas of Catana (about 100) had established, under a constitution democratic but modified by a high census, which placed the power in the hands of a council of members selected from the wealthiest men—a constitution which proved lasting and kept these cities free, upon the whole, from the tyranny alike of usurpers and of the mob. We know little as to the external relations of these Campanian Greeks. They remained, whether from necessity or from choice, confined to a district of even narrower limits than the Tarentines; and issuing from it not for purposes of conquest and oppression, but for the holding of peaceful commercial intercourse with the natives, they created the means of a prosperous existence for themselves, and at the same time took the foremost place among the missionaries of Greek civilization in Italy.

Relations of the Adriatic Regions to the Greeks

While on the one side of the straits of Rhegium the whole southern coast of the mainland and its western coast as far as Vesuvius, and on the other the larger eastern half of the island of Sicily, were Greek territory, the west coast of Italy northward of Vesuvius and the whole of the east coast were in a position essentially different. No Greek settlements arose on the Italian seaboard of the Adriatic; and with this we may evidently connect the comparatively small number and subordinate importance of the Greek colonies planted on the opposite Illyrian shore and on the numerous adjacent islands. Two considerable mercantile towns, Epidamnus or Dyrrachium (now Durazzo, 127), and Apollonia (near Avlona, about 167), were founded upon the portion of this coast nearest to Greece during the regal period of Rome; but no old Greek colony can be pointed out further to the north, with the exception perhaps of the insignificant settlement at Black Corcyra (Curzola, about 174?). No adequate explanation has yet been given why the Greek colonization developed itself in this direction to so meagre an extent. Nature herself appeared to direct the Hellenes thither, and in fact from the earliest times there existed a regular traffic to that region from Corinth and still more from the settlement at Corcyra (Corfu) founded not long after Rome (about 44); a traffic, which had as its emporia on the Italian coast the towns of Spina and Atria, situated at the mouth of the Po. The storms of the Adriatic, the inhospitable character at least of the Illyrian coasts, and the barbarism of the natives are manifestly not in themselves sufficient to explain this fact. But it was a circumstance fraught with the most momentous consequences for Italy, that the elements of civilization which came from the east did not exert their influence on its eastern provinces directly, but reached them only through the medium of those that lay to the west. The Adriatic commerce carried on by Corinth and Corcyra was shared by the most easterly mercantile city of Magna Graecia, the Doric Tarentum, which by the possession of Hydrus (Otranto) had the command, on the Italian side, of the entrance of the Adriatic. Since, with the exception of the ports at the mouth of the Po, there were in those times no emporia worthy of mention along the whole east coast—the rise of Ancona belongs to a far later period, and later still the rise of Brundisium—it may well be conceived that the mariners of Epidamnus and Apollonia frequently discharged their cargoes at Tarentum. The Tarentines had also much intercourse with Apulia by land; all the Greek civilization to be met with in the south-east of Italy owed its existence to them. That civilization, however, was during the present period only in its infancy; it was not until a later epoch that the Hellenism of Apulia was developed.

Relations of the Western Italians to the Greeks

It cannot be doubted, on the other hand, that the west coast of Italy northward of Vesuvius was frequented in very early times by the Hellenes, and that there were Hellenic factories on its promontories and islands. Probably the earliest evidence of such voyages is the localizing of the legend of Odysseus on the coasts of the Tyrrhene Sea.(4) When men discovered the isles of Aeolus in the Lipari islands, when they pointed out at the Lacinian cape the isle of Calypso, at the cape of Misenum that of the Sirens, at the cape of Circeii that of Circe, when they recognized in the steep promontory of Terracina the towering burial-mound of Elpenor, when the Laestrygones were provided with haunts near Caieta and Formiae, when the two sons of Ulysses and Circe, Agrius, that is the "wild," and Latinus, were made to rule over the Tyrrhenians in the "inmost recess of the holy islands," or, according to a more recent version, Latinus was called the son of Ulysses and Circe, and Auson the son of Ulysses and Calypso—we recognize in these legends ancient sailors' tales of the seafarers of Ionia, who thought of their native home as they traversed the Tyrrhene Sea. The same noble vividness of feeling, which pervades the Ionic poem of the voyages of Odysseus, is discernible in this fresh localization of the same legend at Cumae itself and throughout the regions frequented by the Cumaean mariners.

Other traces of these very ancient voyages are to be found in the Greek name of the island Aethalia (Ilva, Elba), which appears to have been (after Aenaria) one of the places earliest occupied by Greeks, perhaps also in that of the seaport Telamon in Etruria; and further in the two townships on the Caerite coast, Pyrgi (near S. Severa) and Alsium (near Palo), the Greek origin of which is indicated beyond possibility of mistake not only by their names, but also by the peculiar architecture of the walls of Pyrgi, which differs essentially in character from that of the walls of Caere and the Etruscan cities generally. Aethalia, the "fire-island," with its rich mines of copper and especially of iron, probably sustained the chief part in this commerce, and there in all likelihood the foreigners had their central settlement and seat of traffic with the natives; the more especially as they could not have found the means of smelting the ores on the small and not well-wooded island without intercourse with the mainland. The silver mines of Populonia also on the headland opposite to Elba were perhaps already known to the Greeks and wrought by them.

If, as was undoubtedly the case, the foreigners, ever in those times intent on piracy and plunder as well as trade, did not fail, when opportunity offered, to levy contributions on the natives and to carry them off as slaves, the natives on their part exercised the right of retaliation; and that the Latins and Tyrrhenes retaliated with greater energy and better fortune than their neighbours in the south of Italy, is attested not merely by the legends to that effect, but by the actual results. In these regions the Italians succeeded in resisting the foreigners and in retaining, or at any rate soon resuming, the mastery not merely of their own mercantile cities and mercantile ports, but also of their own sea. The same Hellenic invasion which crushed and denationalized the races of the south of Italy, directed the energies of the peoples of Central Italy—very much indeed against the will of their instructors—

towards navigation and the founding of towns. It must have been in this quarter that the Italians first exchanged the raft and the boat for the oared galley of the Phoenicians and Greeks. Here too we first encounter great mercantile cities, particularly Caere in southern Etruria and Rome on the Tiber, which, if we may judge from their Italian names as well as from their being situated at some distance from the sea, were—like the exactly similar commercial towns at the mouth of the Po, Spina and Atria, and Ariminum further to the south—certainly not Greek, but Italian foundations. It is not in our power, as may easily be supposed, to exhibit the historical course of this earliest reaction of Italian nationality against foreign aggression; but we can still recognize the fact, which was of the greatest importance as bearing upon the further development of Italy, that this reaction took a different course in Latium and in southern Etruria from that which it exhibited in the properly Tuscan and adjoining provinces.

Hellenes and Latins

Legend itself contrasts in a significant manner the Latin with the "wild Tyrrhenian," and the peaceful beach at the mouth of the Tiber with the inhospitable shore of the Volsci. This cannot mean that Greek colonization was tolerated in some of the provinces of Central Italy, but not permitted in others. Northward of Vesuvius there existed no independent Greek community at all in historical times; if Pyrgi once was such, it must have already reverted, before the period at which our tradition begins, into the hands of the Italians or in other words of the Caerites. But in southern Etruria, in Latium, and likewise on the east coast, peaceful intercourse with the foreign merchants was protected and encouraged; and such was not the case elsewhere. The position of Caere was especially remarkable. "The Caerites," says Strabo, "were held in much repute among the Hellenes for their bravery and integrity, and because, powerful though they were, they abstained from robbery." It is not piracy that is thus referred to, for in this the merchant of Caere must have indulged like every other. But Caere was a sort of free port for Phoenicians as well as Greeks. We have already mentioned the Phoenician station—subsequently called Punicum—and the two Hellenic stations of Pyrgi and Alsium.(5) It was these ports that the Caerites refrained from robbing, and it was beyond doubt through this tolerant attitude that Caere, which possessed but a wretched roadstead and had no mines in its neighbourhood, early attained so great prosperity and acquired, in reference to the earliest Greek commerce, an importance even greater than the cities of the Italians destined by nature as emporia at the mouths of the Tiber and Po. The cities we have just named are those which appear as holding primitive religious intercourse with Greece. The first of all barbarians to present gifts to the Olympian Zeus was the Tuscan king Arimnus, perhaps a ruler of Ariminum. Spina and Caere had their special treasuries in the temple of the Delphic Apollo, like other communities that had regular dealings with the shrine; and the sanctuary at Delphi, as well as the Cumaean oracle, is interwoven with the earliest traditions of Caere and of Rome. These cities, where the Italians held peaceful sway and carried on friendly traffic with the foreign merchant, became preeminently wealthy and powerful, and were genuine marts not only for Hellenic merchandise, but also for the germs of Hellenic civilization.

Hellenes and Etruscans—Etruscan Maritime Power

Matters stood on a different footing with the "wild Tyrrhenians." The same causes, which in the province of Latium, and in the districts on the right bank of the Tiber and along the lower course of the Po that were perhaps rather subject to Etruscan supremacy than strictly Etruscan, had led to the emancipation of the natives from the maritime power of the foreigner, led in Etruria proper to the development of piracy and maritime ascendency, in consequence possibly of the difference of national character disposing the people to violence and pillage, or it may be for other reasons with which we are not acquainted. The Etruscans were not content with dislodging the Greeks from Aethalia and Populonia; even the individual trader was apparently not tolerated by them, and soon Etruscan privateers roamed over the sea far and wide, and rendered the name of the Tyrrhenians a terror to the Greeks. It was not without reason that the Greeks reckoned the grapnel as an Etruscan invention, and called the western sea of Italy the sea of the Tuscans. The rapidity with which these wild corsairs multiplied and the violence of their proceedings in the Tyrrhene Sea in particular, are very clearly shown by their establishment on the Latin and Campanian coasts. The Latins indeed maintained their ground in Latium proper, and the Greeks at Vesuvius; but between them and by their side the Etruscans held sway in Antium and in Surrentum. The Volscians became clients of the Etruscans; their forests contributed the keels for the Etruscan galleys; and seeing that the piracy of the Antiates was only terminated by the Roman occupation, it is easy to understand why the coast of the southern Volscians bore among Greek mariners the name of the Laestrygones. The high promontory of Sorrento with the cliff of Capri which is still more precipitous but destitute of any harbour—a station thoroughly adapted for corsairs on the watch, commanding a prospect of the Tyrrhene Sea between the bays of Naples and Salerno—was early occupied by the Etruscans. They are affirmed even to have founded a "league of twelve towns" of their own in Campania, and communities speaking Etruscan still existed in its inland districts in times quite historical. These settlements were probably indirect results of the maritime dominion of the Etruscans in the Campanian sea, and of their rivalry with the Cumaeans at Vesuvius.

Etruscan Commerce

The Etruscans however by no means confined themselves to robbery and pillage. The peaceful intercourse which they held with Greek towns is attested by the gold and silver coins which, at least from the year 200, were struck by the Etruscan cities, and in particular by Populonia, after a Greek model and a Greek standard. The circumstance, moreover, that these coins are modelled not upon those of Magna Graecia, but rather upon those of Attica and even Asia Minor, is perhaps an indication of the hostile attitude in which the Etruscans stood towards the Italian Greeks. For commerce they in fact enjoyed the most favourable position, far more advantageous than that of the inhabitants of Latium. Inhabiting the country from sea to sea, they commanded the great Italian free ports on the western waters, the mouths of the Po and the Venice of that time on the eastern sea, and the land route which from ancient times led from Pisa on the Tyrrhene Sea to Spina on the Adriatic, while in the south of Italy they commanded the rich plains of Capua and Nola. They were the holders of the most important Italian articles of export, the iron of Aethalia, the copper of Volaterrae and Campania, the silver of Populonia, and even the amber which was brought to them from the Baltic.(6) Under the protection of their piracy, which constituted as it were a rude navigation act, their own commerce could not fail to flourish. It need not surprise us to find Etruscan and Milesian merchants competing in the market of Sybaris, nor need we be astonished to learn that the combination of privateering and commerce on a great scale generated the unbounded and senseless luxury, in which the vigour of Etruria early wasted away.

Rivalry between the Phoenicians and Hellenes

While in Italy the Etruscans and, although in a lesser degree, the Latins thus stood opposed to the Hellenes, warding them off and partly treating them as enemies, this antagonism to some extent necessarily affected the rivalry which then above all dominated the commerce and navigation of the Mediterranean—the rivalry between the Phoenicians and Hellenes. This is not the place to set forth in detail how, during the regal period of Rome, these two great nations contended for supremacy on all the shores of the Mediterranean, in Greece even and Asia Minor, in Crete and Cyprus, on the African, Spanish, and Celtic coasts. This struggle did not take place directly on Italian soil, but its effects were deeply and permanently felt in Italy. The fresh energies and more universal endowments of the younger competitor had at first the advantage everywhere. Not only did the Hellenes rid themselves of the Phoenician factories in their own European and Asiatic homes, but they dislodged the Phoenicians also from Crete and Cyprus, gained a footing in Egypt and Cyrene, and possessed themselves of Lower Italy and the larger eastern half of the island of Sicily. On all hands the small trading stations of the Phoenicians gave way before the more energetic colonization of the Greeks. Selinus (126) and Agrigentum (174) were founded in western Sicily; the more remote western sea was traversed, Massilia was built on the Celtic coast (about 150), and the shores of Spain were explored, by the bold Phocaeans from Asia Minor. But about the middle of the second century the progress of Hellenic colonization was suddenly arrested; and there is no doubt that the cause of this arrest was the contemporary rapid rise of Carthage, the most powerful of the Phoenician cities in Libya—a rise manifestly due to the danger with which Hellenic aggression threatened the whole Phoenician race. If the nation which had opened up maritime commerce on the Mediterranean had been already dislodged by its younger rival from the sole command of the western half, from the possession of both lines of communication between the eastern and western basins of the Mediterranean, and from the monopoly of the carrying trade between east and west, the sovereignty at least of the seas to the west of Sardinia and Sicily might still be saved for the Orientals; and to its maintenance Carthage applied all the tenacious and circumspect energy peculiar to the Aramaean race. Phoenician colonization and Phoenician resistance assumed an entirely different character. The earlier Phoenician settlements, such as those in Sicily described by Thucydides, were mercantile factories: Carthage subdued extensive territories with numerous subjects and powerful fortresses. Hitherto the Phoenician settlements had stood isolated in opposition to the Greeks; now the powerful Libyan city centralized within its sphere the whole warlike resources of those akin to it in race with a vigour to which the history of the Greeks can produce nothing parallel.

Phoenicians and Italians in Opposition to the Hellenes

Perhaps the element in this reaction which exercised the most momentous influence in the sequel was the close relation into which the weaker Phoenicians entered with the natives of Sicily and Italy in order to resist the Hellenes. When the Cnidians and Rhodians made an attempt about 175 to establish themselves at Lilybaeum, the centre of the Phoenician settlements in Sicily, they were expelled by the natives—the Elymi of Segeste—in concert with the Phoenicians. When the Phocaeans settled about 217 at Alalia (Aleria) in Corsica opposite to Caere, there appeared for the purpose of expelling them a combined fleet of Etruscans and Carthaginians, numbering a hundred and twenty sail; and although in the naval battle that ensued—one of the earliest known in history-the fleet of the Phocaeans, which was only half as strong, claimed the victory, the Carthaginians and Etruscans gained the object which they had in view in the attack; the Phocaeans abandoned Corsica, and preferred to settle at Hyde (Velia) on the less exposed coast of Lucania. A treaty between Etruria and Carthage not only established regulations regarding the import of goods and the giving due effect to rights, but included also an alliance-in-arms (—summachia—), the serious import of which is shown by that very battle of Alalia. It is a significant indication of the position of the Caerites, that they stoned the Phocaean captives in the market at Caere and then sent an embassy to the Delphic Apollo to atone for the crime.

Latium did not join in these hostilities against the Hellenes; on the contrary, we find friendly relations subsisting in very ancient times between the Romans and the Phocaeans in Velia as well as in Massilia, and the Ardeates are even said to have founded in concert with the Zacynthians a colony in Spain, the later Saguntum. Much less, however, did the Latins range themselves on the side of the Hellenes: the neutrality of their position in this respect is attested by the close relations maintained between Caere and Rome, as well as by the traces of ancient intercourse between the Latins and the Carthaginians. It was through the medium of the Hellenes that the Cannanite race became known to the Romans, for, as we have already seen,(7) they always designated it by its Greek name; but the fact that they did not borrow from the Greeks either the name for the city of Carthage(8) or the national name of the -Afri-,(9) and the circumstance that among the earlier Romans Tyrian wares were designated by the adjective -Sarranus-,(10) which in like manner precludes the idea of Greek intervention, demonstrate—what the treaties of a later period concur in proving—the direct commercial intercourse anciently subsisting between Latium and Carthage.

The combined power of the Italians and Phoenicians actually succeeded in substantially retaining the western half of the Mediterranean in their hands. The northwestern portion of Sicily, with the important ports of Soluntum and Panormus on the north coast, and Motya at the point which looks towards Africa, remained in the direct or indirect possession of the Carthaginians. About the age of Cyrus and Croesus, just when the wise Bias was endeavouring to induce the Ionians to emigrate in a body from Asia Minor and settle in Sardinia (about 200), the Carthaginian general Malchus anticipated them, and subdued a considerable portion of that important island by force of arms; half a century later, the whole coast of Sardinia appears in the undisputed possession of the Carthaginian community. Corsica on the other hand, with the towns of Alalia and Nicaea, fell to the Etruscans, and the natives paid to these tribute of the products of their poor island, pitch, wax, and honey. In the Adriatic sea, moreover, the allied Etruscans and Carthaginians ruled, as in the waters to the west of Sicily and Sardinia. The Greeks, indeed, did not give up the struggle. Those Rhodians and Cnidians, who had been driven out of Lilybaeum, established themselves on the islands between Sicily and Italy and founded there the town of Lipara (175). Massilia flourished in spite of its isolation, and soon monopolized the trade of the region from Nice to the Pyrénées. At the Pyrénées themselves Rhoda (now Rosas) was established as an offset from Lipara, and it is affirmed that Zacynthians settled in Saguntum, and even that Greek dynasts ruled at Tingis (Tangiers) in Mauretania. But the Hellenes no longer gained ground; after the foundation of Agrigentum they did not succeed in acquiring any important additions of territory on the Adriatic or on the western sea, and they remained excluded from the Spanish waters as well as from the Atlantic Ocean. Every year the Liparaeans had their conflicts with the Tuscan "sea-robbers," and the Carthaginians with the Massiliots, the Cyrenaeans, and above all with the Sicilian Greeks; but no results of permanent moment were on either side achieved, and the issue of struggles which lasted for centuries was, on the whole, the simple maintenance of the -status quo-.

Thus Italy was—if but indirectly—indebted to the Phoenicians for the exemption of at least her central and northern provinces from colonization, and for the counter-development of a national maritime power there, especially in Etruria. But there are not wanting indications that the Phoenicians already found it worth while to manifest that jealousy which is usually associated with naval domination, if not in reference to their Latin allies, at any rate in reference to their Etruscan confederates, whose naval power was greater. The statement as to the Carthaginians having prohibited the sending forth of an Etruscan colony to the Canary islands, whether true or false, reveals the existence of a rivalry of interests in the matter.

Notes for Book I Chapter X

1. Whether the name of Graeci was originally associated with the interior of Epirus and the region of Dodona, or pertained rather to the Aetolians who perhaps earlier reached the western sea, may be left an open question; it must at a remote period have belonged to a prominent stock or aggregate of stocks of Greece proper and have passed over from these to the nation as a whole. In the Eoai of Hesiod it appears as the older collective name for the nation, although it is manifest that it is intentionally thrust aside and subordinated to that of Hellenes. The latter does not occur in Homer, but, in addition to Hesiod, it is found in Archilochus about the year 50, and it may very well have come into use considerably earlier (Duncker, Gesch. d. Alt. iii. 18, 556). Already before this period, therefore, the Italians were so widely acquainted with the Greeks that that name, which early fell into abeyance in Hellas, was retained by them as a collective name for the Greek nation, even when the latter itself adopted other modes of self-designation. It was withal only natural that foreigners should have attained to an earlier and clearer consciousness of the fact that the Hellenic stocks belonged to one race than the latter themselves, and that hence the collective designation should have become more definitely fixed among the former than with the latter—not the less, that it was not taken directly from the well-known Hellenes who dwelt the nearest to them. It is difficult to see how we can reconcile with this fact the statement that a century before the foundation of Rome Italy was still quite unknown to the Greeks of Asia Minor. We shall speak of the alphabet below; its history yields entirely similar results. It may perhaps be characterized as a rash step to reject the statement of Herodotus respecting the age of Homer on the strength of such considerations; but is there no rashness in following implicitly the guidance of tradition in questions of this kind?

2. Thus the three old Oriental forms of the —"id:i" (—"id:S"), —"id:l" (—"id:Λ") and —"id:r" (—"id:P"), for which as apt to be confounded with the forms of the —-"id:s", —"id:g", and —"id:p" the signs —"id:I") —"id:L" —"id:R") were early proposed to be substituted, remained either in exclusive or in very preponderant use among the Achaean colonies, while the other Greeks of Italy and Sicily without distinction of race used exclusively or at any rate chiefly the more recent forms.

3. E. g. the inscription on an earthen vase of Cumae runs thus:——Tataies emi lequthos Fos d' an me klephsei thuphlos estai—.

4. Among Greek writers this Tyrrhene legend of Odysseus makes its earliest appearance in the Theogony of Hesiod, in one of its more recent sections, and thereafter in authors of the period shortly before Alexander, Ephorus (from whom the so-called Scymnus drew his materials), and the writer known as Scylax. The first of these sources belongs to an age when Italy was still regarded by the Greeks as a group of islands, and is certainly therefore very old; so that the origin of these legends may, on the whole, be confidently placed in the regal period of Rome.

5. I. X. Phoenicians in Italy, I. X. Relations of the Western Italians to the Greeks

6. I. X. Relations of Italy with Other Lands

7. I. X. Phoenicians in Italy

8. The Phoenician name was Karthada; the Greek, Karchedon; the Roman, Cartago.

9. The name -Afri-, already current in the days of Ennius and Cato (comp. -Scipio Africanus-), is certainly not Greek, and is most probably cognate with that of the Hebrews.

10. The adjective -Sarranus- was from early times applied by the Romans to the Tyrian purple and the Tyrian flute; and -Sarranus-was in use also as a surname, at least from the time of the war with Hannibal. -Sarra-, which occurs in Ennius and Plautus as the name of the city, was perhaps formed from -Sarranus-, not directly from the native name -Sor-. The Greek form, -Tyrus-, -Tyrius-, seems not to occur in any Roman author anterior to Afranius (ap. Fest. p. 355 M.). Compare Movers, Phon. ii. x, 174.

CHAPTER XI

Law and Justice

Modern Character of Italian Culture

History, as such, cannot reproduce the life of a people in the infinite variety of its details; it must be content with exhibiting the development of that life as a whole. The doings and dealings, the thoughts and imaginings of the individual, however strongly they may reflect the characteristics of the national mind, form no part of history. Nevertheless it seems necessary to make some attempt to indicate—only in the most general outlines—the features of individual life in the case of those earlier ages which are, so far as history is concerned, all but lost in oblivion; for it is in this field of research alone that we acquire some idea of the breadth of the gulf which separates our modes of thinking and feeling from those of the civilized nations of antiquity. Tradition, with its confused mass of national names and its dim legends, resembles withered leaves which with difficulty we recognize to have once been green. Instead of threading that dreary maze and attempting to classify those shreds of humanity, the Chones and Oenotrians, the Siculi and the Pelasgi, it will be more to the purpose to inquire how the real life of the people in ancient Italy expressed itself in their law, and their ideal life in religion; how they farmed and how they traded; and whence the several nations derived the art of writing and other elements of culture. Scanty as our knowledge in this respect is in reference to the Roman people and still more so in reference to the Sabellians and Etruscans, even the slight and very defective information which is attainable will enable the mind to associate with these names some more or less clear glimpse of the once living reality. The chief result of such a view (as we may here mention by way of anticipation) may be summed up in saying that fewer traces comparatively of the primitive state of things have been preserved in the case of the Italians, and of the Romans in particular, than in the case of any other Indo-Germanic race. The bow and arrow, the war-chariot, the incapacity of women to hold property, the acquiring of wives by purchase, the primitive form of burial, blood-revenge, the clan-constitution conflicting with the authority of the community, a vivid natural symbolism —all these, and numerous phenomena of a kindred character, must be presumed to have lain at the foundation of civilization in Italy as well as elsewhere; but at the epoch when that civilization comes clearly into view they have already wholly disappeared, and only the comparison of kindred races informs us that such things once existed. In this respect Italian history begins at a far later stage of civilization than *e.g.* the Greek or the Germanic, and from the first it exhibits a comparatively modern character.

The laws of most of the Italian stocks are lost in oblivion. Some information regarding the law of the Latin land alone has survived in Roman tradition.

Jurisdiction

All jurisdiction was vested in the community or, in other words, in the king, who administered justice or "command" (-ius-) on the "days of utterance" (-dies fasti-) at the "judgment platform" (-tribunal-) in the place of public assembly, sitting on the "chariot-seat" (-sella curulis-);(1) by his side stood his "messengers" (-lictores-), and before him the person accused or the "parties" (-rei-). No doubt in the case of slaves the decision lay primarily with the master, and in the case of women with the father, husband, or nearest male relative;(2) but slaves and women were not primarily reckoned as members of the community. Over sons and grandsons who were -in potestate- the power of the -pater familias- subsisted concurrently with the royal jurisdiction; that power, however, was not a jurisdiction in the proper sense of the term, but simply a consequence of the father's inherent right of property in his children. We find no traces of any jurisdiction appertaining to the clans as such, or of any judicature at all that did not derive its authority from the king. As regards the right of self-redress and in particular the avenging of blood, we still find perhaps in legends an echo of the original principle that a murderer, or any one who should illegally protect a murderer, might justifiably be slain by the kinsmen of the person murdered; but these very legends characterize this principle as objectionable,(3) and from their statements blood-revenge would appear to have been very early suppressed in Rome through the energetic assertion of the authority of the community. In like manner we perceive in the earliest Roman law no trace of that influence which under the oldest Germanic institutions the comrades of the accused and the people present were entitled to exercise over the pronouncing of judgment; nor do we find in the former any evidence of the usage so frequent in the latter, by which the mere will and power to maintain a claim with arms in hand were treated as judicially necessary or at any rate admissible.

Crimes

Judicial procedure took the form of a public or a private process, according as the king interposed of his own motion or only when appealed to by the injured party. The former course was taken only in cases which involved a breach of the public peace. First of all, therefore, it was applicable in the case of public treason or communion with the public enemy (-proditio-), and in that of violent rebellion against the magistracy (-perduellio-). But the public peace was also broken by the foul murderer (-parricida-), the sodomite, the violator of a maiden's or matron's chastity, the incendiary, the false witness, by those, moreover, who with evil spells conjured away the harvest, or who without due title cut the corn by night in the field entrusted to the protection of the gods and of the people; all of these were therefore dealt with as though they had been guilty of high treason. The king opened and conducted the process, and pronounced sentence after conferring with the senators whom he had called in to advise with him. He was at liberty, however, after he had initiated the process, to commit the further handling and the adjudication of the matter to deputies who were, as a rule, taken from the senate. The later extraordinary deputies, the two men for adjudicating on rebellion (-duoviri perduellionis-) and the later standing deputies the "trackers of murder" (-quaestores parricidii-) whose primary duty was to search out and arrest murderers, and who therefore exercised in some measure police functions, do not belong to the regal period, but may probably have sprung out of, or been suggested by, certain of its institutions. Imprisonment while the case was undergoing investigation was the rule; the accused might, however, be released on bail. Torture to compel confession was only applied to slaves. Every one convicted of having broken the public peace expiated his offence with his life. The modes of inflicting capital punishment were various: the false witness, for example, was hurled from the stronghold-rock; the harvest-thief was hanged; the incendiary was burnt. The king could not grant pardon, for that power was vested in the community alone; but the king might grant or refuse to the condemned permission to appeal for mercy (-provocatio-). In addition to this, the law recognized an intervention of the gods in favour of the condemned criminal. He who had made a genuflection before the priest of Jupiter might not be scourged on the same day; any one under fetters who set foot in his house had to be released from his bonds; and the life of a criminal was spared, if on his way to execution he accidentally met one of the sacred virgins of Vesta.

Punishment of Offenses against Order

The king inflicted at his discretion fines payable to the state for trespasses against order and for police offences; they consisted in a definite number (hence the name - multa-) of cattle or sheep. It was in his power also to pronounce sentence of scourging.

Law of Private Offenses

In all other cases, where the individual alone was injured and not the public peace, the state only interposed upon the appeal of the party injured, who caused his opponent, or in case of need by laying violent hands on him compelled him, to appear personally along with himself before the king. When both parties had appeared and the plaintiff had orally stated his demand, while the defendant had in similar fashion refused to comply with it, the king might either investigate the cause himself or have it disposed of by a deputy acting in his name. The regular form of satisfaction for such an injury was a compromise arranged between the injurer and the injured; the state only interfered supplementarily, when the aggressor did not satisfy the party aggrieved by an adequate expiation (-poena-), when any one had his property detained or his just demand was not fulfilled.

Theft

Under what circumstances during this epoch theft was regarded as at all expiable, and what in such an event the person injured was entitled to demand from the thief, cannot be ascertained. But the injured party with reason demanded heavier compensation from a thief caught in the very act than from one detected afterwards, since the feeling of exasperation which had to be appeased was more vehement in the case of the former than in that of the latter. If the theft appeared incapable of expiation, or if the thief was not in a position to pay the value demanded by the injured party and approved by the judge, he was by the judge assigned as a bondsman to the person from whom he had stolen.

Injuries

In cases of damage (-iniuria-) to person or to property, where the injury was not of a very serious description, the aggrieved party was probably obliged unconditionally to accept compensation; if, on the other hand, any member was lost in consequence of it, the maimed person could demand eye for eye and tooth for tooth.

Property

Since the arable land among the Romans was long cultivated upon the system of joint possession and was not distributed until a comparatively late age, the idea of property was primarily associated not with immoveable estate, but with "estate in slaves and cattle" (-familia pecuniaque-). It was not the right of the stronger that was regarded as the foundation of a title to it; on the contrary, all property was considered as conferred by the community upon the individual burgess for his exclusive possession and use; and therefore it was only the burgess, and such as the community accounted in this respect as equal to burgesses, that were capable of holding property. All property passed freely from hand to hand. The Roman law made no substantial distinction between moveable and immoveable estate (from the time that the latter was regarded as private property at all), and recognized no absolute vested interest of children or other relatives in the paternal or family property. Nevertheless it was not in the power of the father arbitrarily to deprive his children of their right of inheritance, because he could neither dissolve the paternal power nor execute a testament except with consent of the whole community, which might be, and certainly under such circumstances often was, refused. In his lifetime no doubt the father might make dispositions disadvantageous to his children; for the law was sparing of personal restrictions on the proprietor and allowed, upon the whole, every grown-up man freely to dispose of his property. The regulation, however, under which he who alienated his hereditary property and deprived his children of it was placed by order of the magistrate under guardianship like a lunatic, was probably as ancient as the period when the arable land was first divided and thereby private property generally acquired greater importance for the commonwealth. In this way the two antagonistic principles—the unlimited right of the owner to dispose of his own, and the preservation of the family property unbroken—were as far as possible harmonized in the Roman law. Permanent restrictions on property were in no case allowed, with the exception of servitudes such as those indispensable in husbandry. Heritable leases and ground-rents charged upon property could not legally exist. The law as little recognized mortgaging; but the same purpose was served by the immediate delivery of the property in pledge to the creditor as if he were its purchaser, who thereupon gave his word of honour (-fiducia-) that he would not alienate the object pledged until the payment fell due, and would restore it to his debtor when the sum advanced had been repaid.

Contracts

Contracts concluded between the state and a burgess, particularly the obligation given by those who became sureties for a payment to the state (-praevides-, -praedes-), were valid without further formality. On the other hand, contracts between private persons under ordinary circumstances gave no claim for legal aid on the part of the state. The only protection of the creditor was the debtor's word of honour which was held in high esteem after the wont of merchants, and possibly also, in those frequent cases where an oath had been added, the fear of the gods who avenged perjury. The only contracts legally actionable were those of betrothal (the effect of which was that the father, in the event of his failing to give the promised bride, had to furnish satisfaction and compensation), of purchase (-mancipatio-), and of loan (-nexum-). A purchase was held to be legally concluded when the seller delivered the article purchased into the hand of the buyer (-mancipare-) and the buyer at the same time paid to the seller the stipulated price in presence of witnesses. This was done, after copper superseded sheep and cattle as the regular standard of value, by weighing out the stipulated quantity of copper in a balance adjusted by a neutral person.(4) These conditions having been complied with, the seller had to answer for his being the owner, and in addition seller and purchaser had to fulfil every stipulation specially agreed on; the party failing to do so made reparation to the other, just as if he had deprived him of the article in question. But a purchase only founded an action in the event of its being a transaction for ready money: a purchase on credit neither gave nor took away the right of property, and constituted no ground of action. A loan was negotiated in a similar way; the creditor weighed over to the debtor in presence of witnesses the stipulated quantity of copper under the obligation (-nexum-) of repayment. In addition to the capital the debtor had to pay interest, which under ordinary circumstances probably amounted to ten per cent per annum.(5) The repayment of the loan took place, when the time came, with similar forms.

Private Process

If a debtor to the state did not fulfil his obligations, he was without further ceremony sold with all that he had; the simple demand on the part of the state was sufficient to establish the debt. If on the other hand a private person informed the king of any violation of his property (-vindiciae-) or if repayment of the loan received did not duly take place, the procedure depended on whether the facts relating to the cause needed to be established, which was ordinarily the case with actions as to property, or were already clearly apparent, which in the case of actions as to loans could easily be accomplished according to the current rules of law by means of the witnesses. The establishment of the facts assumed the form of a wager, in which each party made a deposit (-sacramentum-) against the contingency of his being worsted; in important causes when the value involved was greater than ten oxen, a deposit of five oxen, in causes of less amount, a deposit of five sheep. The judge then decided who had gained the wager, whereupon the deposit of the losing party fell to the priests for behoof of the public sacrifices. The party who lost the wager and allowed thirty days to elapse without giving due satisfaction to his opponent, and the party whose obligation to pay was established from the first—consequently, as a rule, the debtor who had got a loan and had not witnesses to attest its repayment—became liable to proceedings in execution "by laying on of hands" (-manus iniectio-); the plaintiff seized him wherever he found him, and brought him to the bar of the judge simply to satisfy the acknowledged debt. The party seized was not allowed to defend himself; a third person might indeed intercede for him and represent this act of violence as unwarranted (-vindex-), in which case the proceedings were stayed; but such an intercession rendered the intercessor personally responsible, for which reason the proletarian could not be intercessor for the tribute-paying burgess. If neither satisfaction nor intercession took place, the king adjudged the party seized to his creditor, so that the latter could lead him away and keep him like a slave. After the expiry of sixty days during which the debtor had been three times exposed in the market-place and proclamation had been made to ascertain whether any one would have compassion upon him, if these steps were without effect, his creditors had the right to put him to death and to divide his carcase, or to sell him with his children and his effects into foreign slavery, or to keep him at home in a slave's stead; for such an one could not by the Roman law, so long as he remained within the bounds of the Roman community, become completely a slave.(6) Thus the Roman community protected every man's estate and effects with unrelenting rigour as well from the thief and the injurer, as from the unauthorized possessor and the insolvent debtor.

Guardianship

Protection was in like manner provided for the estate of persons not capable of bearing arms and therefore not capable of protecting their own property, such as minors and lunatics, and above all for that of women; in these cases the nearest heirs were called to undertake the guardianship.

Law of Inheritance

After a man's death his property fell to the nearest heirs: in the division all who were equal in proximity of relationship—women included—shared alike, and the widow along with her children was admitted to her proportional share. A dispensation from the legal order of succession could only be granted by the assembly of the people; previous to which the consent of the priests had to be obtained on account of the ritual obligations attaching to succession. Such dispensations appear nevertheless to have become at an early period very frequent. In the event of a dispensation not being procured, the want of it might be in some measure remedied by means of the completely free control which every one had over his property during his lifetime. His whole property was transferred to a friend, who distributed it after death according to the wishes of the deceased.

Manumission

Manumission was unknown to the law of very early times. The owner might indeed refrain from exercising his proprietary rights; but this did not cancel the existing impossibility of master and slave coming under mutual obligations; still less did it enable the slave to acquire, in relation to the community, the rights of a guest or of a burgess. Accordingly manumission must have been at first simply -de facto-, not -de jure-; and the master cannot have been debarred from the possibility of again at pleasure treating the freedman as a slave. But there was a departure from this principle in cases where the master came under obligation not merely towards the slave, but towards the community, to leave him in possession of freedom. There was no special legal form, however, for thus binding the master—the best proof that there was at first no such thing as a manumission,—but those methods were employed for this object which the law otherwise presented, testament, action, or census. If the master had either declared his slave free when executing his last will in the assembly of the people, or had allowed his slave to claim freedom in his own presence before a judge or to get his name inscribed in the valuation-roll, the freedman was regarded not indeed as a burgess, but as personally free in relation to his former master and his heirs, and was accordingly looked upon at first as a client, and in later times as a plebeian.(7)

The emancipation of a son encountered greater difficulties than that of a slave; for while the relation of master to slave was accidental and therefore capable of being dissolved at will, the father could never cease to be father. Accordingly in later times the son was obliged, in order to get free from the father, first to enter into slavery and then to be set free out of this latter state; but in the period now before us no emancipation of sons can have as yet existed.

Clients and Foreigners

Such were the laws under which burgesses and clients lived in Rome. Between these two classes, so far as we can see, there subsisted from the beginning complete equality of private rights. The foreigner on the other hand, if he had not submitted to a Roman patron and thus lived as a client, was beyond the pale of the law both in person and in property. Whatever the Roman burgess took from him was as rightfully acquired as was the shellfish, belonging to nobody, which was picked up by the sea-shore; but in the case of ground lying beyond the Roman bounds, while the Roman burgess might take practical possession, he could not be regarded as in a legal sense its proprietor; for the individual burgess was not entitled to advance the bounds of the community. The case was different in war: whatever the soldier who was fighting in the ranks of the levy gained, whether moveable or immoveable property, fell not to him, but to the state, and accordingly here too it depended upon the state whether it would advance or contract its bounds.

Exceptions from these general rules were created by special state-treaties, which secured certain rights to the members of foreign communities within the Roman state. In particular, the perpetual league between Rome and Latium declared all contracts between Romans and Latins to be valid in law, and at the same time instituted in their case an accelerated civil process before sworn "recoverers" (-reciperatores-). As, contrary to Roman usage, which in other instances committed the decision to a single judge, these always sat in plural number and that number uneven, they are probably to be conceived as a court for the cognizance of commercial dealings, composed of arbiters from both nations and an umpire. They sat in judgment at the place where the contract was entered into, and were obliged to have the process terminated at latest in ten days. The forms, under which the dealings between Romans and Latins were conducted, were of course the general forms which regulated the mutual dealings of patricians and plebeians; for the -mancipatio- and the -nexum- were originally not at all formal acts, but the significant expression of legal ideas which held a sway at least as extensive as the range of the Latin language.

Dealings with countries strictly foreign were carried on in a different fashion and by means of other forms. In very early times treaties as to commerce and legal redress must have been entered into with the Caerites and other friendly peoples, and must have formed the basis of the international private law (-ius gentium-), which gradually became developed in Rome alongside of the law of the land. An indication of the formation of such a law is found in the remarkable -mutuum-, "the exchange" (from -mutare- like -dividuus-)—a form of loan, which was not based like the -nexum-upon a binding declaration of the debtor expressly emitted before witnesses, but upon the mere transit of the money from one hand to another, and which as evidently originated in dealings with foreigners as the -nexum- in business dealings at home. It is accordingly a significant fact that the word reappears in Sicilian Greek as —moiton—; and with this is to be connected the reappearance of the Latin -carcer- in the Sicilian —karkaron—. Since it is philologically certain that both words were originally Latin, their occurrence in the local dialect of Sicily becomes an important testimony to the frequency of the dealings of Latin traders in the island, which led to their borrowing money there and becoming liable to that imprisonment for debt, which was everywhere in the earlier systems of law the consequence of the non-repayment of a loan. Conversely, the name of the Syracusan prison, "stone-quarries" or —latomiai—, was transferred at an early period to the enlarged Roman state-prison, the -lautumiae-.

Character of the Roman Law

We have derived our outline of these institutions mainly from the earliest record of the Roman common law prepared about half a century after the abolition of the monarchy; and their existence in the regal period, while doubtful perhaps as to particular points of detail, cannot be doubted in the main. Surveying them as a whole, we recognize the law of a far-advanced agricultural and mercantile city, marked alike by its liberality and its consistency. In its case the conventional language of symbols, such as e. g. the Germanic laws exhibit, has already quite disappeared. There is no doubt that such a symbolic language must have existed at one time among the Italians. Remarkable instances of it are to be found in the form of searching a house, wherein the searcher must, according to the Roman as well as the Germanic custom, appear without upper garment merely in his shirt; and especially in the primitive Latin formula for declaring war, in which we meet with two symbols occurring at least also among the Celts and the Germans—the "pure herb" (-herba pura-, Franconian -chrene chruda-) as a symbol of the native soil, and the singed bloody staff as a sign of commencing war. But with a few exceptions, in which reasons of religion protected the ancient usages—to which class the -confarreatio-as well as the declaration of war by the college of Fetiales belonged—the Roman law, as we know it, uniformly and on principle rejects the symbol, and requires in all cases neither more nor less than the full and pure expression of will. The delivery of an article, the summons to bear witness, the conclusion of marriage, were complete as soon as the parties had in an intelligible manner declared their purpose; it was usual, indeed, to deliver the article into the hand of the new owner, to pull the person summoned as a witness by the ear, to veil the bride's head and to lead her in solemn procession to her husband's house; but all these primitive practices were already, under the oldest national law of the Romans, customs legally worthless. In a way entirely analogous to the setting aside of allegory and along with it of personification in religion, every sort of symbolism was on principle expelled from their law. In like manner that earliest state of things presented to us by the Hellenic as well as the Germanic institutions, wherein the power of the community still contends with the authority of the smaller associations of clans or cantons that are merged in it, is in Roman law wholly superseded; there is no alliance for the vindication of rights within the state, to supplement the state's imperfect aid, by mutual offence and defence; nor is there any serious trace of vengeance for bloodshed, or of the family property restricting the individual's power of disposal. Such institutions must probably at one time have existed among the Italians; traces of them may perhaps be found in particular institutions of ritual, e. g. in the expiatory goat, which the involuntary homicide was obliged to give to the nearest of kin to the slain; but even at the earliest period of Rome which we can conceive this stage had long been transcended. The clan and the family doubtless were not annihilated in the Roman community; but the theoretical as well as the practical omnipotence of the state in its own sphere was no more limited by them than by the freedom which the state granted and guaranteed to the burgess. The ultimate foundation of law was in all cases the state; freedom was simply another expression for the right of citizenship in its widest sense; all property was based on express or tacit transference by the community to the individual; a contract was valid only so far as the community by its representatives attested it, a testament only so far as the community confirmed it.

The provinces of public and private law were definitely and clearly discriminated: the former having reference to crimes against the state, which immediately called for the judgment of the state and always involved capital punishment; the latter having reference to offences against a fellow-burgess or a guest, which were mainly disposed of in the way of compromise by expiation or satisfaction made to the party injured, and were never punished with the forfeit of life, but, at most, with the loss of freedom. The greatest liberality in the permission of commerce and the most rigorous procedure in execution went hand in hand; just as in commercial states at the present day the universal right to draw bills of exchange appears in conjunction with a strict procedure in regard to them. The burgess and the client stood in their dealings on a footing of entire equality; state-treaties conceded a comprehensive equality of rights also to the guest; women were placed completely on a level in point of legal capacity with men, although restricted in action; the boy had scarcely grown up when he received at once the most comprehensive powers in the disposal of his estate, and every one who could dispose at all was as sovereign in his own sphere as was the state in public affairs. A feature eminently characteristic was the system of credit. There did not exist any credit on landed security, but instead of a debt on mortgage the step which constitutes at present the final stage in mortgage-procedure —the delivery of the property from the debtor to the creditor—took place at once. On the other hand personal credit was guaranteed in the most summary, not to say extravagant fashion; for the lawgiver entitled the creditor to treat his insolvent debtor like a thief, and granted to him in entire legislative earnest what Shylock, half in jest, stipulated for from his mortal enemy, guarding indeed by special clauses the point as to the cutting off too much more carefully than did the Jew. The law could not have more clearly expressed its design, which was to establish at once an independent agriculture free of debt and a mercantile credit, and to suppress with stringent energy all merely nominal ownership and all breaches of fidelity. If we further take into consideration the right of settlement recognized at an early date as belonging to all the Latins,(8) and the validity which was likewise early pronounced to belong to civil marriage,(9) we shall perceive that this state, which made the highest demands on its burgesses and carried the idea of subordinating the individual to the interest of the whole further than any state before or since has done, only did and only could do so by itself removing the barriers to intercourse and unshackling liberty quite as much as it subjected it to restriction. In permission or in prohibition the law was always absolute. As the foreigner who had none to intercede for him was like the hunted deer, so the guest was on a footing of equality with the burgess. A contract did not ordinarily furnish a ground of action, but where the right of the creditor was acknowledged, it was so all-powerful that there was no deliverance for the poor debtor, and no humane or equitable consideration was shown towards him. It seemed as if the law found a pleasure in presenting on all sides its sharpest spikes, in drawing the most extreme consequences, in forcibly obtruding on the bluntest understanding the tyrannic nature of the idea of right. The poetical form and the genial symbolism, which so pleasingly prevail in the Germanic legal ordinances, were foreign to the Roman; in his law all was clear and precise; no symbol was employed, no institution was superfluous. It was not cruel; everything necessary was performed without much ceremony, even the punishment of death; that a free man could not be tortured was a primitive maxim of Roman law, to obtain which other peoples have had to struggle for thousands of years. Yet this law was frightful in its inexorable severity, which we cannot suppose to have been very greatly mitigated by humanity in practice, for it was really the law of the people; more terrible than Venetian -piombi- and chambers of torture was that series of living entombments which the poor man saw yawning before him in the debtors' towers of the rich. But the greatness of Rome was involved in, and was based upon, the fact that the Roman people ordained for itself and endured a system of law, in which the eternal principles of freedom and of subordination, of property and of legal redress, reigned and still at the present day reign unadulterated and unmodified.

Notes for Book I Chapter XI

1. This "chariot-seat"—philologically no other explanation can well be given (comp. Servius ad Aen. i. 16)—is most simply explained by supposing that the king alone was entitled to ride in a chariot within the city (v. The King)—whence originated the privilege subsequently accorded to the chief magistrate on solemn occasions—and that originally, so long as there was no elevated tribunal, he gave judgment, at the comitium or wherever else he wished, from the chariot-seat.

2. I. V. The Housefather and His Household

3. The story of the death of king Tatius, as given by Plutarch (Rom. 23, 24), *viz.* that kinsmen of Tatius had killed envoys from Laurentum; that Tatius had refused the complaint of the kinsmen of the slain for redress; that they then put Tatius to death; that Romulus acquitted the murderers of Tatius, on the ground that murder had been expiated by murder; but that, in consequence of the penal judgments of the gods that simultaneously fell upon Rome and Laurentum, the perpetrators of both murders were in the sequel subjected to righteous punishment—this story looks quite like a historical version of the abolition of blood-revenge, just as the introduction of the -provocatio- lies at the foundation of the myth of the Horatii. The versions of the same story that occur elsewhere certainly present considerable variations, but they seem to be confused or dressed up.

4. The -mancipatio- in its developed form must have been more recent than the Servian reform, as the selection of mancipable objects, which had for its aim the fixing of agricultural property, shows, and as even tradition must have assumed, for it makes Servius the inventor of the balance. But in its origin the -mancipatio- must be far more ancient; for it primarily applies only to objects which are acquired by grasping with the hand, and must therefore in its earliest form have belonged to the epoch when property consisted essentially in slaves and cattle (-familia pecuniaque-). The enumeration of those objects which had to be acquired by -mancipatio-, falls accordingly to be ranked as a Servian innovation; the -mancipatio-itself, and consequently the use also of the balance and of copper, are older. Beyond doubt -mancipatio- was originally the universal form of purchase, and occurred in the case of all articles even after the Servian reform; it was only a misunderstanding of later ages which put upon the rule, that certain articles had to be transferred by -mancipatio-, the construction that these articles only and no others could be so transferred.

5. Viz. for the year of ten months one twelfth part of the capital (-uncia-), which amounts to 8 1/3 per cent for the year of ten, and 10 per cent for the fear of twelve, months.

6. I. VII. Relation of Rome to Latium

7. I. VI. Dependents and Guests.

CHAPTER XII

Religion

Roman Religion

The Roman world of gods, as we have already indicated,(1) was a higher counterpart, an ideal reflection, of the earthly Rome, in which the little and the great were alike repeated with painstaking exactness. The state and the clan, the individual phenomenon of nature as well as the individual mental operation, every man, every place and object, every act even falling within the sphere of Roman law, reappeared in the Roman world of gods; and, as earthly things come and go in perpetual flux, the circle of the gods underwent a corresponding fluctuation. The tutelary spirit, which presided over the individual act, lasted no longer than that act itself: the tutelary spirit of the individual man lived and died with the man; and eternal duration belonged to divinities of this sort only in so far as similar acts and similarly constituted men and therefore spirits of a similar kind were ever coming into existence afresh. As the Roman gods ruled over the Roman community, so every foreign community was presided over by its own gods; but sharp as was the distinction between the burgess and non-burgess, between the Roman and the foreign god, both foreign men and foreign divinities could be admitted by resolution of the community to the freedom of Rome, and when the citizens of a conquered city were transported to Rome, the gods of that city were also invited to take up their new abode there.

Oldest Table of Roman Festivals

We obtain information regarding the original cycle of the gods, as it stood in Rome previous to any contact with the Greeks, from the list of the public and duly named festival-days (-feriae publicae-) of the Roman community, which is preserved in its calendar and is beyond all question the oldest document which has reached us from Roman antiquity. The first place in it is occupied by the gods Jupiter and Mars along with the duplicate of the latter, Quirinus. To Jupiter all the days of full moon (-idus-) are sacred, besides all the wine-festivals and various other days to be mentioned afterwards; the 21st May (-agonalia-) is dedicated to his counterpart, the "bad Jovis" (-Ve-diovis-). To Mars belongs the new-year of the 1st March, and generally the great warrior-festival in this month which derived its very name from the god; this festival, introduced by the horse-racing (-equirria-) on the 27th February, had during March its principal solemnities on the days of the shield-forging (-equirria- or -Mamuralia-, March 14), of the armed dance at the Comitium (-quinquatrus-, March 19), and of the consecration of trumpets (-tubilustrium-, March 23). As, when a war was to be waged, it began with this festival, so after the close of the campaign in autumn there followed a further festival of Mars, that of the consecration of arms (-armilustrium-, October 19). Lastly, to the second Mars, Quirinus, the 17th February was appropriated (-Quirinalia-). Among the other festivals those which related to the culture of corn and wine hold the first place, while the pastoral feasts play a subordinate part. To this class belongs especially the great series of spring-festivals in April, in the course of which sacrifices were offered on the 15th to Tellus, the nourishing earth (-fordicidia-, sacrifice of the pregnant cow), on the 19th to Ceres, the goddess of germination and growth (-Cerialia-) on the 21st to Pales, the fecundating goddess of the flocks (-Parilia-), on the 23rd to Jupiter, as the protector of the vines and of the vats of the previous year's vintage which were first opened on this day (-Vinalia-), and on the 25th to the bad enemy of the crops, rust (-Robigus-: -Robigalia-). So after the completion of the work of the fields and the fortunate ingathering of their produce double festivals were celebrated in honour of the god and goddess of inbringing and harvest, Census (from -condere-) and Ops; the first, immediately after the completion of cutting (August 21, -Consualia-; August 25, -Opiconsiva-); and the second, in the middle of winter, when the blessings of the granary are especially manifest (December 15, -Consualia-; December 19, -Opalia-); between these two latter days the thoughtfulness of the old arrangers of the festivals inserted that of seed-sowing (Saturnalia from -Saeturnus- or -Saturnus-, December 17). In like manner the festival of must or of healing (-meditrinalia-, October 11), so called because a healing virtue was attributed to the fresh must, was dedicated to Jovis as the wine-god after the completion of the vintage; the original reference of the third wine-feast (-Vinalia-, August 19) is not clear. To these festivals were added at the close of the year the wolf-festival (-Lupercalia-, February 17) of the shepherds in honour of the good god, Faunus, and the boundary-stone festival (-Terminalia-, February 23) of the husbandmen, as also the summer grove-festival of two days (-Lucaria-, July 19, 21) which may have had reference to the forest-gods (-Silvani-), the fountain-festival (-Fontinalia-, October 13), and the festival of the shortest day, which brings in the new sun (-An-geronalia-, -Divalia-, December 21).

200

Of not less importance—as was to be expected in the case of the port of Latium—were the mariner-festivals of the divinities of the sea (-Neptunalia-, July 23), of the harbour (-Portunalia-, August 17), and of the Tiber stream (-Volturnalia-, August 27).

Handicraft and art, on the other hand, are represented in this cycle of the gods only by the god of fire and of smith's work, Vulcanus, to whom besides the day named after him (-Volcanalia-, August 23) the second festival of the consecration of trumpets was dedicated (-tubilustrium-, May 23), and eventually also by the festival of Carmentis (-Carmentalia- January 11, 15), who probably was adored originally as the goddess of spells and of song and only inferentially as protectress of births.

Domestic and family life in general were represented by the festival of the goddess of the house and of the spirits of the storechamber, Vesta and the Penates (-Vestalia-, June 9); the festival of the goddess of birth(2) (-Matralia-, June 11); the festival of the blessing of children, dedicated to Liber and Libera (-Liberalia-, March 17), the festival of departed spirits (-Feralia-, February 21), and the three days' ghost-celebration (-Lemuria- May 9, 11, 13); while those having reference to civil relations were the two—otherwise to us somewhat obscure—festivals of the king's flight (-Regifugium-, February 24) and of the people's flight (-Poplifugia-, July 5), of which at least the last day was devoted to Jupiter, and the festival of the Seven Mounts (-Agonia- or -Septimontium-, December 11). A special day (-agonia-, January 9) was also consecrated to Janus, the god of beginning. The real nature of some other days—that of Furrina (July 25), and that of the Larentalia devoted to Jupiter and Acca Larentia, perhaps a feast of the Lares (December 23)—is no longer known.

This table is complete for the immoveable public festivals; and—although by the side of these standing festal days there certainly occurred from the earliest times changeable and occasional festivals—this document, in what it says as well as in what it omits, opens up to us an insight into a primitive age otherwise almost wholly lost to us. The union of the Old Roman community and the Hill-Romans had indeed already taken place when this table of festivals was formed, for we find in it Quirinus alongside of Mars; but, when this festival-list was drawn up, the Capitoline temple was not yet in existence, for Juno and Minerva are absent; nor was the temple of Diana erected on the Aventine; nor was any notion of worship borrowed from the Greeks.

Mars and Jupiter

The central object not only of Roman but of Italian worship generally in that epoch when the Italian stock still dwelt by itself in the peninsula was, according to all indications, the god Maurs or Mars, the killing god,(3) preeminently regarded as the divine champion of the burgesses, hurling the spear, protecting the flock, and overthrowing the foe. Each community of course possessed its own Mars, and deemed him to be the strongest and holiest of all; and accordingly every "-ver sacrum-" setting out to found a new community marched under the protection of its own Mars. To Mars was dedicated the first month not only in the Roman calendar of the months, which in no other instance takes notice of the gods, but also probably in all the other Latin and Sabellian calendars: among the Roman proper names, which in like manner contain no allusion to any gods, Marcus, Mamercus, and Mamurius appear in prevailing use from very early times; with Mars and his sacred woodpecker was connected the oldest Italian prophecy; the wolf, the animal sacred to Mars, was the badge of the Roman burgesses, and such sacred national legends as the Roman imagination was able to produce referred exclusively to the god Mars and to his duplicate Quirinus. In the list of festivals certainly Father Diovis—a purer and more civil than military reflection of the character of the Roman community—occupies a larger space than Mars, just as the priest of Jupiter has precedence over the two priests of the god of war; but the latter still plays a very prominent part in the list, and it is even quite likely that, when this arrangement of festivals was established, Jovis stood by the side of Mars like Ahuramazda by the side of Mithra, and that the worship of the warlike Roman community still really centred at this time in the martial god of death and his March festival, while it was not the "care-destroyer" afterwards introduced by the Greeks, but Father Jovis himself, who was regarded as the god of the heart-gladdening wine.

Nature of the Roman Gods

It is no part of our present task to consider the Roman deities in detail; but it is important, even in an historical point of view, to call attention to the peculiar character at once of shallowness and of fervour that marked the Roman faith. Abstraction and personification lay at the root of the Roman as well as of the Hellenic mythology: the Hellenic as well as the Roman god was originally suggested by some natural phenomenon or some mental conception, and to the Roman just as to the Greek every divinity appeared a person. This is evident from their apprehending the individual gods as male or female; from their style of appeal to an unknown deity,—"Be thou god or goddess, man or woman;" and from the deeply cherished belief that the name of the proper tutelary spirit of the community ought to remain for ever unpronounced, lest an enemy should come to learn it and calling the god by his name should entice him beyond the bounds. A remnant of this strongly sensuous mode of apprehension clung to Mars in particular, the oldest and most national form of divinity in Italy. But while abstraction, which lies at the foundation of every religion, elsewhere endeavoured to rise to wider and more enlarged conceptions and to penetrate ever more deeply into the essence of things, the forms of the Roman faith remained at, or sank to, a singularly low level of conception and of insight. While in the case of the Greek every influential motive speedily expanded into a group of forms and gathered around it a circle of legends and ideas, in the case of the Roman the fundamental thought remained stationary in its original naked rigidity. The religion of Rome had nothing of its own presenting even a remote resemblance to the religion of Apollo investing earthly morality with a halo of glory, to the divine intoxication of Dionysus, or to the Chthonian and mystical worships with their profound and hidden meanings. It had indeed its "bad god" (-Ve-diovis-), its apparitions and ghosts (-lemures-), and afterwards its deities of foul air, of fever, of diseases, perhaps even of theft (-laverna-); but it was unable to excite that mysterious awe after which the human heart has always a longing, or thoroughly to embody the incomprehensible and even the malignant elements in nature and in man, which must not be wanting in religion if it would reflect man as a whole. In the religion of Rome there was hardly anything secret except possibly the names of the gods of the city, the Penates; the real character, moreover, even of these gods was manifest to every one.

The national Roman theology sought on all hands to form distinct conceptions of important phenomena and qualities, to express them in its terminology, and to classify them systematically—in the first instance, according to that division of persons and things which also formed the basis of private law—that it might thus be able in due fashion to invoke the gods individually or by classes, and to point out (-indigitare-) to the multitude the modes of appropriate invocation. Of such notions, the products of outward abstraction—of the homeliest simplicity, sometimes venerable, sometimes ridiculous—Roman theology was in substance made up. Conceptions such as sowing (-saeturnus-) and field-labour (-ops-) ground (-tellus-) and boundary-stone (-terminus-), were among the oldest and most sacred of Roman divinities. Perhaps the most peculiar of all the forms of deity in Rome, and probably the only one for whose worship there was devised an effigy peculiarly Italian, was the double-headed Ianus; and yet it was simply suggestive of the idea so characteristic of the scrupulous spirit of Roman religion, that at the commencement of every act the "spirit of opening" should first be invoked, while it above all betokened the deep conviction that it was as indispensable to combine the Roman gods in sets as it was necessary that the more personal gods of the Hellenes should stand singly and apart.(4) Of all the worships of Rome that which perhaps had the deepest hold was the worship of the tutelary spirits that presided in and over the household and the storechamber: these were in public worship Vesta and the Penates, in family worship the gods of forest and field, the Silvani, and above all the gods of the household in its strict sense, the Lases or Lares, to whom their share of the family meal was regularly assigned, and before whom it was, even in the time of Cato the Elder, the first duty of the father of the household on returning home to perform his devotions. In the ranking of the gods, however, these spirits of the house and of the field occupied the lowest rather than the highest place; it was—and it could not be otherwise with a religion which renounced all attempts to idealize—not the broadest and most general, but the simplest and most individual abstraction, in which the pious heart found most nourishment.

This indifference to ideal elements in the Roman religion was accompanied by a practical and utilitarian tendency, as is clearly enough apparent in the table of festivals which has been already explained. Increase of substance and of prosperity by husbandry and the rearing of flocks and herds, by seafaring and commerce—this was what the Roman desired from his gods; and it very well accords with this view, that the god of good faith (-deus fidius-), the goddess of chance and good luck (-fors fortuna-), and the god of traffic (-mercurius-), all originating out of their daily dealings, although not occurring in that ancient table of festivals, appear very early as adored far and near by the Romans. Strict frugality and mercantile speculation were rooted in the Roman character too deeply not to find their thorough reflection in its divine counterpart.

Spirits

Respecting the world of spirits little can be said. The departed souls of mortal men, the "good" (-manes-) continued to exist as shades haunting the spot where the body reposed (-dii inferi-), and received meat and drink from the survivors. But they dwelt in the depths beneath, and there was no bridge that led from the lower world either to men ruling on earth or upward to the gods above. The hero-worship of the Greeks was wholly foreign to the Romans, and the late origin and poor invention of the legend as to the foundation of Rome are shown by the thoroughly unRoman transformation of king Romulus into the god Quirinus. Numa, the oldest and most venerable name in Roman tradition, never received the honours of a god in Rome as Theseus did in Athens.

Priests

The most ancient priesthoods in the community bore reference to Mars; especially the priest of the god of the community, nominated for life, "the kindler of Mars" (-flamen Martialis-) as he was designated from presenting burnt-offerings, and the twelve "leapers" (-salii-), a band of young men who in March performed the war-dance in honour of Mars and accompanied it by song. We have already explained(5) how the amalgamation of the Hill-community with that of the Palatine gave rise to the duplication of the Roman Mars, and thereby to the introduction of a second priest of Mars—the -flamen Quirinalis- —and a second guild of dancers—the -salii collini- .

To these were added other public worships (some of which probably had an origin far earlier than that of Rome), for which either single priests were appointed—as those of Carmentis, of Volcanus, of the god of the harbour and the river—or the celebration of which was committed to particular colleges or clans in name of the people. Such a college was probably that of the twelve "field-brethren" (-fratres arvales-) who invoked the "creative goddess" (-dea dia-) in May to bless the growth of the seed; although it is very doubtful whether they already at this period enjoyed that peculiar consideration which we find subsequently accorded to them in the time of the empire. These were accompanied by the Titian brotherhood, which had to preserve and to attend to the distinctive -cultus- of the Roman Sabines,(6) and by the thirty "curial kindlers" (-flamines curiales-), instituted for the hearth of the thirty curies. The "wolf festival" (-lupercalia-) already mentioned was celebrated for the protection of the flocks and herds in honour of the "favourable god" (-faunus-) by the Quinctian clan and the Fabii who were associated with them after the admission of the Hill-Romans, in the month of February—a genuine shepherds' carnival, in which the "Wolves" (-luperci-) jumped about naked with a girdle of goatskin, and whipped with thongs those whom they met. In like manner the community may be conceived as represented and participating in the case of other gentile worships.

To this earliest worship of the Roman community new rites were gradually added. The most important of these worships had reference to the city as newly united and virtually founded afresh by the construction of the great wall and stronghold. In it the highest and best Iovis of the Capitol—that is, the genius of the Roman people—-was placed at the head of all the Roman divinities, and his "kindler" thenceforth appointed, the -flamen Dialis-, formed in conjunction with the two priests of Mars the sacred triad of high-priests. Contemporaneously began the -cultus- of the new single city-hearth—Vesta—and the kindred -cultus- of the Penates of the community.(7) Six chaste virgins, daughters as it were of the household of the Roman people, attended to that pious service, and had to maintain the wholesome fire of the common hearth always blazing as an example(8) and an omen to the burgesses. This worship, half-domestic, half-public, was the most sacred of all in Rome, and it accordingly was the latest of all the heathen worships there to give way before the ban of Christianity. The Aventine, moreover, was assigned to Diana as the representative of the Latin confederacy,(9) but for that very reason no special Roman priesthood was appointed for her; and the community gradually became accustomed to render definite homage to numerous other deified abstractions by means of general festivals or by representative priesthoods specially destined for their service; in particular instances—such as those of the goddess of flowers (-Flora-) and of fruits (-Pomona-)—it appointed also special -flamines-, so that the number of these was at length fifteen. But among them they carefully distinguished those three "great kindlers" (-flamines maiores-), who down to the latest times could only be taken from the ranks of the old burgesses, just as the old incorporations of the Palatine and Quirinal -Salii-always asserted precedence over all the other colleges of priests. Thus the necessary and stated observances due to the gods of the community were entrusted once for all by the state to fixed colleges or regular ministers; and the expense of sacrifices, which was presumably not inconsiderable, was covered partly by the assignation of certain lands to particular temples, partly by the fines.(10)

It cannot be doubted that the public worship of the other Latin, and presumably also of the Sabellian, communities was essentially similar in character. At any rate it can be shown that the Flamines, Salii, Luperci, and Vestales were institutions not special to Rome, but general among the Latins, and at least the first three colleges appear to have been formed in the kindred communities independently of the Roman model.

Lastly, as the state made arrangements for the cycle of its gods, so each burgess might make similar arrangements within his individual sphere, and might not only present sacrifices, but might also consecrate set places and ministers, to his own divinities.

Colleges of Sacred Lore

There was thus enough of priesthood and of priests in Rome. Those, however, who had business with a god resorted to the god, and not to the priest. Every suppliant and inquirer addressed himself directly to the divinity—the community of course by the king as its mouthpiece, just as the -curia- by the -curio- and the -equites-by their colonels; no intervention of a priest was allowed to conceal or to obscure this original and simple relation. But it was no easy matter to hold converse with a god. The god had his own way of speaking, which was intelligible only to the man acquainted with it; but one who did rightly understand it knew not only how to ascertain, but also how to manage, the will of the god, and even in case of need to overreach or to constrain him. It was natural, therefore, that the worshipper of the god should regularly consult such men of skill and listen to their advice; and thence arose the corporations or colleges of men specially skilled in religious lore, a thoroughly national Italian institution, which had a far more important influence on political development than the individual priests and priesthoods. These colleges have been often, but erroneously, confounded with the priesthoods. The priesthoods were charged with the worship of a specific divinity; the skilled colleges, on the other hand, were charged with the preservation of traditional rules regarding those more general religious observances, the proper fulfilment of which implied a certain amount of knowledge and rendered it necessary that the state in its own interest should provide for the faithful transmission of that knowledge. These close corporations supplying their own vacancies, of course from the ranks of the burgesses, became in this way the depositaries of skilled arts and sciences.

Augurs—Pontifices

Under the Roman constitution and that of the Latin communities in general there were originally but two such colleges; that of the augurs and that of the Pontifices.(11)

The six "bird-carriers" (-augures-) were skilled in interpreting the language of the gods from the flight of birds; an art which was prosecuted with great earnestness and reduced to a quasi-scientific system. The six "bridge-builders" (-Pontifices-) derived their name from their function, as sacred as it was politically important, of conducting the building and demolition of the bridge over the Tiber. They were the Roman engineers, who understood the mystery of measures and numbers; whence there devolved upon them also the duty of managing the calendar of the state, of proclaiming to the people the time of new and full moon and the days of festivals, and of seeing that every religious and every judicial act took place on the right day. As they had thus an especial supervision of all religious observances, it was to them in case of need—on occasion of marriage, testament, and -adrogatio- —that the preliminary question was addressed, whether the business proposed did not in any respect offend against divine law; and it was they who fixed and promulgated the general exoteric precepts of ritual, which were known under the name of the "royal laws." Thus they acquired (although not probably to the full extent till after the abolition of the monarchy) the general oversight of Roman worship and of whatever was connected with it—and what was there that was not so connected? They themselves described the sum of their knowledge as "the science of things divine and human." In fact the rudiments of spiritual and temporal jurisprudence as well as of historical recording proceeded from this college. For all writing of history was associated with the calendar and the book of annals; and, as from the organization of the Roman courts of law no tradition could originate in these courts themselves, it was necessary that the knowledge of legal principles and procedure should be traditionally preserved in the college of the Pontifices, which alone was competent to give an opinion respecting court-days and questions of religious law.

Fetiales

By the side of these two oldest and most eminent corporations of men versed in spiritual lore may be to some extent ranked the college of the twenty state-heralds (-fetiales-, of uncertain derivation), destined as a living repository to preserve traditionally the remembrance of the treaties concluded with neighbouring communities, to pronounce an authoritative opinion on alleged infractions of treaty-rights, and in case of need to attempt reconciliation or declare war. They had precisely the same position with reference to international, as the Pontifices had with reference to religious, law; and were therefore, like the latter, entitled to point out the law, although not to administer it.

But in however high repute these colleges were, and important and comprehensive as were the functions assigned to them, it was never forgotten—least of all in the case of those which held the highest position—that their duty was not to command, but to tender skilled advice, not directly to obtain the answer of the gods, but to explain the answer when obtained to the inquirer. Thus the highest of the priests was not merely inferior in rank to the king, but might not even give advice to him unasked. It was the province of the king to determine whether and when he would take an observation of birds; the "bird-seer" simply stood beside him and interpreted to him, when necessary, the language of the messengers of heaven. In like manner the Fetialis and the Pontifex could not interfere in matters of international or common law except when those concerned therewith desired it. The Romans, notwithstanding all their zeal for religion, adhered with unbending strictness to the principle that the priest ought to remain completely powerless in the state and—excluded from all command— ought like any other burgess to render obedience to the humblest magistrate.

Character of the -Cultus-

The Latin worship was grounded essentially on man's enjoyment of earthly pleasures, and only in a subordinate degree on his fear of the wild forces of nature; it consisted pre-eminently therefore in expressions of joy, in lays and songs, in games and dances, and above all in banquets. In Italy, as everywhere among agricultural tribes whose ordinary food consists of vegetables, the slaughter of cattle was at once a household feast and an act of worship: a pig was the most acceptable offering to the gods, just because it was the usual roast for a feast. But all extravagance of expense as well as all excess of rejoicing was inconsistent with the solid character of the Romans. Frugality in relation to the gods was one of the most prominent traits of the primitive Latin worship; and the free play of imagination was repressed with iron severity by the moral self-discipline which the nation maintained. In consequence the Latins remained strangers to the excesses which grow out of unrestrained indulgence. At the very core of the Latin religion there lay that profound moral impulse which leads men to bring earthly guilt and earthly punishment into relation with the world of the gods, and to view the former as a crime against the gods, and the latter as its expiation. The execution of the criminal condemned to death was as much an expiatory sacrifice offered to the divinity as was the killing of an enemy in just war; the thief who by night stole the fruits of the field paid the penalty to Ceres on the gallows just as the enemy paid it to mother earth and the good spirits on the field of battle. The profound and fearful idea of substitution also meets us here: when the gods of the community were angry and nobody could be laid hold of as definitely guilty, they might be appeased by one who voluntarily gave himself up (-devovere se-); noxious chasms in the ground were closed, and battles half lost were converted into victories, when a brave burgess threw himself as an expiatory offering into the abyss or upon the foe. The "sacred spring" was based on a similar view; all the offspring whether of cattle or of men within a specified period were presented to the gods. If acts of this nature are to be called human sacrifices, then such sacrifices belonged to the essence of the Latin faith; but we are bound to add that, far back as our view reaches into the past, this immolation, so far as life was concerned, was limited to the guilty who had been convicted before a civil tribunal, or to the innocent who voluntarily chose to die. Human sacrifices of a different description run counter to the fundamental idea of a sacrificial act, and, wherever they occur among the Indo-Germanic stocks at least, are based on later degeneracy and barbarism. They never gained admission among the Romans; hardly in a single instance were superstition and despair induced, even in times of extreme distress, to seek an extraordinary deliverance through means so revolting. Of belief in ghosts, fear of enchantments, or dealing in mysteries, comparatively slight traces are to be found among the Romans. Oracles and prophecy never acquired the importance in Italy which they obtained in Greece, and never were able to exercise a serious control over private or public life. But on the other hand the Latin religion sank into an incredible insipidity and dulness, and early became shrivelled into an anxious and dreary round of ceremonies. The god of the Italian was, as we have already said, above all things an instrument for helping him to the attainment of very substantial earthly aims; this turn was given to the religious views of the Italian by his tendency towards the palpable and the real, and is no less distinctly apparent in the saint-worship of the modern inhabitants of Italy. The gods confronted man just as a creditor confronted his debtor; each of them had a duly acquired right to certain performances and payments; and as the number of the gods was as great as the number of the incidents in earthly life, and the neglect or wrong performance of the worship of each god revenged itself in the corresponding incident, it was a laborious and difficult task even to gain a knowledge of a man's religious obligations, and the priests who were skilled in the law of divine things and pointed out its requirements—the -Pontifices- —could not fail to attain an extraordinary influence. The upright man fulfilled the requirements of sacred ritual with the same mercantile punctuality with which he met his earthly obligations, and at times did more than was due, if the god had done so on his part. Man even dealt in speculation with his god; a vow was in reality as in name a formal contract between the god and the man, by which the latter promised to the former for a certain service to be rendered a certain equivalent return; and the Roman legal principle that no contract could be concluded by deputy was not the least important of the reasons on account of which all priestly mediation remained excluded from the religious concerns of man in Latium. Nay, as the Roman merchant was entitled, without injury to his conventional rectitude, to fulfil his contract merely in the letter, so in dealing with the gods, according to the teaching of Roman theology, the copy of an object was given and received instead of the object itself. They presented to the lord of the sky heads of onions and poppies, that he might launch his lightnings at these rather than at the heads of men. In payment of the offering annually demanded by father Tiber, thirty puppets plaited of rushes were annually thrown into the stream.(12) The ideas of divine mercy and placability were in these instances inseparably mixed up with a pious cunning, which tried to delude and to pacify so formidable a master by means of a sham satisfaction. The Roman fear of the gods accordingly exercised powerful influence over the minds of the multitude; but it was by no means that sense of awe in the presence of an all-controlling nature or of an almighty God, that lies at the foundation of the views of pantheism and monotheism respectively; on the contrary, it was of a very earthly character, and scarcely different in any material respect from the trembling with which the Roman debtor approached his just, but very strict and very powerful creditor. It is plain that such a religion was fitted rather to stifle than to foster artistic and speculative views. When the Greek had clothed the simple thoughts of primitive times with human flesh and blood, the ideas of the gods so formed not only became the elements of plastic and poetic art, but acquired also that universality and elasticity which are the profoundest characteristics of human nature and for this very reason are essential to all religions that aspire to rule the world. Through such means the simple view of nature became expanded into the conception of a cosmogony, the homely moral notion became enlarged into a principle of universal humanity; and for a long period the Greek religion was enabled to embrace within it the physical and metaphysical views—the whole ideal development of the nation—and to expand in depth and breadth with the increase of its contents, until imagination and speculation rent asunder the vessel which had nursed them. But in Latium the embodiment of the conceptions of deity continued so wholly transparent that it afforded no opportunity for the training either of artist or poet, and the Latin religion always held a distant and even hostile attitude towards art As the god was not and could not be aught else than the spiritualizattion of an earthly phenomenon, this same earthly counterpart naturally formed his place of abode (-templum-) and his image; walls and effigies made by the hands of men seemed only to obscure and to embarrass the spiritual conception. Accordingly the original Roman worship had no images of the gods or houses set apart for them; and although the god was at an early period worshipped in Latium, probably in imitation of the Greeks, by means of an image, and had a little chapel (-aedicula-) built for him, such a figurative representation was reckoned contrary to the laws of Numa and was generally regarded as an impure and foreign innovation. The Roman religion could exhibit no image of a god peculiar to it, with the exception, perhaps, of the double-headed Ianus; and Varro even in his time derided the desire of the multitude for puppets and effigies. The utter want of productive power in the Roman religion was likewise the ultimate cause of the thorough poverty which always marked Roman poetry and still more Roman speculation.

The same distinctive character was manifest, moreover, in the domain of its practical use. The practical gain which accrued to the Roman community from their religion was a code of moral law gradually developed by the priests, and the -Pontifices- in particular, which on the one hand supplied the place of police regulations at a time when the state was still far from providing any direct police-guardianship for its citizens, and on the other hand brought to the bar of the gods and visited with divine penalties the breach of moral obligations. To the regulations of the former class belonged the religious inculcation of a due observance of holidays and of a cultivation of the fields and vineyards according to the rules of good husbandry—which we shall have occasion to notice more fully in the sequel—as well as the worship of the heath or of the Lares which was connected with considerations of sanitary police,(13) and above all the practice of burning the bodies of the dead, adopted among the Romans at a singularly early period, far earlier than among the Greeks—a practice implying a rational conception of life and of death, which was foreign to primitive times and is even foreign to ourselves at the present day. It must be reckoned no small achievement that the national religion of the Latins was able to carry out these and similar improvements. But the civilizing effect of this law was still more important. If a husband sold his wife, or a father sold his married son; if a child struck his father, or a daughter-in-law her father-in-law; if a patron violated his obligation to keep faith with his guest or dependent; if an unjust neighbour displaced a boundary-stone, or the thief laid hands by night on the grain entrusted to the common good faith; the burden of the curse of the gods lay thenceforth on the head of the offender. Not that the person thus accursed (-sacer-) was outlawed; such an outlawry, inconsistent in its nature with all civil order, was only an exceptional occurrence—an aggravation of the religious curse in Rome at the time of the quarrels between the orders. It was not the province of the individual burgess, or even of the wholly powerless priest, to carry into effect such a divine curse. Primarily the person thus accursed became liable to the divine penal judgment, not to human caprice; and the pious popular faith, on which that curse was based, must have had power even over natures frivolous and wicked. But the banning was not confined to this; the king was in reality entitled and bound to carry the ban into execution, and, after the fact, on which the law set its curse, had been according to his conscientious conviction established, to slay the person under ban, as it were, as a victim offered up to the injured deity (-supplicium-), and thus to purify the community from the crime of the individual. If the crime was of a minor nature, for the slaying of the guilty there was substituted a ransom through the presenting of a sacrificial victim or of similar gifts. Thus the whole criminal law rested as to its ultimate basis on the religious idea of expiation.

But religion performed no higher service in Latium than the furtherance of civil order and morality by such means as these. In this field Hellas had an unspeakable advantage over Latium; it owed to its religion not merely its whole intellectual development, but also its national union, so far as such an union was attained at all; the oracles and festivals of the gods, Delphi and Olympia, and the Muses, daughters of faith, were the centres round which revolved all that was great in Hellenic life and all in it that was the common heritage of the nation. And yet even here Latium had, as compared with Hellas, its own advantages. The Latin religion, reduced as it was to the level of ordinary perception, was completely intelligible to every one and accessible in common to all; and therefore the Roman community preserved the equality of its citizens, while Hellas, where religion rose to the level of the highest thought, had from the earliest times to endure all the blessing and curse of an aristocracy of intellect. The Latin religion like every other had its origin in the effort of faith to fathom the infinite; it is only to a superficial view, which is deceived as to the depth of the stream because it is clear, that its transparent spirit-world can appear to be shallow. This fervid faith disappeared with the progress of time as necessarily as the dew of morning disappears before the rising sun, and thus the Latin religion came subsequently to wither; but the Latins preserved their simplicity of belief longer than most peoples and longer especially than the Greeks. As colours are effects of light and at the same time dim it, so art and science are not merely the creations but also the destroyers of faith; and, much as this process at once of development and of destruction is swayed by necessity, by the same law of nature certain results have been reserved to the epoch of early simplicity—results which subsequent epochs make vain endeavours to attain. The mighty intellectual development of the Hellenes, which created their religious and literary unity (ever imperfect as that unity was), was the very thing that made it impossible for them to attain to a genuine political union; they sacrificed thereby the simplicity, the flexibility, the self-devotion, the power of amalgamation, which constitute the conditions of any such union. It is time therefore to desist from that childish view of history which believes that it can commend the Greeks only at the expense of the Romans, or the Romans only at the expense of the Greeks; and, as we allow the oak to hold its own beside the rose, so should we abstain from praising or censuring the two noblest organizations which antiquity has produced, and comprehend the truth that their distinctive excellences have a necessary connection with their respective defects. The deepest and ultimate reason of the diversity between the two nations lay beyond doubt in the fact that Latium did not, and that Hellas did, during the season of growth come into contact with the East. No people on earth was great enough by its own efforts to create either the marvel of Hellenic or at a later period the marvel of Christian culture; history has produced these most brilliant results only where the ideas of Aramaic religion have sunk into an Indo-Germanic soil. But if for this reason Hellas is the prototype of purely human, Latium is not less for all time the prototype of national, development; and it is the duty of us their successors to honour both and to learn from both.

Foreign Worships

Such was the nature and such the influence of the Roman religion in its pure, unhampered, and thoroughly national development. Its national character was not infringed by the fact that, from the earliest times, modes and systems of worship were introduced from abroad; no more than the bestowal of the rights of citizenship on individual foreigners denationalized the Roman state. An exchange of gods as well as of goods with the Latins in older time must have been a matter of course; the transplantation to Rome of gods and worships belonging to less cognate races is more remarkable. Of the distinctive Sabine worship maintained by the Tities we have already spoken.(14) Whether any conceptions of the gods were borrowed from Etruria is more doubtful: for the Lases, the older designation of the genii (from -lascivus-), and Minerva the goddess of memory (-mens-, -menervare-), which it is customary to describe as originally Etruscan, were on the contrary, judging from philological grounds, indigenous to Latium. It is at any rate certain, and in keeping with all that we otherwise know of Roman intercourse that the Greek worship received earlier and more extensive attention in Rome than any other of foreign origin. The Greek oracles furnished the earliest occasion of its introduction. The language of the Roman gods was on the whole confined to Yea and Nay or at the most to the making their will known by the method of casting lots, which appears in its origin Italian;(15) while from very ancient times—although not apparently until the impulse was received from the East—the more talkative gods of the Greeks imparted actual utterances of prophecy. The Romans made efforts, even at an early period, to treasure up such counsels, and copies of the leaves of the soothsaying priestess of Apollo, the Cumaean Sibyl, were accordingly a highly valued gift on the part of their Greek guest-friends from Campania. For the reading and interpretation of the fortune-telling book a special college, inferior in rank only to the augurs and Pontifices, was instituted in early times, consisting of two men of lore (-duoviri sacris faciundis-), who were furnished at the expense of the state with two slaves acquainted with the Greek language. To these custodiers of oracles the people resorted in cases of doubt, when an act of worship was needed in order to avoid some impending evil and they did not know to which of the gods or with what rites it was to be performed. But Romans in search of advice early betook themselves also to the Delphic Apollo himself. Besides the legends relating to such an intercourse already mentioned,(16) it is attested partly by the reception of the word -thesaurus- so closely connected with the Delphic oracle into all the Italian languages with which we are acquainted, and partly by the oldest Roman form of the name of Apollo, -Aperta-, the "opener," an etymologizing alteration of the Doric Apellon, the antiquity of which is betrayed by its very barbarism. The Greek Herakles was naturalized in Italy as Herclus, Hercoles, Hercules, at an early period and under a peculiar conception of his character, apparently in the first instance as the god of gains of adventure and of any extraordinary increase of wealth; for which reason the general was wont to present the tenth of the spoil which he had procured, and the merchant the tenth of the substance which he had obtained, to Hercules at the chief altar (-ara maxima-) in the cattle-market. Accordingly he became the god of mercantile covenants generally, which in early times were frequently concluded at this altar and confirmed by oath, and in so far was identified with the old Latin god of good faith (-deus fidius-). The worship of Hercules was from an early date among the most widely diffused; he was, to use the words of an ancient author, adored in every hamlet of Italy, and altars were everywhere erected to him in the streets of the cities and along the country roads. The gods also of the mariner, Castor and Polydeukes or, in Roman form, Pollux, the god of traffic Hermes—the Roman Mercurius—and the god of healing, Asklapios or Aesculapius, became early known to the Romans, although their public worship only began at a later period. The name of the festival of the "good goddess" (-bona dea-) -damium-, corresponding to the Greek —damion— or —deimion—, may likewise reach back as far as this epoch. It must be the result also of ancient borrowing, that the old -Liber pater- of the Romans was afterwards conceived as "father deliverer" and identified with the wine-god of the Greeks, the "releaser" (-Lyaeos-), and that the Roman god of the lower regions was called the "dispenser of riches" (-Pluto- — -Dis pater-), while his spouse Persephone became converted at once by change of the initial sound and by transference of the idea into the Roman Proserpina, that is, "germinatrix." Even the goddess of the Romano-Latin league, Diana of the Aventine, seems to have been copied from the federal goddess of the Ionians of Asia Minor, the Ephesian Artemis; at least her carved image in the Roman temple was formed after the Ephesian type.(17) It was in this way alone, through the myths of Apollo, Dionysus, Pluto, Herakles, and Artemis, which were early pervaded by Oriental ideas, that the Aramaic religion exercised at this period a remote and indirect influence on Italy. We clearly perceive from these facts that the introduction of the Greek religion was especially due to commercial intercourse, and that it was traders and mariners who primarily brought the Greek gods to Italy.

These individual cases however of derivation from abroad were but of secondary moment, while the remains of the natural symbolism of primeval times, of which the legend of the oxen of Cacus may perhaps be a specimen,(18) had virtually disappeared. In all its leading features the Roman religion was an organic creation of the people among whom we find it.

Religion of the Sabellians

The Sabellian and Umbrian worship, judging from the little we know of it, rested upon quite the same fundamental views as the Latin with local variations of colour and form. That it was different from the Latin is very distinctly apparent from the founding of a special college at Rome for the preservation of the Sabine rites;(19) but that very fact affords an instructive illustration of the nature of the difference. Observation of the flight of birds was with both stocks the regular mode of consulting the gods; but the Tities observed different birds from the Ramnian augurs. Similar relations present themselves, wherever we have opportunity of comparing them. Both stocks in common regarded the gods as abstractions of the earthly and as of an impersonal nature; they differed in expression and ritual. It was natural that these diversities should appear of importance to the worshippers of those days; we are no longer able to apprehend what was the characteristic distinction, if any really existed.

Religion of the Etruscans

But the remains of the sacred ritual of the Etruscans that have reached us are marked by a different spirit. Their prevailing characteristics are a gloomy and withal tiresome mysticism, ringing the changes on numbers, soothsaying, and that solemn enthroning of pure absurdity which at all times finds its own circle of devotees. We are far from knowing the Etruscan worship in such completeness and purity as we know the Latin; and it is not improbable—indeed it cannot well be doubted—that several of its features were only imported into it by the minute subtlety of a later period, and that the gloomy and fantastic principles, which were most alien to the Latin worship, are those that have been especially handed down to us by tradition. But enough still remains to show that the mysticism and barbarism of this worship had their foundation in the essential character of the Etruscan people.

With our very unsatisfactory knowledge we cannot grasp the intrinsic contrast subsisting between the Etruscan conceptions of deity and the Italian; but it is clear that the most prominent among the Etruscan gods were the malignant and the mischievous; as indeed their worship was cruel, and included in particular the sacrifice of their captives; thus at Caere they slaughtered the Phocaean, and at Traquinii the Roman, prisoners. Instead of a tranquil world of departed "good spirits" ruling peacefully in the realms beneath, such as the Latins had conceived, the Etruscan religion presented a veritable hell, in which the poor souls were doomed to be tortured by mallets and serpents, and to which they were conveyed by the conductor of the dead, a savage semi-brutal figure of an old man with wings and a large hammer—a figure which afterwards served in the gladiatorial games at Rome as a model for the costume of the man who removed the corpses of the slain from the arena. So fixed was the association of torture with this condition of the shades, that there was even provided a redemption from it, which after certain mysterious offerings transferred the poor soul to the society of the gods above. It is remarkable that, in order to people their lower world, the Etruscans early borrowed from the Greeks their gloomiest notions, such as the doctrine of Acheron and Charon, which play an important part in the Etruscan discipline.

But the Etruscan occupied himself above all in the interpretation of signs and portents. The Romans heard the voice of the gods in nature; but their bird-seer understood only the signs in their simplicity, and knew only in general whether the occurrence boded good or ill. Disturbances of the ordinary course of nature were regarded by him as boding evil, and put a stop to the business in hand, as when for example a storm of thunder and lightning dispersed the comitia; and he probably sought to get rid of them, as, for example, in the case of monstrous births, which were put to death as speedily as possible. But beyond the Tiber matters were carried much further. The profound Etruscan read off to the believer his future fortunes in detail from the lightning and from the entrails of animals offered in sacrifice; and the more singular the language of the gods, the more startling the portent or prodigy, the more confidently did he declare what they foretold and the means by which it was possible to avert the mischief. Thus arose the lore of lightning, the art of inspecting entrails, the interpretation of prodigies—all of them, and the science of lightning especially, devised with the hair-splitting subtlety which characterizes the mind in pursuit of absurdities. A dwarf called Tages with the figure of a child but with gray hairs, who had been ploughed up by a peasant in a field near Tarquinii—we might almost fancy that practices at once so childish and so drivelling had sought to present in this figure a caricature of themselves—betrayed the secret of this lore to the Etruscans, and then straightway died. His disciples and successors taught what gods were in the habit of hurling the lightning; how the lightning of each god might be recognized by its colour and the quarter of the heavens whence it came; whether the lightning boded a permanent state of things or a single event; and in the latter case whether the event was one unalterably fixed, or whether it could be up to a certain limit artificially postponed: how they might convey the lightning away when it struck, or compel the threatening lightning to strike, and various marvellous arts of the like kind, with which there was incidentally conjoined no small desire of pocketing fees. How deeply repugnant this jugglery was to the Roman character is shown by the fact that, even when people came at a later period to employ the Etruscan lore in Rome, no attempt was made to naturalize it; during our present period the Romans were probably still content with their own, and with the Greek oracles.

The Etruscan religion occupied a higher level than the Roman, in so far as it developed at least the rudiments of what was wholly wanting among the Romans—a speculation veiled under religious forms. Over the world and its gods there ruled the veiled gods (-Dii involuti-), consulted by the Etruscan Jupiter himself; that world moreover was finite, and, as it had come into being, so was it again to pass away after the expiry of a definite period of time, whose sections were the -saecula-. Respecting the intellectual value which may once have belonged to this Etruscan cosmogony and philosophy, it is difficult to form a judgment; they appear however to have been from the very first characterized by a dull fatalism and an insipid play upon number.

Notes for Book I Chapter XII

1. I. II. Religion

2. This was, to all appearance, the original nature of the "morning-mother" or -Mater matuta-; in connection with which we may recall the circumstance that, as the names Lucius and especially -Manius- show, the morning hour was reckoned as lucky for birth. -Mater matuta-probably became a goddess of sea and harbour only at a later epoch under the influence of the myth of Leucothea; the fact that the goddess was chiefly worshipped by women tells against the view that she was originally a harbour-goddess.

3. From -Maurs-, which is the oldest form handed down by tradition, there have been developed by different treatment of the -u -Mars-, -Mavors-, -Mors-; the transition to -o (similar to -Paula-, -Pola-, and the like) appears also in the double form Mar-Mor (comp. -Ma-murius-) alongside of -Mar-Mor- and -Ma-Mers-.

4. The facts, that gates and doors and the morning (-ianus matutinus-) were sacred to Ianus, and that he was always invoked before any other god and was even represented in the series of coins before Jupiter and the other gods, indicate unmistakeably that he was the abstraction of opening and beginning. The double-head looking both ways was connected with the gate that opened both ways. To make him god of the sun and of the year is the less justifiable, because the month that bears his name was originally the eleventh, not the first; that month seems rather to have derived its name from the circumstance, that at this season after the rest of the middle of winter the cycle of the labours of the field began afresh. It was, however, a matter of course that the opening of the year should also be included in the sphere of Ianus, especially after Ianuarius came to be placed at its head.

5. I. IV. Tities and Luceres

6. I. VI. Amalgamation of the Palatine and Quirinal Cities

7. I. VII. Servian Wall

8. I. III. Latium

9. I. VII. Relation of Rome to Latium

10. I. V. Burdens of the Burgesses, I. XI. Crimes

11. The clearest evidence of this is the fact, that in the communities organized on the Latin scheme augurs and Pontifices occur everywhere (e. g. Cic. de Lege Agr. ii. 35, 96, and numerous inscriptions), as does likewise the -pater patratus- of the Fetiales in Laurentum (Orelli, 2276), but the other colleges do not. The former, therefore, stand

on the same footing with the constitution of ten curies and the Flamines, Salii, and Luperci, as very ancient heirlooms of the Latin stock; whereas the Duoviri -sacris faciundis-, and the other colleges, like the thirty curies and the Servian tribes and centuries, originated in, and remained therefore confined to, Rome. But in the case of the second college—the pontifices—the influence of Rome probably led to the introduction of that name into the general Latin scheme instead of some earlier— perhaps more than one—designation; or—a hypothesis which philologically has much in its favour— -pons- originally signified not "bridge," but "way" generally, and -pontifex- therefore meant "constructor of ways."

The statements regarding the original number of the augurs in particular vary. The view that it was necessary for the number to be an odd one is refuted by Cicero (de Lege Agr. ii. 35, 96); and Livy (x. 6) does not say so, but only states that the number of Roman augurs had to be divisible by three, and so must have had an odd number as its basis. According to Livy (l. c.) the number was six down to the Ogulnian law, and the same is virtually affirmed by Cicero (de Rep. ii. 9, 14) when he represents Romulus as instituting four, and Numa two, augural stalls. On the number of the pontifices comp. Staatsrecht, ii. 20.

12. It is only an unreflecting misconception that can discover in this usage a reminiscence of ancient human sacrifices.

13. I. XII. Nature of the Roman Gods

14. I. XII. Priests

15. -Sors- from -serere-, to place in row. The -sortes- were probably small wooden tablets arranged upon a string, which when thrown formed figures of various kinds; an arrangement which puts one in mind of the Runic characters.

16. I. X. Hellenes and Latins

17. I. VII. Servian Wall

18. I. II. Indo-Germanic Culture

19. I. IV. Tities and Luceres

CHAPTER XIII

Agriculture, Trade, and Commerce

Agriculture and commerce are so intimately bound up with the constitution and the external history of states, that the former must frequently be noticed in the course of describing the latter. We shall here endeavour to supplement the detached notices which we have already given, by exhibiting a summary view of Italian and particularly of Roman economics.

Agriculture

It has been already observed(1) that the transition from a pastoral to an agricultural economy preceded the immigration of the Italians into the peninsula. Agriculture continued to be the main support of all the communities in Italy, of the Sabellians and Etruscans no less than of the Latins. There were no purely pastoral tribes in Italy during historical times, although of course the various races everywhere combined pastoral husbandry, to a greater or less extent according to the nature of the locality, with the cultivation of the soil. The beautiful custom of commencing the formation of new cities by tracing a furrow with the plough along the line of the future ring-wall shows how deeply rooted was the feeling that every commonwealth is dependent on agriculture. In the case of Rome in particular—and it is only in its case that we can speak of agrarian relations with any sort of certainty—the Servian reform shows very clearly not only that the agricultural class originally preponderated in the state, but also that an effort was made permanently to maintain the collective body of freeholders as the pith and marrow of the community. When in the course of time a large portion of the landed property in Rome had passed into the hands of non-burgesses and thus the rights and duties of burgesses were no longer bound up with freehold property, the reformed constitution obviated this incongruous state of things, and the perils which it threatened, not merely temporarily but permanently, by treating the members of the community without reference to their political position once for all according to their freeholding, and imposing the common burden of war-service on the freeholders—a step which in the natural course of things could not but be followed by the concession of public rights. The whole policy of Roman war and conquest rested, like the constitution itself, on the basis of the freehold system; as the freeholder alone was of value in the state, the aim of war was to increase the number of its freehold members. The vanquished community was either compelled to merge entirely into the yeomanry of Rome, or, if not reduced to this extremity, it was required, not to pay a war-contribution or a fixed tribute, but to cede a portion, usually a third part, of its domain, which was thereupon regularly occupied by Roman farms. Many nations have gained victories and made conquests as the Romans did; but none has equalled the Roman in thus making the ground he had won his own by the sweat of his brow, and in securing by the ploughshare what had been gained by the lance. That which is gained by war may be wrested from the grasp by war again, but it is not so with the conquests made by the plough; while the Romans lost many battles, they scarcely ever on making peace ceded Roman soil, and for this result they were indebted to the tenacity with which the farmers clung to their fields and homesteads. The strength of man and of the state lies in their dominion over the soil; the greatness of Rome was built on the most extensive and immediate mastery of her citizens over her soil, and on the compact unity of the body which thus acquired so firm a hold.

System of Joint Cultivation

We have already indicated(2) that in the earliest times the arable land was cultivated in common, probably by the several clans; each clan tilled its own land, and thereafter distributed the produce among the several households belonging to it. There exists indeed an intimate connection between the system of joint tillage and the clan form of society, and even subsequently in Rome joint residence and joint management were of very frequent occurrence in the case of co-proprietors.(3) Even the traditions of Roman law furnish the information that wealth consisted at first in cattle and the usufruct of the soil, and that it was not till later that land came to be distributed among the burgesses as their own special property.(4) Better evidence that such was the case is afforded by the earliest designation of wealth as "cattle-stock" or "slave-and-cattle-stock" (-pecunia-, -familia pecuniaque-), and of the separate possessions of the children of the household and of slaves as "small cattle" (-peculium-) also by the earliest form of acquiring property through laying hold of it with the hand (-mancipatio-), which was only appropriate to the case of moveable articles;(5) and above all by the earliest measure of "land of one's own" (-heredium-, from -herus-lord), consisting of two -jugera-(about an acre and a quarter), which can only have applied to garden-ground, and not to the hide.(6) When and how the distribution of the arable land took place, can no longer be ascertained. This much only is certain, that the oldest form of the constitution was based not on freehold settlement, but on clanship as a substitute for it, whereas the Servian constitution presupposes the distribution of the land. It is evident from the same constitution that the great bulk of the landed property consisted of middle-sized farms, which provided work and subsistence for a family and admitted of the keeping of cattle for tillage as well as of the application of the plough. The ordinary extent of such a Roman full hide has not been ascertained with precision, but can scarcely, as has already been shown,(7) be estimated at less than twenty -jugera-(12 1/2 acres nearly).

Culture of Grain

Their husbandry was mainly occupied with the culture of the cereals. The usual grain was spelt (-far-);(8) but different kinds of pulse, roots, and vegetables were also diligently cultivated.

Culture of the Vine

That the culture of the vine was not introduced for the first time into Italy by Greek settlers,(9) is shown by the list of the festivals of the Roman community which reaches back to a time preceding the Greeks, and which presents three wine-festivals to be celebrated in honour of "father Jovis," not in honour of the wine-god of more recent times who was borrowed from the Greeks, the "father deliverer." The very ancient legend which represents Mezentius king of Caere as levying a wine-tax from the Latins or the Rutuli, and the various versions of the widely-spread Italian story which affirms that the Celts were induced to cross the Alps in consequence of their coming to the knowledge of the noble fruits of Italy, especially of the grape and of wine, are indications of the pride of the Latins in their glorious vine, the envy of all their neighbours. A careful system of vine-husbandry was early and generally inculcated by the Latin priests. In Rome the vintage did not begin until the supreme priest of the community, the -flamen- of Jupiter, had granted permission for it and had himself made a beginning; in like manner a Tusculan ordinance forbade the sale of new wine, until the priest had proclaimed the festival of opening the casks. The early prevalence of the culture of the vine is likewise attested not only by the general adoption of wine-libations in the sacrificial ritual, but also by the precept of the Roman priests promulgated as a law of king Numa, that men should present in libation to the gods no wine obtained from uncut grapes; just as, to introduce the beneficial practice of drying the grain, they prohibited the offering of grain undried.

Culture of the Olive

The culture of the olive was of later introduction, and certainly was first brought to Italy by the Greeks.(10) The olive is said to have been first planted on the shores of the western Mediterranean towards the close of the second century of the city; and this view accords with the fact that the olive-branch and the olive occupy in the Roman ritual a place very subordinate to the juice of the vine. The esteem in which both noble trees were held by the Romans is shown by the vine and the olive-tree which were planted in the middle of the Forum, not far from the Curtian lake.

The Fig

The principal fruit-tree planted was the nutritious fig, which was probably a native of Italy. The legend of the origin of Rome wove its threads most closely around the old fig-trees, several of which stood near to and in the Roman Forum.(11)

Management of the Farm

It was the farmer and his sons who guided the plough, and performed generally the labours of husbandry: it is not probable that slaves or free day-labourers were regularly employed in the work of the ordinary farm. The plough was drawn by the ox or by the cow; horses, asses, and mules served as beasts of burden. The rearing of cattle for the sake of meat or of milk did not exist at all as a distinct branch of husbandry, or was prosecuted only to a very limited extent, at least on the land which remained the property of the clan; but, in addition to the smaller cattle which were driven out together to the common pasture, swine and poultry, particularly geese, were kept at the farm-yard. As a general rule, there was no end of ploughing and re-ploughing: a field was reckoned imperfectly tilled, in which the furrows were not drawn so close that harrowing could be dispensed with; but the management was more earnest than intelligent, and no improvement took place in the defective plough or in the imperfect processes of reaping and of threshing. This result is probably attributable rather to the scanty development of rational mechanics than to the obstinate clinging of the farmers to use and wont; for mere kindly attachment to the system of tillage transmitted with the patrimonial soil was far from influencing the practical Italian, and obvious improvements in agriculture, such as the cultivation of fodder-plants and the irrigation of meadows, may have been early adopted from neighbouring peoples or independently developed—Roman literature itself in fact began with the discussion of the theory of agriculture. Welcome rest followed diligent and judicious labour; and here too religion asserted her right to soothe the toils of life even to the humble by pauses for recreation and for freer human movement and intercourse. Every eighth day (-nonae-), and therefore on an average four times a month, the farmer went to town to buy and sell and transact his other business. But rest from labour, in the strict sense, took place only on the several festival days, and especially in the holiday-month after the completion of the winter sowing (-feriae sementivae-): during these set times the plough rested by command of the gods, and not the farmer only, but also his slave and his ox, reposed in holiday idleness.

Such, probably, was the way in which the ordinary Roman farm was cultivated in the earliest times. The next heirs had no protection against bad management except the right of having the spendthrift who squandered his inherited estate placed under wardship as if he were a lunatic.(12) Women moreover were in substance divested of their personal right of disposal, and, if they married, a member of the same clan was ordinarily assigned as husband, in order to retain the estate within the clan. The law sought to check the overburdening of landed property with debt partly by ordaining, in the case of a debt secured over the land, the provisional transference of the ownership of the object pledged from the debtor to the creditor, partly, in the case of a simple loan, by the rigour of the proceedings in execution which speedily led to actual bankruptcy; the latter means however, as the sequel will show, attained its object but very imperfectly. No restriction was imposed by law on the free divisibility of property. Desirable as it might be that co-heirs should remain in the undivided possession of their heritage, even the oldest law was careful to keep the power of dissolving such a partnership open at any time to any partner; it was good that brethren should dwell together in peace, but to compel them to do so was foreign to the liberal spirit of Roman law. The Servian constitution moreover shows that even in the regal period of Rome there were not wanting cottagers and garden-proprietors, with whom the mattock took the place of the plough. It was left to custom and the sound sense of the population to prevent excessive subdivision of the soil; and that their confidence in this respect was not misplaced and the landed estates ordinarily remained entire, is proved by the universal Roman custom of designating them by permanent individual names. The community exercised only an indirect influence in the matter by the sending forth of colonies, which regularly led to the establishment of a number of new full hides, and frequently doubtless also to the suppression of a number of cottage holdings, the small landholders being sent forth as colonists.

Landed Proprietors

It is far more difficult to perceive how matters stood with landed property on a larger scale. The fact that such larger properties existed to no inconsiderable extent, cannot be doubted from the early development of the -equites-, and may be easily explained partly by the distribution of the clan-lands, which of itself could not but call into existence a class of larger landowners in consequence of the necessary inequality in the numbers of the persons belonging to the several clans and participating in the distribution, and partly by the abundant influx of mercantile capital to Rome. But farming on a large scale in the proper sense, implying a considerable establishment of slaves, such as we afterwards meet with at Rome, cannot be supposed to have existed during this period. On the contrary, to this period we must refer the ancient definition, which represents the senators as called fathers from the fields which they parcelled out among the common people as a father among his children; and originally the landowner must have distributed that portion of his land which he was unable to farm in person, or even his whole estate, into little parcels among his dependents to be cultivated by them, as is the general practice in Italy at the present day. The recipient might be the house-child or slave of the granter; if he was a free man, his position was that which subsequently went by the name of "occupancy on sufferance" (-precarium-). The recipient retained his occupancy during the pleasure of the granter, and had no legal means of protecting himself in possession against him; on the contrary, the granter could eject him at any time when he pleased. The relation did not necessarily involve any payment on the part of the person who had the usufruct of the soil to its proprietor; but such a payment beyond doubt frequently took place and may, as a rule, have consisted in the delivery of a portion of the produce. The relation in this case approximated to the lease of subsequent times, but remained always distinguished from it partly by the absence of a fixed term for its expiry, partly by its non-actionable character on either side and the legal protection of the claim for rent depending entirely on the lessor's right of ejection. It is plain that it was essentially a relation based on mutual fidelity, which could not subsist without the help of the powerful sanction of custom consecrated by religion; and this was not wanting. The institution of clientship, altogether of a moral-religious nature, beyond doubt rested fundamentally on this assignation of the profits of the soil. Nor was the introduction of such an assignation dependent on the abolition of the system of common tillage; for, just as after this abolition the individual, so previous to it the clan might grant to dependents a joint use of its lands; and beyond doubt with this very state of things was connected the fact that the Roman clientship was not personal, but that from the outset the client along with his clan entrusted himself for protection and fealty to the patron and his clan. This earliest form of Roman landholding serves to explain how there sprang from the great landlords in Rome a landed, and not an urban, nobility. As the pernicious institution of middlemen remained foreign to the Romans, the Roman landlord found himself not much less chained to his land than was the tenant and the farmer; he inspected and took part in everything himself, and the wealthy Roman esteemed it his highest praise to be reckoned a good landlord. His house was in the country; in the city he had only a lodging for the purpose of attending to his business there, and perhaps of breathing the purer air that prevailed there during the hot season. Above all, however, these arrangements furnished a moral basis for the relation between the upper class and the common people, and so materially lessened its dangers. The free tenants-on-sufferance, sprung from families of decayed farmers, dependents, and freedmen, formed the great bulk of the proletariate,(13) and were not much more dependent on the landlord than the petty leaseholder inevitably is with reference to the great proprietor. The slaves tilling the fields for a master were beyond doubt far less numerous than the free tenants. In all cases where an immigrant nation has not at once reduced to slavery a population -en masse-, slaves seem to have existed at first only to a very limited amount, and consequently free labourers seem to have played a very different part in the state from that in which they subsequently appear. In Greece "day-labourers" (—theites—) in various instances during the earlier period occupy the place of the slaves of a later age, and in some communities, among the Locrians for instance, there was no slavery down to historical times. Even the slave, moreover, was ordinarily of Italian descent; the Volscian, Sabine, or Etruscan war-captive must have stood in a different relation towards his master from the Syrian and the Celt of later times. Besides as a tenant he had in fact, though not in law, land and cattle, wife and child, as the landlord had, and after manumission was introduced(14) there was a possibility, not remote, of working out his freedom. If such then was the footing on which landholding on a large scale stood in the earliest times, it was far from being an open sore in the commonwealth; on the contrary, it was of most material service to it. Not only did it provide subsistence, although scantier upon the whole, for as many families in proportion as the intermediate and smaller properties; but the landlords moreover, occupying a comparatively elevated and free position, supplied the community with its natural leaders and rulers, while the agricultural and unpropertied tenants-on-sufferance furnished the genuine material for the Roman policy of colonization, without which it never would have succeeded; for while the state may furnish land to him who has none, it cannot impart to one who knows nothing of agriculture the spirit and the energy to wield the plough.

232

Pastoral Husbandry

Ground under pasture was not affected by the distribution of the land. The state, and not the clanship, was regarded as the owner of the common pastures. It made use of them in part for its own flocks and herds, which were intended for sacrifice and other purposes and were always kept up by means of the cattle-fines; and it gave to the possessors of cattle the privilege of driving them out upon the common pasture for a moderate payment (-scriptura-). The right of pasturage on the public domains may have originally borne some relation -de facto- to the possession of land, but no connection -de jure- can ever have subsisted in Rome between the particular hides of land and a definite proportional use of the common pasture; because property could be acquired even by the —metoikos—, but the right to use the common pasture was only granted exceptionally to the —metoikos— by the royal favour. At this period, however, the public land seems to have held but a subordinate place in the national economy generally, for the original common pasturage was not perhaps very extensive, and the conquered territory was probably for the most part distributed immediately as arable land among the clans or at a later period among individuals.

Handicrafts

While agriculture was the chief and most extensively prosecuted occupation in Rome, other branches of industry did not fail to accompany it, as might be expected from the early development of urban life in that emporium of the Latins. In fact eight guilds of craftsmen were numbered among the institutions of king Numa, that is, among the institutions that had existed in Rome from time immemorial. These were the flute-blowers, the goldsmiths, the coppersmiths, the carpenters, the fullers, the dyers, the potters, and the shoemakers—a list which would substantially exhaust the class of tradesmen working to order on account of others in the very early times, when the baking of bread and the professional art of healing were not yet known and wool was spun into clothing by the women of the household themselves. It is remarkable that there appears no special guild of workers in iron. This affords a fresh confirmation of the fact that the manufacture of iron was of comparatively late introduction in Latium; and on this account in matters of ritual down to the latest times copper alone might be used, *e.g.* for the sacred plough and the shear-knife of the priests. These bodies of craftsmen must have been of great importance in early times for the urban life of Rome and for its position towards the Latin land—an importance not to be measured by the depressed condition of Roman handicraft in later times, when it was injuriously affected by the multitude of artisan-slaves working for their master or on his account, and by the increased import of articles of luxury. The oldest lays of Rome celebrated not only the mighty war-god Mamers, but also the skilled armourer Mamurius, who understood the art of forging for his fellow-burgesses shields similar to the divine model shield that had fallen from heaven; Volcanus the god of fire and of the forge already appears in the primitive list of Roman festivals.(15) Thus in the earliest Rome, as everywhere, the arts of forging and of wielding the ploughshare and the sword went hand in hand, and there was nothing of that arrogant contempt for handicrafts which we afterwards meet with there. After the Servian organization, however, imposed the duty of serving in the army exclusively on the freeholders, the industrial classes were excluded not by any law, but practically in consequence of their general want of a freehold qualification, from the privilege of bearing arms, except in the case of special subdivisions chosen from the carpenters, coppersmiths, and certain classes of musicians and attached with a military organization to the army; and this may perhaps have been the origin of the subsequent habit of depreciating the manual arts and of the position of political inferiority assigned to them. The institution of guilds doubtless had the same object as the colleges of priests that resembled them in name; the men of skill associated themselves in order more permanently and securely to preserve the tradition of their art. That there was some mode of excluding unskilled persons is probable; but no traces are to be met with either of monopolizing tendencies or of protective steps against inferior manufactures. There is no aspect, however, of the life of the Roman people respecting which our information is so scanty as that of the Roman trades.

Inland Commerce of the Italians

Italian commerce must, it is obvious, have been limited in the earliest epoch to the mutual dealings of the Italians themselves. Fairs (-mercatus-), which must be distinguished from the usual weekly markets (-nundinae-) were of great antiquity in Latium. Probably they were at first associated with international gatherings and festivals, and so perhaps were connected in Rome with the festival at the federal temple on the Aventine; the Latins, who came for this purpose to Rome every year on the 13th August, may have embraced at the same time the opportunity of transacting their business in Rome and of purchasing what they needed there. A similar and perhaps still greater importance belonged in the case of Etruria to the annual general assembly at the temple of Voltumna (perhaps near Montefiascone) in the territory of Volsinii; it served at the same time as a fair and was regularly frequented by Roman traders. But the most important of all the Italian fairs was that which was held at Soracte in the grove of Feronia, a situation than which none could be found more favourable for the exchange of commodities among the three great nations. That high isolated mountain, which appears to have been set down by nature herself in the midst of the plain of the Tiber as a goal for the traveller, lay on the boundary which separated the Etruscan and Sabine lands (to the latter of which it appears mostly to have belonged), and it was likewise easily accessible from Latium and Umbria. Roman merchants regularly made their appearance there, and the wrongs of which they complained gave rise to many a quarrel with the Sabines.

Beyond doubt dealings of barter and traffic were carried on at these fairs long before the first Greek or Phoenician vessel entered the western sea. When bad harvests had occurred, different districts supplied each other at these fairs with grain; there, too, they exchanged cattle, slaves, metals, and whatever other articles were deemed needful or desirable in those primitive times. Oxen and sheep formed the oldest medium of exchange, ten sheep being reckoned equivalent to one ox. The recognition of these objects as universal legal representatives of value or in other words as money, as well as the scale of proportion between the large and smaller cattle, may be traced back—as the recurrence of both especially among the Germans shows—not merely to the Graeco-Italian period, but beyond this even to the epoch of a purely pastoral economy.(16) In Italy, where metal in considerable quantity was everywhere required especially for agricultural purposes and for armour, but few of its provinces themselves produced the requisite metals, copper (-aes-) very early made its appearance alongside of cattle as a second medium of exchange; and so the Latins, who were poor in copper, designated valuation itself as "coppering" (-aestimatio-). This establishment of copper as a general equivalent recognized throughout the whole peninsula, as well as the simplest numeral signs of Italian invention to be mentioned more particularly below(17) and the Italian duodecimal system, may be regarded as traces of this earliest international intercourse of the Italian peoples while they still had the peninsula to themselves.

Transmarine Traffic of the Italians

We have already indicated generally the nature of the influence exercised by transmarine commerce on the Italians who continued independent. The Sabellian stocks remained almost wholly unaffected by it. They were in possession of but a small and inhospitable belt of coast, and received whatever reached them from foreign nations—the alphabet for instance—only through the medium of the Tuscans or Latins; a circumstance which accounts for their want of urban development. The intercourse of Tarentum with the Apulians and Messapians appears to have been at this epoch still unimportant. It was otherwise along the west coast. In Campania the Greeks and Italians dwelt peacefully side by side, and in Latium, and still more in Etruria, an extensive and regular exchange of commodities took place. What were the earliest articles of import, may be inferred partly from the objects found in the primitive tombs, particularly those at Caere, partly from indications preserved in the language and institutions of the Romans, partly and chiefly from the stimulus given to Italian industry; for of course they bought foreign manufactures for a considerable time before they began to imitate them. We cannot determine how far the development of handicrafts had advanced before the separation of the stocks, or what progress it thereafter made while Italy remained left to its own resources; it is uncertain how far the Italian fullers, dyers, tanners, and potters received their impulse from Greece or Phoenicia or had their own independent development But certainly the trade of the goldsmiths, which existed in Rome from time immemorial, can only have arisen after transmarine commerce had begun and ornaments of gold had to some extent found sale among the inhabitants of the peninsula. We find, accordingly, in the oldest sepulchral chambers of Caere and Vulci in Etruria and of Praeneste in Latium, plates of gold with winged lions stamped upon them, and similar ornaments of Babylonian manufacture. It may be a question in reference to the particular object found, whether it has been introduced from abroad or is a native imitation; but on the whole it admits of no doubt that all the west coast of Italy in early times imported metallic wares from the East. It will be shown still more clearly in the sequel, when we come to speak of the exercise of art, that architecture and modelling in clay and metal received a powerful stimulus in very early times through Greek influence, or, in other words, that the oldest tools and the oldest models came from Greece. In the sepulchral chambers just mentioned, besides the gold ornaments, there were deposited vessels of bluish enamel or greenish clay, which, judging from the materials and style as well as from the hieroglyphics impressed upon them, were of Egyptian origin;(18) perfume-vases of Oriental alabaster, several of them in the form of Isis; ostrich-eggs with painted or carved sphinxes and griffins; beads of glass and amber. These last may have come by the land-route from the north; but the other objects prove the import of perfumes and articles of ornament of all sorts from the East. Thence came linen and purple, ivory and frankincense, as is proved by the early use of linen fillets, of the purple dress and ivory sceptre for the king, and of frankincense in sacrifice, as well as by the very ancient borrowed names for them (—linon—, -linum-; —porphura—, -purpura-; —-skeiptron—, —skipon—, -scipio-; perhaps also —elephas—, -ebur-; —thuos—, -thus-). Of similar significance is the derivation of a number of words relating to articles used in eating and drinking, particularly the names of oil,(19) of jugs (—-amphoreus—, -amp(h)ora-, -ampulla-, —krateir—, -cratera-), of feasting (—-

komazo—, -comissari-), of a dainty dish (—opsonion—, -opsonium-) of dough (—maza—, -massa-), and various names of cakes (—glukons—, -lucuns-; —plakons—, -placenta-; —turons—, -turunda-); while conversely the Latin names for dishes (-patina-, —patanei—) and for lard (-arvina-, —arbinei—) have found admission into Sicilian Greek. The later custom of placing in the tomb beside the dead Attic, Corcyrean, and Campanian vases proves, what these testimonies from language likewise show, the early market for Greek pottery in Italy. That Greek leather-work made its way into Latium at least in the shape of armour is apparent from the application of the Greek word for leather —skutos— to signify among the Latins a shield (-scutum-; like -lorica-, from -lorum-). Finally, we deduce a similar inference from the numerous nautical terms borrowed from the Greek (although it is remarkable that the chief technical expressions in navigation—the terms for the sail, mast, and yard—are pure Latin forms);(20) and from the recurrence in Latin of the Greek designations for a letter (—epistolei—, -epistula-), a token (-tessera-, from —tessara—(21)), a balance (—stateir—, -statera-), and earnest-money (—arrabon—, -arrabo-, -arra-); and conversely from the adoption of Italian law-terms in Sicilian Greek,(22) as well as from the exchange of the proportions and names of coins, weights, and measures, which we shall notice in the sequel. The character of barbarism which all these borrowed terms obviously present, and especially the characteristic formation of the nominative from the accusative (-placenta- = —plakounta—; -ampora- = —amphorea—; -statera-= —stateira—), constitute the clearest evidence of their great antiquity. The worship of the god of traffic (-Mercurius-) also appears to have been from the first influenced by Greek conceptions; and his annual festival seems even to have been fixed on the ides of May, because the Hellenic poets celebrated him as the son of the beautiful Maia.

Commerce, in Latium Passive, in Etruria Active

It thus appears that Italy in very ancient times derived its articles of luxury, just as imperial Rome did, from the East, before it attempted to manufacture for itself after the models which it imported. In exchange it had nothing to offer except its raw produce, consisting especially of its copper, silver, and iron, but including also slaves and timber for shipbuilding, amber from the Baltic, and, in the event of bad harvests occurring abroad, its grain. From this state of things as to the commodities in demand and the equivalents to be offered in return, we have already explained why Italian traffic assumed in Latium a form so differing from that which it presented in Etruria. The Latins, who were deficient in all the chief articles of export, could carry on only a passive traffic, and were obliged even in the earliest times to procure the copper of which they had need from the Etruscans in exchange for cattle or slaves—-we have already mentioned the very ancient practice of selling the latter on the right bank of the Tiber.(23) On the other hand the Tuscan balance of trade must have been necessarily favourable in Caere as in Populonia, in Capua as in Spina. Hence the rapid development of prosperity in these regions and their powerful commercial position; whereas Latium remained preeminently an agricultural country. The same contrast recurs in all their individual relations. The oldest tombs constructed and furnished in the Greek fashion, but with an extravagance to which the Greeks were strangers, are to be found at Caere, while—with the exception of Praeneste, which appears to have occupied a peculiar position and to have been very intimately connected with Falerii and southern Etruria—the Latin land exhibits only slight ornaments for the dead of foreign origin, and not a single tomb of luxury proper belonging to the earlier times; there as among the Sabellians a simple turf ordinarily sufficed as a covering for the dead. The most ancient coins, of a time not much later than those of Magna Graecia, belong to Etruria, and to Populonia in particular: during the whole regal period Latium had to be content with copper by weight, and had not even introduced foreign coins, for the instances are extremely rare in which such coins (e.g. one of Posidonia) have been found there. In architecture, plastic art, and embossing, the same stimulants acted on Etruria and on Latium, but it was only in the case of the former that capital was everywhere brought to bear on them and led to their being pursued extensively and with growing technical skill. The commodities were upon the whole the same, which were bought, sold, and manufactured in Latium and in Etruria; but the southern land was far inferior to its northern neighbours in the energy with which its commerce was plied. The contrast between them in this respect is shown in the fact that the articles of luxury manufactured after Greek models in Etruria found a market in Latium, particularly at Praeneste, and even in Greece itself, while Latium hardly ever exported anything of the kind.

Etrusco-Attic, and Latino-Sicilian Commerce

A distinction not less remarkable between the commerce of the Latins and that of the Etruscans appears in their respective routes or lines of traffic. As to the earliest commerce of the Etruscans in the Adriatic we can hardly do more than express the conjecture that it was directed from Spina and Atria chiefly to Corcyra. We have already mentioned(24) that the western Etruscans ventured boldly into the eastern seas, and trafficked not merely with Sicily, but also with Greece proper. An ancient intercourse with Attica is indicated by the Attic clay vases, which are so numerous in the more recent Etruscan tombs, and had been perhaps even at this time introduced for other purposes than the already-mentioned decoration of tombs, while conversely Tyrrhenian bronze candlesticks and gold cups were articles early in request in Attica. Still more definitely is such an intercourse indicated by the coins. The silver pieces of Populonia were struck after the pattern of a very old silver piece stamped on one side with the Gorgoneion, on the other merely presenting an incuse square, which has been found at Athens and on the old amber-route in the district of Posen, and which was in all probability the very coin struck by order of Solon in Athens. We have mentioned already that the Etruscans had also dealings, and perhaps after the development of the Etrusco-Carthaginian maritime alliance their principal dealings, with the Carthaginians. It is a remarkable circumstance that in the oldest tombs of Caere, besides native vessels of bronze and silver, there have been found chiefly Oriental articles, which may certainly have come from Greek merchants, but more probably were introduced by Phoenician traders. We must not, however, attribute too great importance to this Phoenician trade, and in particular we must not overlook the fact that the alphabet, as well as the other influences that stimulated and matured native culture, were brought to Etruria by the Greeks, and not by the Phoenicians.

Latin commerce assumed a different direction. Rarely as we have opportunity of instituting comparisons between the Romans and the Etruscans as regards the reception of Hellenic elements, the cases in which such comparisons can be instituted exhibit the two nations as completely independent of each other. This is most clearly apparent in the case of the alphabet. The Greek alphabet brought to the Etruscans from the Chalcidico-Doric colonies in Sicily or Campania varies not immaterially from that which the Latins derived from the same quarter, so that, although both peoples have drawn from the same source, they have done so at different times and different places. The same phenomenon appears in particular words: the Roman Pollux and the Tuscan Pultuke are independent corruptions of the Greek Polydeukes; the Tuscan Utuze or Uthuze is formed from Odysseus, the Roman Ulixes is an exact reproduction of the form of the name usual in Sicily; in like manner the Tuscan Aivas corresponds to the old Greek form of this name, the Roman Aiax to a secondary form that was probably also Sicilian; the Roman Aperta or Apello and the Samnite Appellun have sprung from the Doric Apellon, the Tuscan Apulu from Apollon. Thus the language and writing of Latium indicate that the direction of Latin commerce was exclusively towards the Cumaeans and Siceliots. Every other trace which has survived from so remote an age leads to the same conclusion: such as, the coin of Posidonia found in Latium; the purchase of grain, when a failure of the harvest occurred in Rome, from the Volscians, Cumaeans, and Siceliots (and, as was natural, from the Etruscans as well); above all, the relations subsisting between the Latin and Sicilian monetary systems. As the local Dorico-Chalcidian designation of silver coin —nomos—, and the Sicilian measure —-eimina—, were transferred with the same meaning to Latium as -nummus- and -hemina-, so conversely the Italian designations of weight, -libra-, -triens-, -quadrans-, -sextans-, -uncia-, which arose in Latium for the measurement of the copper which was used by weight instead of money, had found their way into the common speech of Sicily in the third century of the city under the corrupt and hybrid forms, —litra—, —trias—, —tetras—, —exas—, —ougkia—. Indeed, among all the Greek systems of weights and moneys, the Sicilian alone was brought into a determinate relation to the Italian copper-system; not only was the value of silver set down conventionally and perhaps legally as two hundred and fifty times that of copper, but the equivalent on this computation of a Sicilian pound of copper (1/120th of the Attic talent, 2/3 of the Roman pound) was in very early times struck, especially at Syracuse, as a silver coin (—litra argurion—, *i.e.* "copper-pound in silver"). Accordingly it cannot be doubted that Italian bars of copper circulated also in Sicily instead of money; and this exactly harmonizes with the hypothesis that the commerce of the Latins with Sicily was a passive commerce, in consequence of which Latin money was drained away thither. Other proofs of ancient intercourse between Sicily and Italy, especially the adoption in the Sicilian dialect of the Italian expressions for a commercial loan, a prison, and a dish, and the converse reception of Sicilian terms in Italy, have been already mentioned.(25) We meet also with several, though less definite, traces of an ancient intercourse of the Latins with the Chalcidian cities in Lower Italy, Cumae and Neapolis, and with the Phocaeans in Velia and Massilia. That it was however far less active than that with the Siceliots is shown by the well-known fact that all the Greek words which made their way in earlier times to Latium exhibit Doric forms—-we need only recall -Aesculapius-, -Latona-, -Aperta-, -machina-. Had their dealings with the originally Ionian cities, such as Cumae(26) and the Phocaean settlements, been even merely on a similar scale with those which they had with the Sicilian Dorians, Ionic forms would at least have made their appearance along with the others; although certainly Dorism early penetrated even into these Ionic colonies themselves, and their dialect varied greatly. While all the facts thus combine to attest the stirring traffic of the Latins with the Greeks of the western main generally, and especially with the Sicilians, there hardly occurred any immediate intercourse with the Asiatic Phoenicians, and the intercourse with those of Africa, which is sufficiently attested by statements of authors and by articles found, can only have occupied a secondary position as affecting the state of culture in Latium; in particular it is significant that—if we leave out of account some local names—there is an utter absence of any evidence from language as to ancient intercourse between the Latins and the nations speaking the Aramaic tongue.(27)

If we further inquire how this traffic was mainly carried on, whether by Italian merchants abroad or by foreign merchants in Italy, the former supposition has all the probabilities in its favour, at least so far as Latium is concerned. It is scarcely conceivable that those Latin terms denoting the substitute for money and the commercial loan could have found their way into general use in the language of the inhabitants of Sicily through the mere resort of Sicilian merchants to Ostia and their receipt of copper in exchange for ornaments. Lastly, in regard to the persons and classes by whom this traffic was carried on in Italy, no special superior class of merchants distinct from and independent of the class of landed proprietors developed itself in Rome. The reason of this surprising phenomenon was, that the wholesale commerce of Latium was from the beginning in the hands of the large landed proprietors—a hypothesis which is not so singular as it seems. It was natural that in a country intersected by several navigable rivers the great landholder, who was paid by his tenants their quotas of produce in kind, should come at an early period to possess barks; and there is evidence that such was the case. The transmarine traffic conducted on the trader's own account must therefore have fallen into the hands of the great landholder, seeing that he alone possessed the vessels for it and—in his produce—the articles for export.(28) In fact the distinction between a landed and a moneyed aristocracy was unknown to the Romans of earlier times; the great landholders were at the same time the speculators and the capitalists. In the case of a very energetic commerce such a combination certainly could not have been maintained; but, as the previous representation shows, while there was a comparatively vigorous traffic in Rome in consequence of the trade of the Latin land being there concentrated, Rome was by no means essentially a commercial city like Caere or Tarentum, but was and continued to be the centre of an agricultural community.

Notes for Book I Chapter XIII

1. I. II. Agriculture

2. I. III. Clan Villages, I. V. The Community

3. The system which we meet with in the case of the Germanic joint tillage, combining a partition of the land in property among the clansmen with its joint cultivation by the clan, can hardly ever have existed in Italy. Had each clansman been regarded in Italy, as among the Germans, in the light of proprietor of a particular spot in each portion of the collective domain that was marked off for tillage, the separate husbandry of later times would probably have set out from a minute subdivision of hides. But the very opposite was the case; the individual names of the Roman hides (-fundus Cornelianus-) show clearly that the Roman proprietor owned from the beginning a possession not broken up but united.

4. Cicero (de Rep. ii. 9, 14, comp. Plutarch, Q. Rom. 15) states: -Tum (in the time of Romulus) erat res in pecore et locorum possessionibus, ex quo pecuniosi et locupletes vocabantur—(Numa) primum agros, quos bello Romulus ceperat, divisit viritim civibus-. In like manner Dionysius represents Romulus as dividing the land into thirty curial districts, and Numa as establishing boundary-stones and introducing the festival of the Terminalia (i. 7, ii. 74; and thence Plutarch, -Numa-, 16).

5. I. XI. Contracts

6. Since this assertion still continues to be disputed, we shall let the numbers speak for themselves. The Roman writers on agriculture of the later republic and the imperial period reckon on an average five -modii- of wheat as sufficient to sow a -jugerum-, and the produce as fivefold. The produce of a -heredium- accordingly (even when, without taking into view the space occupied by the dwelling-house and farm-yard, we regard it as entirely arable land, and make no account of years of fallow) amounts to fifty, or deducting the seed forty, modii. For an adult hard-working slave Cato (c. 56) reckons fifty-one -modii-of wheat as the annual consumption. These data enable any one to answer for himself the question whether a Roman family could or could not subsist on the produce of a -heredium-. The attempted proof to the contrary is based on the ground that the slave of later times subsisted more exclusively on corn than the free farmer of the earlier epoch, and that the assumption of a fivefold return is one too low for this earlier epoch; both assumptions are probably correct, but for both there is a limit. Doubtless the subsidiary produce yielded by the arable land itself and by the common pasture, such as figs, vegetables, milk, flesh (especially as derived from the old and zealously pursued rearing of swine), and the like, are specially to be taken into account for the older period; but the older Roman pastoral husbandry, though not unimportant, was withal of subordinate importance, and the chief subsistence of the people was always notoriously grain. We may, moreover, on account of the thoroughness of the earlier cultivation obtain a very considerable increase, especially of the gross produce—and beyond doubt the farmers of this period drew a larger produce from their lands than

the great landholders of the later republic and the empire obtained (iii. Latium); but moderation must be exercised in forming such estimates, because we have to deal with a question of averages and with a mode of husbandry conducted neither methodically nor with large capital. The assumption of a tenfold instead of a fivefold return will be the utmost limit, and yet it is far from sufficing. In no case can the enormous deficit, which is left even according to those estimates between the produce of the -heredium- and the requirements of the household, be covered by mere superiority of cultivation. In fact the counter-proof can only be regarded as successful, when it shall have produced a methodical calculation based on rural economics, according to which among a population chiefly subsisting on vegetables the produce of a piece of land of an acre and a quarter proves sufficient on an average for the subsistence of a family.

It is indeed asserted that instances occur even in historical times of colonies founded with allotments of two -jugera-; but the only instance of the kind (Liv. iv. 47) is that of the colony of Labici in the year 336—an instance, which will certainly not be reckoned (by such scholars as are worth the arguing with) to belong to the class of traditions that are trustworthy in their historical details, and which is beset by other very serious difficulties (see book ii. ch. 5, note). It is no doubt true that in the non-colonial assignation of land to the burgesses collectively (-adsignatio viritana-) sometimes only a few -jugera- were granted (as e. g. Liv. viii. ii, 21). In these cases however it was the intention not to create new farms with the allotments, but rather, as a rule, to add to the existing farms new parcels from the conquered lands (comp. C. I. L. i. p. 88). At any rate, any supposition is better than a hypothesis which requires us to believe as it were in a miraculous multiplication of the food of the Roman household. The Roman farmers were far less modest in their requirements than their historiographers; they themselves conceived that they could not subsist even on allotments of seven -jugera- or a produce of one hundred and forty -modii-.

7. I. VI. Time and Occasion of the Reform

8. Perhaps the latest, although probably not the last, attempt to prove that a Latin farmer's family might have subsisted on two -jugera- of land, finds its chief support in the argument that Varro (de R. R. i. 44, i) reckons the seed requisite for the -jugerum-at five -modii- of wheat but ten -modii- of spelt, and estimates the produce as corresponding to this, whence it is inferred that the cultivation of spelt yielded a produce, if not double, at least considerably higher than that of wheat. But the converse is more correct, and the nominally higher quantity sown and reaped is simply to be explained by the fact that the Romans garnered and sowed the wheat already shelled, but the spelt still in the husk (Pliny, H. N. xviii. 7, 61), which in this case was not separated from the fruit by threshing. For the same reason spelt is at the present day sown twice as thickly as wheat, and gives a produce twice as great by measure, but less after deduction of the husks. According to Wurtemberg estimates furnished to me by G. Hanssen, the average produce of the Wurtemberg -morgen- is reckoned in the case of wheat (with a sowing of 1/4 to 1/2 -scheffel-) at 3 -scheffel- of the medium weight of 275 Ibs. (= 825 Ibs.); in the case of spelt (with a sowing of 1/2 to 1 1/2 -scheffel-) at least 7 -scheffel- of the medium weight of 150 lbs. (= 1050

Ibs.), which are reduced by shelling to about 4 -scheffel-. Thus spelt compared with wheat yields in the gross more than double, with equally good soil perhaps triple the crop, but—by specific weight—before the shelling not much above, after shelling (as "kernel") less than, the half. It was not by mistake, as has been asserted, but because it was fitting in computations of this sort to start from estimates of a like nature handed down to us, that the calculation instituted above was based on wheat; it may stand, because, when transferred to spelt, it does not essentially differ and the produce rather falls than rises. Spelt is less nice as to soil and climate, and exposed to fewer risks than wheat; but the latter yields on the whole, especially when we take into account the not inconsiderable expenses of shelling, a higher net produce (on an average of fifty years in the district of Frankenthal in Rhenish Bavaria the -malter- of wheat stands at 11 -gulden- 3 krz., the -malter- of spelt at 4 -gulden-30 krz.), and, as in South Germany, where the soil admits, the growing of wheat is preferred and generally with the progress of cultivation comes to supersede that of spelt, so the analogous transition of Italian agriculture from the culture of spelt to that of wheat was undeniably a progress.

9. I. II. Agriculture

10. -Oleum- and -oliva- are derived from —elaion—, —elaia—, and -amurca- (oil-less) from —amorgei—.

11. But there is no proper authority for the statement that the fig-tree which stood in front of the temple of Saturn was cut down in the year 260 (Plin. H. N. xv. 18, 77); the date CCLX. is wanting in all good manuscripts, and has been interpolated, probably with reference to Liv. ii. 21.

12. I. XI. Property

13. I. VI. Class of —Metoeci— Subsisting by the Side of the Community

14. I. XI. Guardianship

15. I. XII. Oldest Table of Roman Festivals

16. The comparative legal value of sheep and oxen, as is well known, is proved by the fact that, when the cattle-fines were converted into money-fines, the sheep was rated at ten, and the ox at a hundred asses (Festus, v. -peculatus-, p. 237, comp. pp. 34, 144; Gell. xi. i; Plutarch, Poplicola, ii). By a similar adjustment the Icelandic law makes twelve rams equivalent to a cow; only in this as in other instances the Germanic law has substituted the duodecimal for the older decimal system.

It is well known that the term denoting cattle was transferred to denote money both among the Latins (-pecunia-) and among the Germans (English fee).

17. I. XIV. Decimal System

18. There has lately been found at Praeneste a silver mixing-jug, with a Phoenician and a hieroglyphic inscription (Mon. dell Inst. x. plate 32), which directly proves that such Egyptian wares as come to light in Italy have found their way thither through the medium of the Phoenicians.

19. comp. I. XIII. Culture of the Olive

20. -Velum- is certainly of Latin origin; so is -malus-, especially as that term denotes not merely the mast, but the tree in general: -antenna- likewise may come from —ana— (-anhelare-, -antestari-), and -tendere- = -supertensa-. Of Greek origin, on the other hand, are -gubenare-, to steer (—kubernan—); -ancora-, anchor (—agkura—); -prora-, ship's bow (—prora—); -aplustre-, ship's stern (—aphlaston—); -anquina-, the rope fastening the yards (—agkoina—); -nausea-, sea-sickness (—nausia—). The four chief winds of the ancients- -aquilo-, the "eagle-wind," the north-easterly Tramontana; -voltumus- (of uncertain derivation, perhaps the "vulture-wind"), the south-easterly; -auster- the "scorching" southwest wind, the Sirocco; -favonius-, the "favourable" north-west wind blowing from the Tyrrhene Sea—have indigenous names bearing no reference to navigation; but all the other Latin names for winds are Greek (such as -eurus-, -notus-), or translations from the Greek (e.g. -solanus- = —apelioteis—, -Africus- = —lips—).

21. This meant in the first instance the tokens used in the service of the camp, the —xuleiphia kata phulakein brachea teleos echonta charakteira— (Polyb. vi. 35, 7); the four -vigiliae- of the night-service gave name to the tokens generally. The fourfold division of the night for the service of watching is Greek as well as Roman; the military science of the Greeks may well have exercised an influence—possibly through Pyrrhus (Liv. xxxv. 14)—in the organization of the measures for security in the Roman camp. The employment of the non-Doric form speaks for the comparatively late date at which theword was taken over.

22. I. XI. Character of the Roman Law

23. I. VII. Relation of Rome to Latium

24. I. X. Etruscan Commerce

25. I. XI. Clients and Foreigners, I. XIII. Commerce, in Latium Passive, in Etruria Active

26. I. X. Greek Cities Near Vesuvius

27. If we leave out of view -Sarranus-, -Afer-, and other local designations (I. X. Phoenicians and Italians in Opposition to the Hellenes), the Latin language appears not to possess a single word immediately derived in early times from the Phoenician. The very few words from Phoenician roots which occur in it, such as -arrabo-or -arra- and perhaps also -murra-, -nardus-, and the like, are plainly

borrowed proximately from the Greek, which has a considerable number of such words of Oriental extraction as indications of its primitive intercourse with the Aramaeans. That —elephas— and -ebur- should have come from the same Phoenician original with or without the addition of the article, and thus have been each formed independently, is a linguistic impossibility, as the Phoenician article is in reality -ha-, and is not so employed; besides the Oriental primitive word has not as yet been found. The same holds true of the enigmatical word -thesaurus-; whether it may have been originally Greek or borrowed by the Greeks from the Phoenician or Persian, it is at any rate, as a Latin word, derived from the Greek, as the very retaining of its aspiration proves (xii. Foreign Worships).

28. Quintus Claudius, in a law issued shortly before 534, prohibited the senators from having sea-going vessels holding more than 300 -amphorae- (1 amph. = nearly 6 gallons): -id satis habitum ad fructus ex agris vectandos; quaestus omnis patribus indecorus visus- (Liv. xxi. 63). It was thus an ancient usage, and was still permitted, that the senators should possess sea-going vessels for the transport of the produce of their estates: on the other hand, transmarine mercantile speculation (-quaestus-, traffic, fitting-out of vessels, &c.) on their part was prohibited. It is a curious fact that the ancient Greeks as well as the Romans expressed the tonnage of their sea-going ships constantly in amphorae; the reason evidently being, that Greece as well as Italy exported wine at a comparatively early period, and on a larger scale than any other bulky article.

246

CHAPTER XIV

Measuring and Writing

The art of measuring brings the world into subjection to man; the art of writing prevents his knowledge from perishing along with himself; together they make man—what nature has not made him—all-powerful and eternal. It is the privilege and duty of history to trace the course of national progress along these paths also.

Italian Measures

Measurement necessarily presupposes the development of the several ideas of units of time, of space, and of weight, and of a whole consisting of equal parts, or in other words of number and of a numeral system. The most obvious bases presented by nature for this purpose are, in reference to time, the periodic returns of the sun and moon, or the day and the month; in reference to space, the length of the human foot, which is more easily applied in measuring than the arm; in reference to gravity, the burden which a man is able to poise (-librare-) on his hand while he holds his arm stretched out, or the "weight" (-libra-). As a basis for the notion of a whole made up of equal parts, nothing so readily suggests itself as the hand with its five, or the hands with their ten, fingers; upon this rests the decimal system. We have already observed that these elements of all numeration and measuring reach back not merely beyond the separation of the Greek and Latin stocks, but even to the most remote primeval times. The antiquity in particular of the measurement of time by the moon is demonstrated by language;(1) even the mode of reckoning the days that elapse between the several phases of the moon, not forward from the phase on which it had entered last, but backward from that which was next to be expected, is at least older than the separation of the Greeks and Latins.

Decimal System

The most definite evidence of the antiquity and original exclusive use of the decimal system among the Indo-Germans is furnished by the well-known agreement of all Indo-Germanic languages in respect to the numerals as far as a hundred inclusive.(2) In the case of Italy the decimal system pervaded all the earliest arrangements: it may be sufficient to recall the number ten so usual in the case of witnesses, securities, envoys, and magistrates, the legal equivalence of one ox and ten sheep, the partition of the canton into ten curies and the pervading application generally of the decurial system, the -limitatio-, the tenth in offerings and in agriculture, decimation, and the praenomen -Decimus-. Among the applications of this most ancient decimal system in the sphere of measuring and of writing, the remarkable Italian ciphers claim a primary place. When the Greeks and Italians separated, there were still evidently no conventional signs of number. On the other hand we find the three oldest and most indispensable numerals, one, five, and ten, represented by three signs—I, V or $\wedge$, X, manifestly imitations of the outstretched finger, and the open hand single and double—which were not derived either from the Hellenes or the Phoenicians, but were common to the Romans, Sabellians, and Etruscans. They were the first steps towards the formation of a national Italian writing, and at the same time evidences of the liveliness of that earlier inland intercourse among the Italians which preceded their transmarine commerce.(3) Which of the Italian stocks invented, and which of them borrowed, these signs, can of course no longer be ascertained. Other traces of the pure decimal system occur but sparingly in this field; among them are the -versus-, the Sabellian measure of surface of 100 square feet,(4) and the Roman year of 10 months.

The Duodecimal System

Otherwise generally in the case of those Italian measures, which were not connected with Greek standards and were probably developed by the Italians before they came into contact with the Greeks, there prevailed the partition of the "whole" (-as-) into twelve "units" (-unciae-). The very earliest Latin priesthoods, the colleges of the Salii and Arvales,(5) as well as the leagues of the Etruscan cities, were organized on the basis of the number twelve. The same number predominated in the Roman system of weights and in the measures of length, where the pound (-libra-) and the foot (-pes-) were usually subdivided into twelve parts; the unit of the Roman measures of surface was the "driving" (-actus-) of 120 square feet, a combination of the decimal and duodecimal systems.(6) Similar arrangements as to the measures of capacity may have passed into oblivion.

If we inquire into the basis of the duodecimal system and consider how it can have happened that, in addition to ten, twelve should have been so early and universally singled out from the equal series of numbers, we shall probably be able to find no other source to which it can be referred than a comparison of the solar and lunar periods. Still more than the double hand of ten fingers did the solar cycle of nearly twelve lunar periods first suggest to man the profound conception of an unit composed of equal units, and thereby originate the idea of a system of numbers, the first step towards mathematical thought. The consistent duodecimal development of this idea appears to have belonged to the Italian nation, and to have preceded the first contact with the Greeks.

Hellenic Measures in Italy

But when at length the Hellenic trader had opened up the route to the west coast of Italy, the measures of surface remained unaffected, but the measures of length, of weight, and above all of capacity—in other words those definite standards without which barter and traffic are impossible—experienced the effects of the new international intercourse. The oldest Roman foot has disappeared; that which we know, and which was in use at a very early period among the Romans, was borrowed from Greece, and was, in addition to its new Roman subdivision into twelfths, divided after the Greek fashion into four hand-breadths (-palmus-) and sixteen finger-breadths (-digitus-). Further, the Roman weights were brought into a fixed proportional relation to the Attic system, which prevailed throughout Sicily but not in Cumae—another significant proof that the Latin traffic was chiefly directed to the island; four Roman pounds were assumed as equal to three Attic -minae-, or rather the Roman pound was assumed as equal to one and a half of the Sicilian -litrae- or half-minae.(7) But the most singular and chequered aspect is presented by the Roman measures of capacity, as regards both their names and their proportions. Their names have come from the Greek terms either by corruption (-amphora-, -modius- after —medimnos—, -congius- from —choeus—, -hemina-, -cyathus-) or by translation (-acetabulum-from —ozubaphon—); while conversely —zesteis— is a corruption of -sextarius-. All the measures are not identical, but those in most common use are so; among liquid measures the -congius- or -chus-, the -sextarius-, and the -cyathus-, the two last also for dry goods; the Roman -amphora- was equalized in water-weight to the Attic talent, and at the same time stood to the Greek —metretes— in the fixed ratio of 3:2, and to the Greek —medimnos— of 2:1. To one who can decipher the significance of such records, these names and numerical proportions fully reveal the activity and importance of the intercourse between the Sicilians and the Latins. The Greek numeral signs were not adopted; but the Roman probably availed himself of the Greek alphabet, when it reached him, to form ciphers for 50 and 1000, perhaps also for 100, out of the signs for the three aspirated letters which he had no use for. In Etruria the sign for 100 at least appears to have been obtained in a similar way. Afterwards, as usually happens, the systems of notation among the two neighbouring nations became assimilated by the adoption in substance of the Roman system in Etruria.

The Italian Calendar before the Period of Greek Influence in Italy

In like manner the Roman calendar—and probably that of the Italians generally—began with an independent development of its own, but subsequently came under the influence of the Greeks. In the division of time the returns of sunrise and sunset, and of the new and full moon, most directly arrest the attention of man; and accordingly the day and the month, determined not by cyclic calculation but by direct observation, were long the exclusive measures of time. Down to a late age sunrise and sunset were proclaimed in the Roman market-place by the public crier, and in like manner it may be presumed that in earlier times, at each of the four phases of the moon, the number of days that would elapse from that phase until the next was proclaimed by the priests. The mode of reckoning therefore in Latium—and the like mode, it may be presumed, was in use not merely among the Sabellians, but also among the Etruscans—was by days, which, as already mentioned, were counted not forward from the phase that had last occurred, but backward from that which was next expected; by lunar weeks, which varied in length between 7 and 8 days, the average length being 7 3/8; and by lunar months which in like manner were sometimes of 29, sometimes of 30 days, the average duration of the synodical month being 29 days 12 hours 44 minutes. For some time the day continued to be among the Italians the smallest, and the month the largest, division of time. It was not until afterwards that they began to distribute day and night respectively into four portions, and it was much later still when they began to employ the division into hours; which explains why even stocks otherwise closely related differed in their mode of fixing the commencement of day, the Romans placing it at midnight, the Sabellians and the Etruscans at noon. No calendar of the year had, at least when the Greeks separated from the Italians, as yet been organized, for the names for the year and its divisions in the two languages have been formed quite independently of each other. Nevertheless the Italians appear to have already in the pre-Hellenic period advanced, if not to the arrangement of a fixed calendar, at any rate to the institution of two larger units of time. The simplifying of the reckoning according to lunar months by the application of the decimal system, which was usual among the Romans, and the designation of a term of ten months as a "ring" (-annus-) or complete year, bear in them all the traces of a high antiquity. Later, but still at a period very early and undoubtedly previous to the operation of Greek influences, the duodecimal system (as we have already stated) was developed in Italy, and, as it derived its very origin from the observation of the fact that the solar period was equal to twelve lunar periods, it was certainly applied in the first instance to the reckoning of time. This view accords with the fact that the individual names of the months—which can only have originated after the month was viewed as part of a solar year—particularly those of March and of May, were similar among the different branches of the Italian stock, while there was no similarity between the Italian names and the Greek. It is not improbable therefore that the problem of laying down a practical calendar which should correspond at once to the moon and the sun—a problem which may be compared in some sense to the quadrature of the circle, and the solution of which was only recognized as impossible and abandoned after the lapse of many centuries—had already employed the minds of men in Italy before the epoch at which their contact with the Greeks began; these purely national attempts to solve it, however, have passed into oblivion.

The Oldest Italo-Greek Calendar

What we know of the oldest calendar of Rome and of some other Latin cities—as to the Sabellian and Etruscan measurement of time we have no traditional information—is decidedly based on the oldest Greek arrangement of the year, which was intended to answer both to the phases of the moon and to the seasons of the solar year, constructed on the assumption of a lunar period of 29 1/2 days and a solar period of 12 1/2 lunar months or 368 3/4 days, and on the regular alternation of a full month or month of thirty days with a hollow month or month of twenty-nine days and of a year of twelve with a year of thirteen months, but at the same time maintained in some sort of harmony with the actual celestial phenomena by arbitrary curtailments and intercalations. It is possible that this Greek arrangement of the year in the first instance came into use among the Latins without undergoing any alteration; but the oldest form of the Roman year which can be historically recognized varied from its model, not indeed in the cyclical result nor yet in the alternation of years of twelve with years of thirteen months, but materially in the designation and in the measuring off of the individual months. The Roman year began with the beginning of spring; the first month in it and the only one which bears the name of a god, was named from Mars (-Martius-), the three following from sprouting (-aprilis-) growing (-maius-), and thriving (-iunius-), the fifth onward to the tenth from their ordinal numbers (-quinctilis-, -sextilis-, -september-, -october-, -november-, -december), the eleventh from commencing (-ianuarius-),(8) with reference presumably to the renewal of agricultural operations that followed midwinter and the season of rest, the twelfth, and in an ordinary year the last, from cleansing (-februarius-). To this series recurring in regular succession there was added in the intercalary year a nameless "labour-month" (-mercedonius-) at the close of the year, *viz.* after February. And, as the Roman calendar was independent as respected the names of the months which were probably taken from the old national ones, it was also independent as regarded their duration. Instead of the four years of the Greek cycle, each composed of six months of 30 and six of 29 days and an intercalary month inserted every second year alternately of 29 and 30 days (354 + 384 + 354 + 383 = 1475 days), the Roman calendar substituted four years, each containing four months—the first, third, fifth, and eighth—of 31 days and seven of 29 days, with a February of 28 days during three years and of 29 in the fourth, and an intercalary month of 27 days inserted every second year (355 + 383 + 355 + 382 = 1475 days). In like manner this calendar departed from the original division of the month into four weeks, sometimes of 7, sometimes of 8 days; it made the eight-day-week run on through the years without regard to the other relations of the calendar, as our Sundays do, and placed the weekly market on the day with which it began (-noundinae-). Along with this it once for all fixed the first quarter in the months of 31 days on the seventh, in those of 29 on the fifth day, and the full moon in the former on the fifteenth, in the latter on the thirteenth day. As the course of the months was thus permanently arranged, it was henceforth necessary to proclaim only the number of days lying between the new moon and the first quarter; thence the day of the newmoon received the name of "proclamation-day" (-kalendae-). The first day of the second section of the month, uniformly of 8 days, was—in conformity with the Roman custom of reckoning, which included the -terminus ad quem- —designated as "nine-day" (-nonae-). The day of the full moon retained the old name of -idus-

(perhaps "dividing-day"). The motive lying at the bottom of this strange remodelling of the calendar seems chiefly to have been a belief in the salutary virtue of odd numbers;(9) and while in general it is based on the oldest form of the Greek year, its variations from that form distinctly exhibit the influence of the doctrines of Pythagoras, which were then paramount in Lower Italy, and which especially turned upon a mystic view of numbers. But the consequence was that this Roman calendar, clearly as it bears traces of the desire that it should harmonize with the course both of sun and moon, in reality by no means so corresponded with the lunar course as did at least on the whole its Greek model, while, like the oldest Greek cycle, it could only follow the solar seasons by means of frequent arbitrary excisions, and did in all probability follow them but very imperfectly, for it is scarcely likely that the calendar would be handled with greater skill than was manifested in its original arrangement. The retention moreover of the reckoning by months or—which is the same thing—by years of ten months implies a tacit, but not to be misunderstood, confession of the irregularity and untrustworthiness of the oldest Roman solar year. This Roman calendar may be regarded, at least in its essential features, as that generally current among the Latins. When we consider how generally the beginning of the year and the names of the months are liable to change, minor variations in the numbering and designations are quite compatible with the hypothesis of a common basis; and with such a calendar-system, which practically was irrespective of the lunar course, the Latins might easily come to have their months of arbitrary length, possibly marked off by annual festivals—as in the case of the Alban months, which varied between 16 and 36 days. It would appear probable therefore that the Greek — trieteris— had early been introduced from Lower Italy at least into Latium and perhaps also among the other Italian stocks, and had thereafter been subjected in the calendars of the several cities to further subordinate alterations.

For the measuring of periods of more than one year the regnal years of the kings might have been employed: but it is doubtful whether that method of dating, which was in use in the East, occurred in Greece or Italy during earlier times. On the other hand the intercalary period recurring every four years, and the census and lustration of the community connected with it, appear to have suggested a reckoning by -lustra- similar in plan to the Greek reckoning by Olympiads—a method, however, which early lost its chronological significance in consequence of the irregularity that now prevailed as to the due holding of the census at the right time.

Introduction of Hellenic Alphabets into Italy

The art of expressing sounds by written signs was of later origin than the art of measurement. The Italians did not any more than the Hellenes develop such an art of themselves, although we may discover attempts at such a development in the Italian numeral signs,(10) and possibly also in the primitive Italian custom—formed independently of Hellenic influence—of drawing lots by means of wooden tablets. The difficulty which must have attended the first individualizing of sounds—occurring as they do in so great a variety of combinations—is best demonstrated by the fact that a single alphabet propagated from people to people and from generation to generation has sufficed, and still suffices, for the whole of Aramaic, Indian, Graeco-Roman, and modern civilization; and this most important product of the human intellect was the joint creation of the Aramaeans and the Indo-Germans. The Semitic family of languages, in which the vowel has a subordinate character and never can begin a word, facilitates on that very account the individualizing of the consonants; and it was among the Semites accordingly that the first alphabet—in which the vowels were still wanting—was invented. It was the Indians and Greeks who first independently of each other and by very divergent methods created, out of the Aramaean consonantal writing brought to them by commerce, a complete alphabet by the addition of the vowels—which was effected by the application of four letters, which the Greeks did not use as consonantal signs, for the four vowels -a -e -i -o, and by the formation of a new sign for -u —in other words by the introduction of the syllable into writing instead of the mere consonant, or, as Palamedes says in Euripides,

—Ta teis ge leitheis pharmak orthosas monos
Aphona kai phonounta, sullabas te theis,
Ezeupon anthropoisi grammat eidenai.—

This Aramaeo-Hellenic alphabet was accordingly brought to the Italians through the medium, doubtless, of the Italian Hellenes; not, however, through the agricultural colonies of Magna Graecia, but through the merchants possibly of Cumae or Tarentum, by whom it would be brought in the first instance to the very ancient emporia of international traffic in Latium and Etruria—to Rome and Caere. The alphabet received by the Italians was by no means the oldest Hellenic one; it had already experienced several modifications, particularly the addition of the three letters —"id:xi", —"id:phi", —"id:chi" and the alteration of the signs for —"id:iota", —"id:gamma", —"id:lambda".(11) We have already observed(12) that the Etruscan and Latin alphabets were not derived the one from the other, but both directly from the Greek; in fact the Greek alphabet came to Etruria in a form materially different from that which reached Latium. The Etruscan alphabet has a double sign -s (sigma -"id:s" and san -"id:sh") and only a single -k,(13) and of the -r only the older form -"id:P"; the Latin has, so far as we know, only a single -s, but a double sign for -k (kappa -"id:k" and koppa -"id:q") and of the -r almost solely the more recent form -"id:R". The oldest Etruscan writing shows no knowledge of lines, and winds like the coiling of a snake; the more recent employs parallel broken-off lines from right to left: the Latin writing, as far as our monuments reach back, exhibits only the latter form of parallel lines, which originally perhaps may have run at pleasure from left to right or from right to left, but subsequently ran among the Romans in the former, and among the Faliscans in the latter direction. The model alphabet brought to Etruria must notwithstanding its comparatively remodelled character reach back to an epoch very ancient, though not positively to be determined; for, as the two sibilants sigma and san were always used by the Etruscans as different sounds side by side, the Greek alphabet which came to Etruria must doubtless still have possessed both of them in this way as living signs of sound; but among all the monuments of the Greek language known to us not one presents sigma and san in simultaneous use.

The Latin alphabet certainly, as we know it, bears on the whole a more recent character; and it is not improbable that the Latins did not simply receive the alphabet once for all, as was the case in Etruria, but in consequence of their lively intercourse with their Greek neighbours kept pace for a considerable period with the alphabet in use among these, and followed its variations. We find, for instance, that the forms - "id:/VV", -"id:P",(14) and -"id:*Sigma*" were not unknown to the Romans, but were superseded in common use by the later forms -"id:/V\", -"id:R", and -"id:S" —a circumstance which can only be explained by supposing that the Latins employed for a considerable period the Greek alphabet as such in writing either their mother-tongue or Greek. It is dangerous therefore to draw from the more recent character of the Greek alphabet which we meet with in Rome, as compared with the older character of that brought to Etruria, the inference that writing was practised earlier in Etruria than in Rome.

The powerful impression produced by the acquisition of the treasure of letters on those who received them, and the vividness with which they realized the power that slumbered in those humble signs, are illustrated by a remarkable vase from a sepulchral chamber of Caere built before the invention of the arch, which exhibits the old Greek model alphabet as it came to Etruria, and also an Etruscan syllabarium formed from it, which may be compared to that of Palamedes—evidently a sacred relic of the introduction and acclimatization of alphabetic writing in Etruria.

Development of Alphabets in Italy

Not less important for history than the derivation of the alphabet is the further course of its development on Italian soil: perhaps it is even of more importance; for by means of it a gleam of light is thrown upon the inland commerce of Italy, which is involved in far greater darkness than the commerce with foreigners on its coasts. In the earliest epoch of Etruscan writing, when the alphabet was used without material alteration as it had been introduced, its use appears to have been restricted to the Etruscans on the Po and in what is now Tuscany. In course of time this alphabet, manifestly diffusing itself from Atria and Spina, reached southward along the east coast as far as the Abruzzi, northward to the Veneti and subsequently even to the Celts at the foot of, among, and indeed beyond the Alps, so that its last offshoots reached as far as the Tyrol and Styria. The more recent epoch starts with a reform of the alphabet, the chief features of which were the introduction of writing in broken-off lines, the suppression of the -"id:o", which was no longer distinguished in pronunciation from the -"id:u", and the introduction of a new letter -"id:f" for which the alphabet as received by them had no corresponding sign. This reform evidently arose among the western Etruscans, and while it did not find reception beyond the Apennines, became naturalized among all the Sabellian tribes, and especially among the Umbrians. In its further course the alphabet experienced various fortunes in connection with the several stocks, the Etruscans on the Arno and around Capua, the Umbrians and the Samnites; frequently the mediae were entirely or partially lost, while elsewhere again new vowels and consonants were developed. But that West-Etruscan reform of the alphabet was not merely as old as the oldest tombs found in Etruria; it was considerably older, for the syllabarium just mentioned as found probably in one of these tombs already presents the reformed alphabet in an essentially modified and modernized shape; and, as the reformed alphabet itself is relatively recent as compared with the primitive one, the mind almost fails in the effort to reach back to the time when that alphabet came to Italy. While the Etruscans thus appear as the instruments in diffusing the alphabet in the north, east, and south of the peninsula, the Latin alphabet on the other hand was confined to Latium, and maintained its ground, upon the whole, there with but few alterations; only the letters -"id:gamma" -"id:kappa" and -"id:zeta" -"id:sigma" gradually became coincident in sound, the consequence of which was, that in each case one of the homophonous signs (-"id:kappa" -"id:zeta") disappeared from writing. In Rome it can be shown that these were already laid aside before the end of the fourth century of the city,(15) and the whole monumental and literary tradition that has reached us knows nothing of them, with a single exception.(16) Now when we consider that in the oldest abbreviations the distinction between -"id:gamma" -"id:c" and -"id:kappa" -"id:k" is still regularly maintained;(17) that the period, accordingly, when the sounds became in pronunciation coincident, and before that again the period during which the abbreviations became fixed, lies beyond the beginning of the Samnite wars; and lastly, that a considerable interval must necessarily have elapsed between the introduction of writing and the establishment of a conventional system of abbreviation; we must, both as regards Etruria and Latium, carry back the commencement of the art of writing to an epoch which more closely approximates to the first incidence of the Egyptian Sirius-period within historical times, the year 1321 B.C., than to the year 776, with which the chronology of the Olympiads began in

Greece.(18) The high antiquity of the art of writing in Rome is evinced otherwise by numerous and plain indications. The existence of documents of the regal period is sufficiently attested; such was the special treaty between Rome and Gabii, which was concluded by a king Tarquinius and probably not by the last of that name, and which, written on the skin of the bullock sacrificed on the occasion, was preserved in the temple of Sancus on the Quirinal, which was rich in antiquities and probably escaped the conflagration of the Gauls; and such was the alliance which king Servius Tullius concluded with Latium, and which Dionysius saw on a copper tablet in the temple of Diana on the Aventine. What he saw, however, was probably a copy restored after the fire with the help of a Latin exemplar, for it was not likely that engraving on metal was practised as early as the time of the kings. The charters of foundation of the imperial period still refer to the charter founding this temple as the oldest document of the kind in Rome and the common model for all. But even then they scratched (-exarare-, -scribere-, akin to -scrobes- (19)) or painted (-linere-, thence -littera-) on leaves (-folium-), inner bark (-liber-), or wooden tablets (-tabula-, -album-), afterwards also on leather and linen. The sacred records of the Samnites as well as of the priesthood of Anagnia were inscribed on linen rolls, and so were the oldest lists of the Roman magistrates preserved in the temple of the goddess of recollection (-Iuno moneta-) on the Capitol. It is scarcely necessary to recall further proofs in the primitive marking of the pastured cattle (-scriptura-), in the mode of addressing the senate, "fathers and enrolled" (-patres conscripti-), and in the great antiquity of the books of oracles, the clan-registers, and the Alban and Roman calendars. When Roman tradition speaks of halls in the Forum, where the boys and girls of quality were taught to read and write, already in the earliest times of the republic, the statement may be, but is not necessarily to be deemed, an invention. We have been deprived of information as to the early Roman history, not in consequence of the want of a knowledge of writing, or even perhaps of the lack of documents, but in consequence of the incapacity of the historians of the succeeding age, which was called to investigate the history, to work out the materials furnished by the archives, and of the perversity which led them to desire for the earliest epoch a delineation of motives and of characters, accounts of battles and narratives of revolutions, and while engaged in inventing these, to neglect what the extant written tradition would not have refused to yield to the serious and self-denying inquirer.

Results

The history of Italian writing thus furnishes in the first place a confirmation of the weak and indirect influence exercised by the Hellenic character over the Sabellians as compared with the more western peoples. The fact that the former received their alphabet from the Etruscans and not from the Romans is probably to be explained by supposing that they already possessed it before they entered upon their migration along the ridge of the Apennines, and that therefore the Sabines as well as Samnites carried it along with them from the mother-land to their new abodes. On the other hand this history of writing contains a salutary warning against the adoption of the hypothesis, originated by the later Roman culture in its devotedness to Etruscan mysticism and antiquarian trifling, and patiently repeated by modern and even very recent inquirers, that Roman civilization derived its germ and its pith from Etruria. If this were the truth, some trace of it ought to be more especially apparent in this field; but on the contrary the germ of the Latin art of writing was Greek, and its development was so national, that it did not even adopt the very desirable Etruscan sign for -"id:f".(20) Indeed, where there is an appearance of borrowing, as in the numeral signs, it is on the part of the Etruscans, who took over from the Romans at least the sign for 50.

Corruption of Language and Writing

Lastly it is a significant fact, that among all the Italian stocks the development of the Greek alphabet primarily consisted in a process of corruption. Thus the -mediae- disappeared in the whole of the Etruscan dialects, while the Umbrians lost -"id:gamma" and -"id:d", the Samnites -"id:d", and the Romans -"id:gamma"; and among the latter -"id:d" also threatened to amalgamate with -"id:r". In like manner among the Etruscans -"id:o" and -"id:u" early coalesced, and even among the Latins we meet with a tendency to the same corruption. Nearly the converse occurred in the case of the sibilants; for while the Etruscan retained the three signs -"id:z", -"id:s", -"id:sh", and the Umbrian rejected the last but developed two new sibilants in its room, the Samnite and the Faliscan confined themselves like the Greek to -"id:s" and -"id:z", and the Roman of later times even to -"id:s" alone. It is plain that the more delicate distinctions of sound were duly felt by the introducers of the alphabet, men of culture and masters of two languages; but after the national writing Became wholly detached from the Hellenic mother-alphabet, the -mediae- and their -tenues- gradually came to coincide, and the sibilants and vowels were thrown into disorder— transpositions or rather destructions of sound, of which the first in particular is entirely foreign to the Greek. The destruction of the forms of flexion and derivation went hand in hand with this corruption of sounds. The cause of this barbarization was thus, upon the whole, simply the necessary process of corruption which is continuously eating away every language, where its progress is not stemmed by literature and reason; only in this case indications of what has elsewhere passed away without leaving a trace have been preserved in the writing of sounds. The circumstance that this barbarizing process affected the Etruscans more strongly than any other of the Italian stocks adds to the numerous proofs of their inferior capacity for culture. The fact on the other hand that, among the Italians, the Umbrians apparently were the most affected by a similar corruption of language, the Romans less so, the southern Sabellians least of all, probably finds its explanation, at least in part, in the more lively intercourse maintained by the former with the Etruscans, and by the latter with the Greeks.

Notes for Book I Chapter XIV

1. I. II. Indo-Germanic Culture

2. I. II. Indo-Germanic Culture

3. I. XII. Inland Commerce of the Italians

4. I. II. Agriculture

5. I. XII. Priests

6. Originally both the -actus-, "riving," and its still more frequently occurring duplicate, the -jugerum-, "yoking," were, like the German "morgen," not measures of surface, but measures of labour; the latter denoting the day's work, the former the half-day's work, with reference to the sharp division of the day especially in Italy by the ploughman's rest at noon.

7. I. XIII. Etrusco-Attic and Latino-Sicilian Commerce

8. I. XII. Nature of the Roman Gods

9. From the same cause all the festival-days are odd, as well those recurring every month (-kalendae- on the 1st. -nonae- on the 5th or 7th, -idus- on the 13th or 15th), as also, with but two exceptions, those of the 45 annual festivals mentioned above (xii. Oldest Table Of Roman Festivals). This is carried so far, that in the case of festivals of several days the intervening even days were dropped out, and so, for example, that of Carmentis was celebrated on Jan. 11, 15, that of the Grove-festival (-Lucaria-) on July 19, 21, and that of the Ghosts-festival on May 9, 11, and 13.

10. I. XIV. Decimal System

11. The history of the alphabet among the Hellenes turns essentially on the fact that—assuming the primitive alphabet of 23 letters, that is to say, the Phoenician alphabet vocalized and enlarged by the addition of the -"id:u" —proposals of very various kinds were made to supplement and improve it, and each of these proposals has a history of its own. The most important of these, which it is interesting to keep in view as bearing on the history of Italian writing, are the following:—I. The introduction of special signs for the sounds —"id:xi" —"id:phi" —"id:chi". This proposal is so old that all the Greek alphabets—with the single exception of that of the islands Thera, Melos, and Crete—and all alphabets derived from the Greek without exception, exhibit its influence. At first probably the aim was to append the signs —"id:*Chi*" = —"id:xi iota", —"id:*Phi*" = —"id:phi iota", and —"id:*Psi*"= —-"id:chi iota" to the close of the alphabet, and in this shape it was adopted on the mainland of Hellas—with the exception of Athens and Corinth—and also among the

Sicilian and Italian Greeks. The Greeks of Asia Minor on the other hand, and those of the islands of the Archipelago, and also the Corinthians on the mainland appear, when this proposal reached them, to have already had in use for the sound —"id:xi iota" the fifteenth sign of the Phoenician alphabet —"id:XI" (Samech); accordingly of the three new signs they adopted the —"id:*Phi*" for —"id:phi iota", but employed the —"id:*Chi*" not for —"id:xi iota", but for —"id:chi iota". The third sign originally invented for —"id:chi iota" was probably allowed in most instances to drop; only on the mainland of Asia Minor it was retained, but received the value of —"id:psi iota". The mode of writing adopted in Asia Minor was followed also by Athens; only in its case not merely the —"id:psi iota", but the —"id:xi iota" also, was not received and in their room the two consonants continued to be written as before.—II. Equally early, if not still earlier, an effort was made to obviate the confusion that might so easily occur between the forms for —"id:iota S" and for —- "id:s E"; for all the Greek alphabets known to us bear traces of the endeavour to distinguish them otherwise and more precisely. Already in very early times two such proposals of change must have been made, each of which found a field for its diffusion. In the one case they employed for the sibilant—for which the Phoenician alphabet furnished two signs, the fourteenth (—"id:/\/\") for —"id:sh" and the eighteenth (—"id:E") for —"id:s" —not the latter, which was in sound the more suitable, but the former; and such was in earlier times the mode of writing in the eastern islands, in Corinth and Corcyra, and among the Italian Achaeans. In the other case they substituted for the sign of —"id:i" the simple stroke —"id:I", which was by far the more usual, and at no very late date became at least so far general that the broken —"id:iota S" everywhere disappeared, although individual communities retained the —"id:s" in the form —"id:/\/\" alongside of the —"I".—III. Of later date is the substitution of —"id:V" for —"id:/\" (—"id:lambda") which might readily be confounded with —"id:*Gamma* gamma". This we meet with in Athens and Boeotia, while Corinth and the communities dependent on Corinth attained the same object by giving to the —"id:gamma" the semicircular form —"id:C" instead of the hook-shape.—IV. The forms for —"id:p" —"id:P (with broken-loop)" and —"id:r" —"id:P", likewise very liable to be confounded, were distinguished by transforming the latter into —"id:R"; which more recent form was not used by the Greeks of Asia Minor, the Cretans, the Italian Achaeans, and a few other districts, but on the other hand greatly preponderated both in Greece proper and in Magna Graecia and Sicily. Still the older form of the —"id:r" —"id:P" did not so early and so completely disappear there as the older form of the —"id:l"; this alteration therefore beyond doubt is to be placed later.—V. The differentiating of the long and short -e and the long and short -o remained in the earlier times confined to the Greeks of Asia Minor and of the islands of the Aegean Sea.

All these technical improvements are of a like nature and from a historical point of view of like value, in so far as each of them arose at a definite time and at a definite place and thereafter took its own mode of diffusion and found its special development. The excellent investigation of Kirchhoff (-Studien zur Geschichte des griechischen Alphabets-), which has thrown a clear light on the previously so obscure history of the Hellenic alphabet, and has also furnished essential data for the earliest relations between the Hellenes and Italians—establishing, in particular, incontrovertibly the previously uncertain home of the Etruscan alphabet—is affected by a certain one-sidedness in so far as it lays proportionally too great stress on a single one of these proposals. If systems are here to be distinguished at all, we may not divide the alphabets into two classes according to the value of the —"id:X" as —"id:zeta" or as —"id:chi", but we shall have to distinguish the alphabet of 23 from that of 25 or 26 letters, and perhaps further in this latter case to distinguish the Ionic of Asia Minor, from which the later common alphabet proceeded, from the common Greek of earlier times. In dealing, however, with the different proposals for the modification of the alphabet the several districts followed an essentially eclectic course, so that one was received here and another there; and it is just in this respect that the history of the Greek alphabet is so instructive, because it shows how particular groups of the Greek lands exchanged improvements in handicraft and art, while others exhibited no such reciprocity. As to Italy in particular we have already called attention to the remarkable contrast between the Achaean agricultural towns and the Chalcidic and Doric colonies of a more mercantile character (x. Iono-Dorian Towns); in the former the primitive forms were throughout retained, in the latter the improved forms were adopted, even those which coming from different quarters were somewhat inconsistent, such as the —"id:C" —"id:gamma" alongside of the —"id:V" —"id:l". The Italian alphabets proceed, as Kirchhoff has shown, wholly from the alphabet of the Italian Greeks and in fact from the Chalcidico-Doric; but that the Etruscans and Latins received their alphabet not the one from the other but both directly from the Greeks, is placed beyond doubt especially by the different form of the —"id:r". For, while of the four modifications of the alphabet above described which concern the Italian Greeks (the fifth was confined to Asia Minor) the first three were already carried out before the alphabet passed to the Etruscans and Latins, the differentiation of —"id:p" and —"id:r" had not yet taken place when it came to Etruria, but on the other hand had at least begun when the Latins received it; for which reason the Etruscans do not at all know the form -"id:R" for -"id:r", whereas among the Faliscans and the Latins, with the single exception of the Dressel vase (xiv. Note 14), the younger form is met with exclusively.

12. I. XIII. Etrusco-Attic and Latino-Sicilian Commerce

13. That the Etruscans always were without the koppa, seems not doubtful; for not only is no sure trace of it to be met with elsewhere, but it is wanting in the model alphabet of the Galassi vase. The attempt to show its presence in the syllabarium of the latter is at any rate mistaken, for the syllabarium can and does only take notice of the Etruscan letters that were afterwards in common use, and to these the koppa notoriously did not belong; moreover the sign placed at the close cannot well from its position have any other value than that of the -f, which was in fact the last letter in the Etruscan alphabet, and which could not be omitted in a syllabarium exhibiting the variations of that alphabet from its model. It is certainly surprising that the koppa should be absent from the Greek alphabet that came to Etruria, when it otherwise so long maintained its place in the Chalcidico-Doric ; but this may well have been a local peculiarity of the town whose alphabet first reached Etruria. Caprice and accident have at all times had a share in determining whether a sign becoming superfluous shall be retained or dropped from the alphabet; thus the Attic alphabet lost the eighteenth Phoenician sign, but retained the others which had disappeared from the -u.

14. The golden bracelet of Praeneste recently brought to light (Mitth. der rom. Inst. 1887), far the oldest of the intelligible monuments of the Latin language and Latin writing, shows the older form of the -"id:m"; the enigmatic clay vase from the Quirinal (published by Dressel in the Annali dell Instituto, 1880) shows the older form of the -"id:r".

15. At this period we shall have to place that recorded form of the Twelve Tables, which subsequently lay before the Roman philologues, and of which we possess fragments. Beyond doubt the code was at its very origin committed to writing; but that those scholars themselves referred their text not to the original exemplar, but to an official document written down after the Gallic conflagration, is proved by the story of the Tables having undergone reproduction at that time. This enables us easily to explain how their text by no means exhibited the oldest orthography, which was not unknown to them; even apart from the consideration that in the case of such a written document, employed, moreover, for the purpose of being committed to memory by the young, a philologically exact transmission cannot possibly be assumed.

16. This is the inscription of the bracelet of Praeneste which has been mentioned at xiv, note 14. On the other hand even on the Ficoroni cista -"id:C" has the later form of -"id:K".

17. Thus -"id:C" represents -Gaius-; -"id:CN" -Gnaeus-; while -"id:K" stands for -Kaeso-. With the more recent abbreviations of course this is not the case; in these -"id:gamma" is represented not by -"id:C", but by -"id:G" (-*Gal*- -Galeria-), —— "id:kappa", as a rule, by -"id:C" (-C- -centum- -*Cos*- -consul; -*col* -Collina-), or before -"id:a" by -"id:K" (-*Kar*- -karmetalia-; -*Merk*- -merkatus-). For they expressed for a time the sound —k before the vowels -e -i -o and before all consonants by -"id:C", before -a on the other hand by -"id:K", before -u by the old sign of the koppa -"id:Q".

18. If this view is correct, the origin of the Homeric poems (though of course not exactly that of the redaction in which we now have them) must have been far anterior to the age which Herodotus assigns for the flourishing of Homer (100 before Rome); for the introduction of the Hellenic alphabet into Italy, as well as the beginning of intercourse at all between Hellas and Italy, belongs only to the post-Homeric period.

19. Just as the old Saxon -writan- signifies properly to tear, thence to write.

20. The enigma as to how the Latins came to employ the Greek sign corresponding to -v for the -f quite different in sound, has been solved by the bracelet of Praeneste (xiv. Developments Of Alphabets in Italy, note) with its -fhefhaked- for -fecit-, and thereby at the same time the derivation of the Latin alphabet from the Chalcidian colonies of Lower Italy has been confirmed. For in a Boeotian inscription belonging to the same alphabet we find in the word -fhekadamoe-(Gustav Meyer, Griech. Grammatik, sec. 244, ap. fin.) the same combination of sound, and an aspirated v might certainly approximate in sound to the Latin -f.

20. -Ratio Tuscanica,: cavum aedium Tuscanicum.-

21. When Varro (ap. Augustin. De Civ. Dei, iv. 31; comp. Plutarch Num. 8) affirms that the Romans for more than one hundred and seventy years worshipped the gods without images, he is evidently thinking of this primitive piece of carving, which, according to the conventional chronology, was dedicated between 176 and 219, and, beyond doubt, was the first statue of the gods, the consecration of which was mentioned in the authorities which Varro had before him. Comp, above, *xiv.* Development of Alphabets in Italy.

22. I. XIII. Handicrafts

23. I. XII. Nature of the Roman Gods

24. I. XII. Pontifices

Chapter XV

Art

Artistic Endowment of the Italians

Poetry is impassioned language, and its modulation is melody. While in this sense no people is without poetry and music, some nations have received a pre-eminent endowment of poetic gifts. The Italian nation, however, was not and is not one of these. The Italian is deficient in the passion of the heart, in the longing to idealize what is human and to confer humanity on what is lifeless, which form the very essence of poetic art. His acuteness of perception and his graceful versatility enabled him to excel in irony and in the vein of tale-telling which we find in Horace and Boccaccio, in the humorous pleasantries of love and song which are presented in Catullus and in the good popular songs of Naples, above all in the lower comedy and in farce. Italian soil gave birth in ancient times to burlesque tragedy, and in modern times to mock-heroic poetry. In rhetoric and histrionic art especially no other nation equalled or equals the Italians. But in the more perfect kinds of art they have hardly advanced beyond dexterity of execution, and no epoch of their literature has produced a true epos or a genuine drama. The very highest literary works that have been successfully produced in Italy, divine poems like Dante's Commedia, and historical treatises such as those of Sallust and Macchiavelli, of Tacitus and Colletta, are pervaded by a passion more rhetorical than spontaneous. Even in music, both in ancient and modern times, really creative talent has been far less conspicuous than the accomplishment which speedily assumes the character of virtuosoship, and enthrones in the room of genuine and genial art a hollow and heart-withering idol. The field of the inward in art—so far as we may in the case of art distinguish an inward and an outward at all—is not that which has fallen to the Italian as his special province; the power of beauty, to have its full effect upon him, must be placed not ideally before his mind, but sensuously before his eyes. Accordingly he is thoroughly at home in architecture, painting, and sculpture; in these he was during the epoch of ancient culture the best disciple of the Hellenes, and in modern times he has become the master of all nations.

Dance, Music, and Song in Latium

From the defectiveness of our traditional information it is not possible to trace the development of artistic ideas among the several groups of nations in Italy; and in particular we are no longer in a position to speak of the poetry of Italy; we can only speak of that of Latium. Latin poetry, like that of every other nation, began in the lyrical form, or, to speak more correctly, sprang out of those primitive festal rejoicings, in which dance, music, and song were still inseparably blended. It is remarkable, however, that in the most ancient religious usages dancing, and next to dancing instrumental music, were far more prominent than song. In the great procession, with which the Roman festival of victory was opened, the chief place, next to the images of the gods and the champions, was assigned to the dancers grave and merry. The grave dancers were arranged in three groups of men, youths, and boys, all clad in red tunics with copper belts, with swords and short lances, the men being moreover furnished with helmets, and generally in full armed attire. The merry dancers were divided into two companies—"the sheep" in sheep-skins with a party-coloured over-garment, and "the goats" naked down to the waist, with a buck's skin thrown over them. In like manner the "leapers" (-salii-) were perhaps the most ancient and sacred of all the priesthoods,(1) and dancers (-ludii-, -ludiones-) were indispensable in all public processions, and particularly at funeral solemnities; so that dancing became even in ancient times a common trade. But, wherever the dancers made their appearance, there appeared also the musicians or—which was in the earliest times the same thing—the pipers. They too were never wanting at a sacrifice, at a marriage, or at a funeral; and by the side of the primitive public priesthood of the "leapers" there was ranged, of equal antiquity although of far inferior rank, the guild of the "pipers" (-collegium tibicinum-(2)), whose true character as strolling musicians is evinced by their ancient privilege—maintained even in spite of the strictness of Roman police—of wandering through the streets at their annual festival, wearing masks and full of sweet wine. While dancing thus presents itself as an honourable function and music as one subordinate but still necessary, so that public corporations were instituted for both of them, poetry appears more as a matter incidental and, in some measure, indifferent, whether it may have come into existence on its own account or to serve as an accompaniment to the movements of the dancers.

Religious Chants

The earliest chant, in the view of the Romans, was that which the leaves sang to themselves in the green solitude of the forest. The whispers and pipings of the "favourable spirit" (-faunus-, from -favere-) in the grove were reproduced for men, by those who had the gift of listening to him, in rhythmically measured language (-casmen-, afterwards -carmen-, from -canere-). Of a kindred nature to these soothsaying songs of inspired men and women (-vates-) were the incantations properly so called, the formulae for conjuring away diseases and other troubles, and the evil spells by which they prevented rain and called down lightning or even enticed the seed from one field to another; only in these instances, probably from the outset, formulae of mere sounds appear side by side with formulae of words.(3) More firmly rooted in tradition and equally ancient were the religious litanies which were sung and danced by the Salii and other priesthoods; the only one of which that has come down to us, a dance-chant of the Arval Brethren in honour of Mars probably composed to be sung in alternate parts, deserves a place here.

-Enos, Lases, iuvate!
Ne velue rue, Marmar, sins incurrere in pleores!
Satur fu, fere Mars! limen sali! sta! berber!
Semunis alternei advocapit conctos!
Enos, Marmar, iuvato!
Triumpe!-

Which may be thus interpreted:

To the gods:
-Nos, Lares, iuvate!
Ne veluem (= malam luem) ruem (= ruinam), Mamers,
    sinas incurrere in plures!
Satur esto, fere Mars!

To the individual brethren:
In limen insili! sta! verbera (limen?)!

To all the brethren:
Semones alterni advocate cunctos!

To the god:
Nos, Mamers, iuvato!

To the individual brethren:
Tripudia!-(4)

The Latin of this chant and of kindred fragments of the Salian songs, which were regarded even by the philologues of the Augustan age as the oldest documents of their mother-tongue, is related to the Latin of the Twelve Tables somewhat as the language of the Nibelungen is related to the language of Luther; and we may perhaps compare these venerable litanies, as respects both language and contents, with the Indian Vedas.

Panegyrics and Lampoons

Lyrical panegyrics and lampoons belonged to a later epoch. We might infer from the national character of the Italians that satirical songs must have abounded in Latium in ancient times, even if their prevalence had not been attested by the very ancient measures of police directed against them. But the panegyrical chants became of more importance. When a burgess was borne to burial, the bier was followed by a female relative or friend, who, accompanied by a piper, sang his dirge (-nenia-). In like manner at banquets boys, who according to the fashion of those days attended their fathers even at feasts out of their own houses, sang by turns songs in praise of their ancestors, sometimes to the pipe, sometimes simply reciting them without accompaniment (-assa voce canere-). The custom of men singing in succession at banquets was presumably borrowed from the Greeks, and that not till a later age. We know no further particulars of these ancestral lays; but it is self-evident that they must have attempted description and narration and thus have developed, along with and out of the lyrical element, the features of epic poetry.

The Masked Farce

Other elements of poetry were called into action in the primitive popular carnival, the comic dance or -satura-,(5) which beyond doubt reached back to a period anterior to the separation of the stocks. On such occasions song would never be wanting; and the circumstances under which such pastimes were exhibited, chiefly at public festivals and marriages, as well as the mainly practical shape which they certainly assumed, naturally suggested that several dancers, or sets of dancers, should take up reciprocal parts; so that the singing thus came to be associated with a species of acting, which of course was chiefly of a comical and often of a licentious character. In this way there arose not merely alternative chants, such as afterwards went by the name of Fescennine songs, but also the elements of a popular comedy—which were in this instance planted in a soil admirably adapted for their growth, as an acute sense of the outward and the comic, and a delight in gesticulation and masquerade have ever been leading traits of Italian character.

No remains have been preserved of these -incunabula- of the Roman epos and drama. That the ancestral lays were traditional is self-evident, and is abundantly demonstrated by the fact that they were regularly recited by children; but even in the time of Cato the Elder they had completely passed into oblivion. The comedies again, if it be allowable so to name them, were at this period and long afterwards altogether improvised. Consequently nothing of this popular poetry and popular melody could be handed down but the measure, the accompaniment of music and choral dancing, and perhaps the masks.

Metre

Whether what we call metre existed in the earlier times is doubtful; the litany of the Arval Brethren scarcely accommodates itself to an outwardly fixed metrical system, and presents to us rather the appearance of an animated recitation. On the other hand we find in subsequent times a very ancient rhythm, the so-called Saturnian(6) or Faunian metre, which is foreign to the Greeks, and may be conjectured to have arisen contemporaneously with the oldest Latin popular poetry. The following poem, belonging, it is true, to a far later age, may give an idea of it:—

Quod re sua difeidens—aspere afleicta

```
Parens timens heic vovit—voto hoc soluto
____
Decuma facta poloucta—leibereis lubentis
_____           _____
Donu danunt__hercolei—maxsume—mereto
_____
Semol te orant se voti—crebro con__demnes.
```

$$\_\_ \mathbf{-}' \_\_ \mathbf{-}' \_\_ \mathbf{-}' \_ \wedge / \_\_ \mathbf{-}' \_\_ \mathbf{-}' \_\_ \mathbf{-}' \_ \wedge$$

That which, misfortune dreading—sharply to afflict him, An anxious parent vowed here,—when his wish was granted, A sacred tenth for banquet—gladly give his children to Hercules a tribute—most of all deserving; And now they thee beseech, that—often thou wouldst hear them.

Panegyrics as well as comic songs appear to have been uniformly sung in Saturnian metre, of course to the pipe, and presumably in such a way that the -caesura- in particular in each line was strongly marked; and in alternate singing the second singer probably took up the verse at this point. The Saturnian measure is, like every other occurring in Roman and Greek antiquity, based on quantity; but of all the antique metres perhaps it is the least thoroughly elaborated, for besides many other liberties it allows itself the greatest license in omitting the short syllables, and it is at the same time the most imperfect in construction, for these iambic and trochaic half-lines opposed to each other were but little fitted to develop a rhythmical structure adequate for the purposes of the higher poetry.

Melody

The fundamental elements of the national music and choral dancing in Latium, which must likewise have been established during this period, are buried for us in oblivion; except that the Latin pipe is reported to have been a short and slender instrument, provided with only four holes, and originally, as the name shows, made out of the light thighbone of some animal.

Masks

Lastly, the masks used in after times for the standing characters of the Latin popular comedy or the Atellana, as it was called: Maccus the harlequin, Bucco the glutton, Pappus the good papa, and the wise Dossennus—masks which have been cleverly and strikingly compared to the two servants, the -pantalon- and the -dottore-, in the Italian comedy of Pulcinello—already belonged to the earliest Latin popular art. That they did so cannot of course be strictly proved; but as the use of masks for the face in Latium in the case of the national drama was of immemorial antiquity, while the Greek drama in Rome did not adopt them for a century after its first establishment, as, moreover, those Atellane masks were of decidedly Italian origin, and as, in fine, the origination as well as the execution of improvised pieces cannot well be conceived apart from fixed masks assigning once for all to the player his proper position throughout the piece, we must associate fixed masks with the rudiments of the Roman drama, or rather regard them as constituting those rudiments themselves.

Earliest Hellenic Influences

If our information respecting the earliest indigenous culture and art of Latium is so scanty, it may easily be conceived that our knowledge will be still scantier regarding the earliest impulses imparted in this respect to the Romans from without. In a certain sense we may include under this head their becoming acquainted with foreign languages, particularly the Greek. To this latter language, of course, the Latins generally were strangers, as was shown by their enactment in respect to the Sibylline oracles;(7) but an acquaintance with it must have been not at all uncommon in the case of merchants. The same may be affirmed of the knowledge of reading and writing, closely connected as it was with the knowledge of Greek.(8) The culture of the ancient world, however, was not based either on the knowledge of foreign languages or on elementary technical accomplishments. An influence more important than any thus imparted was exercised over the development of Latium by the elements of the fine arts, which were already in very early times received from the Hellenes. For it was the Hellenes alone, and not the Phoenicians or the Etruscans, that in this respect exercised an influence on the Italians. We nowhere find among the latter any stimulus of the fine arts which can be referred to Carthage or Caere, and the Phoenician and Etruscan forms of civilization may be in general perhaps classed with those that are hybrid, and for that reason not further productive.(9) But the influence of Greece did not fail to bear fruit. The Greek seven-stringed lyre, the "strings" (-fides-, from —sphidei—, gut; also -barbitus-, —barbitos—), was not like the pipe indigenous in Latium, and was always regarded there as an instrument of foreign origin; but the early period at which it gained a footing is demonstrated partly by the barbarous mutilation of its Greek name, partly by its being employed even in ritual.(10) That some of the legendary stores of the Greeks during this period found their way into Latium, is shown by the ready reception of Greek works of sculpture with their representations based so thoroughly upon the poetical treasures of the nation; and the old Latin barbarous conversions of Persephone into Prosepna, Bellerophontes into Melerpanta, Kyklops into Cocles, Laomedon into Alumentus, Ganymedes into Catamitus, Neilos into Melus, Semele into Stimula, enable us to perceive at how remote a period such stories had been heard and repeated by the Latins. Lastly and especially, the Roman chief festival or festival of the city (-ludi maximi-, -Romani-) must in all probability have owed, if not its origin, at any rate its later arrangements to Greek influence. It was an extraordinary thanksgiving festival celebrated in honour of the Capitoline Jupiter and the gods dwelling along with him, ordinarily in pursuance of a vow made by the general before battle, and therefore usually observed on the return home of the burgess-force in autumn. A festal procession proceeded toward the Circus staked off between the Palatine and Aventine, and furnished with an arena and places for spectators; in front the whole boys of Rome, arranged according to the divisions of the burgess-force, on horseback and on foot; then the champions and the groups of dancers which we have described above, each with their own music; thereafter the servants of the gods with vessels of frankincense and other sacred utensils; lastly the biers with the images of the gods themselves. The spectacle itself was the counterpart of war as it was waged in primitive times, a contest on chariots, on horseback, and on foot. First there ran the war-chariots, each of which carried in Homeric fashion a charioteer and a combatant; then the combatants who had leaped off; then the horsemen, each of whom appeared after the Roman style of fighting with a horse which he rode and another led by the hand (-desultor-); lastly, the champions on foot, naked to the girdle round their loins, measured their powers in racing, wrestling, and boxing. In each species of contest there was but one competition, and that between not more than two competitors. A chaplet rewarded the victor, and the honour in which the simple branch which formed the wreath was held is shown by the law permitting it to be laid on the bier of the victor when he died. The festival thus lasted only one day, and the competitions probably still left sufficient time on that day for the carnival proper, at which the groups of dancers may have displayed their art and above all exhibited their farces; and doubtless other representations also, such as competitions in juvenile horsemanship, found a place.(11) The honours won in real war also played their part in this festival; the brave warrior exhibited on this day the equipments of the antagonist whom he had slain, and was decorated with a chaplet by the grateful community just as was the victor in the competition.

Such was the nature of the Roman festival of victory or city-festival; and the other public festivities of Rome may be conceived to have been of a similar character, although less ample in point of resources. At the celebration of a public funeral dancers regularly bore a part, and along with them, if there was to be any further exhibition, horse-racers; in that case the burgesses were specially invited beforehand to the funeral by the public crier.

But this city-festival, so intimately bound up with the manners and exercises of the Romans, coincides in all essentials with the Hellenic national festivals: more especially in the fundamental idea of combining a religious solemnity and a competition in warlike sports; in the selection of the several exercises, which at the Olympic festival, according to Pindar's testimony, consisted from the first in running, wrestling, boxing, chariot-racing, and throwing the spear and stone; in the nature of the prize of victory, which in Rome as well as in the Greek national festivals was a chaplet, and in the one case as well as in the other was assigned not to the charioteer, but to the owner of the team; and lastly in introducing the feats and rewards of general patriotism in connection with the general national festival. This agreement cannot have been accidental, but must have been either a remnant of the primitive connection between the peoples, or a result of the earliest international intercourse; and the probabilities preponderate in favour of the latter hypothesis. The city-festival, in the form in which we are acquainted with it, was not one of the oldest institutions of Rome, for the Circus itself was only laid out in the later regal period;(12) and just as the reform of the constitution then took place under Greek influence,(13) the city-festival may have been at the same time so far transformed as to combine Greek races with, and eventually to a certain extent to substitute them for, an older mode of amusement—the "leap" (-triumpus-,(14)), and possibly swinging, which was a primitive Italian custom and long continued in use at the festival on the Alban mount. Moreover, while there is some trace of the use of the war-chariot in actual warfare in Hellas, no such trace exists in Latium. Lastly, the Greek term —stadion— (Doric —spadion—) was at a very early period transferred to the Latin language, retaining its signification, as -spatium-; and there exists even an express statement that the Romans derived their horse and chariot races from the

278

people of Thurii, although, it is true, another account derives them from Etruria. It thus appears that, in addition to the impulses imparted by the Hellenes in music and poetry, the Romans were indebted to them for the fruitful idea of gymnastic competitions.

Character of Poetry and of Education in Latium

Thus there not only existed in Latium the same fundamental elements out of which Hellenic culture and art grew, but Hellenic culture and art themselves exercised a powerful influence over Latium in very early times. Not only did the Latins possess the elements of gymnastic training, in so far as the Roman boy learned like every farmer's son to manage horses and waggon and to handle the hunting-spear, and as in Rome every burgess was at the same time a soldier; but the art of dancing was from the first an object of public care, and a powerful impulse was further given to such culture at an early period by the introduction of the Hellenic games. The lyrical poetry and tragedy of Hellas grew out of songs similar to the festal lays of Rome; the ancestral lay contained the germs of epos, the masked farce the germs of comedy; and in this field also Grecian influences were not wanting.

In such circumstances it is the more remarkable that these germs either did not spring up at all, or were soon arrested in their growth. The bodily training of the Latin youth continued to be solid and substantial, but far removed from the idea of artistic culture for the body, such as was the aim of Hellenic gymnastics. The public games of the Hellenes when introduced into Italy, changed not so much their formal rules as their essential character. While they were intended to be competitions of burgesses and beyond doubt were so at first in Rome, they became contests of professional riders and professional boxers, and, while the proof of free and Hellenic descent formed the first condition for participating in the Greek festal games, those of Rome soon passed into the hands of freedmen and foreigners and even of persons not free at all. Consequently the circle of fellow-competitors became converted into a public of spectators, and the chaplet of the victorious champion, which has been with justice called the badge of Hellas, was afterwards hardly ever mentioned in Latium.

A similar fate befel poetry and her sisters. The Greeks and Germans alone possess a fountain of song that wells up spontaneously; from the golden vase of the Muses only a few drops have fallen on the green soil of Italy. There was no formation of legend in the strict sense there. The Italian gods were abstractions and remained such; they never became elevated into or, as some may prefer to say, obscured under, a true personal shape. In like manner men, even the greatest and noblest, remained in the view of the Italian without exception mortal, and were not, as in the longing recollection and affectionately cherished tradition of Greece, elevated in the conception of the multitude into god-like heroes. But above all no development of national poetry took place in Latium. It is the deepest and noblest effect of the fine arts and above all of poetry, that they break down the barriers of civil communities and create out of tribes a nation and out of the nations a world. As in the present day by means of our cosmopolitan literature the distinctions of civilized nations are done away, so Greek poetic art transformed the narrow and egoistic sense of tribal relationship into the consciousness of Hellenic nationality, and this again into the consciousness of a common humanity. But in Latium nothing similar occurred. There might be poets in Alba and in Rome, but there arose no Latin epos, nor even— what were still more conceivable—a catechism for the Latin farmer of a kind similar to the "Works and Days" of Hesiod. The Latin federal festival might well have become a national festival of the fine arts, like the Olympian and Isthmian games of the Greeks. A cycle of legends might well have gathered around the fall of Alba, such as was woven around the conquest of Ilion, and every community and every noble clan of Latium might have discovered in it, or imported into it, the story of its own origin. But neither of these results took place, and Italy remained without national poetry or art.

The inference which of necessity follows from these facts, that the development of the fine arts in Latium was rather a shrivelling up than an expanding into bloom, is confirmed in a manner even now not to be mistaken by tradition. The beginnings of poetry everywhere, perhaps, belong rather to women than to men; the spell of incantation and the chant for the dead pertain pre-eminently to the former, and not without reason the spirits of song, the Casmenae or Camenae and the Carmentis of Latium, like the Muses of Hellas, were conceived as feminine. But the time came in Hellas, when the poet relieved the songstress and Apollo took his place at the head of the Muses. In Latium there was no national god of song, and the older Latin language had no designation for the poet.(15) The power of song emerging there was out of all proportion weaker, and was rapidly arrested in its growth. The exercise of the fine arts was there early restricted, partly to women and children, partly to incorporated or unincorporated tradesmen. We have already mentioned that funeral chants were sung by women and banquet-lays by boys; the religious litanies also were chiefly executed by children. The musicians formed an incorporated, the dancers and the wailing women (-praeficae-) unincorporated, trades. While dancing, music, and singing remained constantly in Greece—as they were originally also in Latium—reputable employments redounding to the honour of the burgess and of the community to which he belonged, in Latium the better portion of the burgesses drew more and more aloof from these vain arts, and that the more decidedly, in proportion as art came to be more publicly exhibited and more thoroughly penetrated by the quickening impulses derived from other lands. The use of the native pipe was sanctioned, but the lyre remained despised; and while the national amusement of masks was allowed, the foreign amusements of the -palaestra- were not only regarded with indifference, but esteemed disgraceful. While the fine arts in Greece became more and more the common property of the Hellenes individually and collectively and thereby became the means of developing a universal culture, they gradually disappeared in Latium from the thoughts and feelings of the people; and, as they degenerated into utterly insignificant handicrafts, the idea of a general national culture to be communicated to youth never suggested itself at all. The education of youth remained entirely confined within the limits of the narrowest domesticity. The boy never left his father's side, and accompanied him not only to the field with the plough and the sickle, but also to the house of a friend or to the council-hall, when his father was invited as a guest or summoned to the senate. This domestic education was well adapted to preserve man wholly for the household and wholly for the state. The permanent intercommunion of life between father and son, and the mutual reverence felt by adolescence for ripened manhood and by the mature man for the innocence of youth, lay at the root of the steadfastness of the domestic and political traditions, of the closeness of the family bond, and in general of the grave earnestness (-gravitas-) and character of moral worth in Roman life. This mode of educating youth was in truth one of those institutions of homely and almost unconscious wisdom, which are as simple as they are profound. But amidst the admiration which it awakens we may not overlook the fact that it could only be carried out, and was only carried out, by the sacrifice of true individual culture and by a complete renunciation of the equally charming and perilous gifts of the Muses.

Dance, Music, and Song among the Sabellians and Etruscans

Regarding the development of the fine arts among the Etruscans and Sabellians our knowledge is little better than none.(16) We can only notice the fact that in Etruria the dancers (-histri-, -histriones-) and the pipe-players (-subulones-) early made a trade of their art, probably earlier even than in Rome, and exhibited themselves in public not only at home, but also in Rome for small remuneration and less honour. It is a circumstance more remarkable that at the Etruscan national festival, in the exhibition of which the whole twelve cities were represented by a federal priest, games were given like those of the Roman city-festival; we are, however, no longer in a position to answer the question which it suggests, how far the Etruscans were more successful than the Latins in attaining a national form of fine art beyond that of the individual communities. On the other hand a foundation probably was laid in Etruria, even in early times, for that insipid accumulation of learned lumber, particularly of a theological and astrological nature, by virtue of which afterwards, when amidst the general decay antiquarian dilettantism began to flourish, the Tuscans divided with the Jews, Chaldeans, and Egyptians the honour of being admired as primitive sources of divine wisdom. We know still less, if possible, of Sabellian art; but that of course by no means warrants the inference that it was inferior to that of the neighbouring stocks. On the contrary, it may be conjectured from what we otherwise know of the character of the three chief races of Italy, that in artistic gifts the Samnites approached nearest to the Hellenes and the Etruscans were farthest removed from them; and a sort of confirmation of this hypothesis is furnished by the fact, that the most gifted and most original of the Roman poets, such as Naevius, Ennius, Lucilius, and Horace, belonged to the Samnite lands, whereas Etruria has almost no representatives in Roman literature except the Arretine Maecenas, the most insufferable of all heart-withered and affected(17) court-poets, and the Volaterran Persius, the true ideal of a conceited and languid, poetry-smitten, youth.

Earliest Italian Architecture

The elements of architecture were, as has been already indicated, a primitive common possession of the stocks. The dwelling-house constitutes the first attempt of structural art; and it was the same among Greeks and Italians. Built of wood, and covered with a pointed roof of straw or shingles it formed a square dwelling-chamber, which let out the smoke and let in the light by an opening in the roof corresponding with a hole for carrying off the rain in the ground (-cavum aedium-). Under this "black roof" (-atrium-) the meals were prepared and consumed; there the household gods were worshipped, and the marriage bed and the bier were set out; there the husband received his guests, and the wife sat spinning amid the circle of her maidens. The house had no porch, unless we take as such the uncovered space between the house door and the street, which obtained its name -vestibulum-, i. e. dressing-place, from the circumstance that the Romans were in the habit of going about within doors in their tunics, and only wrapped the toga around them when they went abroad. There was, moreover, no division of apartments except that sleeping and store closets might be provided around the dwelling-room; and still less were there stairs, or stories placed one above another.

Earliest Hellenic Influence

Whether, or to what extent, a national Italian architecture arose o ut of these beginnings can scarcely be determined, for in this field Greek influence, even in the earliest times, had a very powerful effect and almost wholly overgrew such national attempts as possibly had preceded it. The very oldest Italian architecture with which we are acquainted is not much less under the influence of that of Greece than the architecture of the Augustan age. The primitive tombs of Caere and Alsium, and probably the oldest one also of those recently discovered at Praeneste, have been, exactly like the —thesauroi—of Orchomenos and Mycenae, roofed over with courses of stone placed one above another, gradually overlapping, and closed by a large stone cover. A very ancient building at the city wall of Tusculum was roofed in the same way, and so was originally the well-house (-tullianum-) at the foot of the Capitol, till the top was pulled down to make room for another building. The gates constructed on the same system are entirely similar in Arpinum and in Mycenae. The tunnel which drains the Alban lake(18) presents the greatest resemblance to that of lake Copais. What are called Cyclopean ring-walls frequently occur in Italy, especially in Etruria, Umbria, Latium, and Sabina, and decidedly belong in point of design to the most ancient buildings of Italy, although the greater portion of those now extant were probably not executed till a much later age, several of them certainly not till the seventh century of the city. They are, just like those of Greece, sometimes quite roughly formed of large unwrought blocks of rock with smaller stones inserted between them, sometimes disposed in square horizontal courses,(19) sometimes composed of polygonal dressed blocks fitting into each other. The selection of one or other of these systems was doubtless ordinarily determined by the material, and accordingly the polygonal masonry does not occur in Rome, where in the most ancient times tufo alone was employed for building. The resemblance in the case of the two former and simpler styles may perhaps be traceable to the similarity of the materials employed and of the object in view in building; but it can hardly be deemed accidental that the artistic polygonal wall-masonry, and the gate with the path leading up to it universally bending to the left and so exposing the unshielded right side of the assailant to the defenders, belong to the Italian fortresses as well as to the Greek. The facts are significant that in that portion of Italy which was not reduced to subjection by the Hellenes but yet was in lively intercourse with them, the true polygonal masonry was at home, and it is found in Etruria only at Pyrgi and at the towns, not very far distant from it, of Cosa and Saturnia; as the design of the walls of Pyrgi, especially when we take into account the significant name ("towers"), may just as certainly be ascribed to the Greeks as that of the walls of Tiryns, in them most probably there still stands before our eyes one of the models from which the Italians learned how to build their walls. The temple in fine, which in the period of the empire was called the Tuscanic and was regarded as a kind of style co-ordinate with the various Greek temple-structures, not only generally resembled the Greek temple in being an enclosed space (-cello-) usually quadrangular, over which walls and columns raised aloft a sloping roof, but was also in details, especially in the column itself and its architectural features, thoroughly dependent on the Greek system. It is in accordance with all these facts probable, as it is credible of itself, that Italian architecture previous to its contact with the Hellenes was confined to wooden huts, abattis, and mounds of earth and stones, and that construction in stone was only adopted in consequence of the example and the better tools of the Greeks. It is scarcely to be doubted that the Italians first learned from them the use of iron, and derived from them the preparation of mortar (-cal[e]x-, -calecare-, from —chaliz—), the machine (-machina-, —meichanei—), the measuring-rod (-groma-, a corruption from —gnomon—, —gnoma—), and the artificial latticework (-clathri-, —kleithron—). Accordingly we can scarcely speak of an architecture peculiarly Italian. Yet in the woodwork of the Italian dwelling-house—alongside of alterations produced by Greek influence—various peculiarities may have been retained or even for the first time developed, and these again may have exercised a reflex influence on the building of the Italian temples. The architectural development of the house proceeded in Italy from the Etruscans. The Latin and even the Sabellian still adhered to the hereditary wooden hut and to the good old custom of assigning to the god or spirit not a consecrated dwelling, but only a consecrated space, while the Etruscan had already begun artistically to transform his dwelling-house, and to erect after the model of the dwelling-house of man a temple also for the god and a sepulchral chamber for the spirit. That the advance to such luxurious structures in Latium first took place under Etruscan influence, is proved by the designation of the oldest style of temple architecture and of the oldest style of house architecture respectively as Tuscanic.(20) As concerns the character of this transference, the Grecian temple probably imitated the general outlines of the tent or dwelling-house; but it was essentially built of hewn stone and covered with tiles, and the nature of the stone and the baked clay suggested to the Greek the laws of necessity and beauty. The Etruscan on the other hand remained a stranger to the strict Greek distinction between the dwelling of man necessarily erected of wood and the dwelling of the gods necessarily formed of stone. The peculiar characteristics of the Tuscan temple—the outline approaching nearer to a square, the higher gable, the greater breadth of the intervals between the columns, above all, the increased inclination of the roof and the singular projection of the roof-corbels beyond the supporting columns—all arose out of the greater approximation of the temple to the dwelling-house, and out of the peculiarities of wooden architecture.

Plastic Art in Italy

The plastic and delineative arts are more recent than architecture; the house must be built before any attempt is made to decorate gable and walls. It is not probable that these arts really gained a place in Italy during the regal period of Rome; it was only in Etruria, where commerce and piracy early gave rise to a great concentration of riches, that art or handicraft—if the term be preferred—obtained a footing in the earliest times. Greek art, when it acted on Etruria, was still, as its copy shows, at a very primitive stage, and the Etruscans may have learned from the Greeks the art of working in clay and metal at a period not much later than that at which they borrowed from them the alphabet. The silver coins of Populonia, almost the only works that can be with any precision assigned to this period, give no very high idea of Etruscan artistic skill as it then stood; yet the best of the Etruscan works in bronze, to which the later critics of art assigned so high a place, may have belonged to this primitive age; and the Etruscan terra-cottas also cannot have been altogether despicable, for the oldest works in baked clay placed in the Roman temples—the statue of the Capitoline Jupiter, and the four-horse chariot on the roof of his temple—were executed in Veii, and the large ornaments of a similar kind placed on the roofs of temples passed generally among the later Romans under the name of "Tuscanic works."

On the other hand, among the Italians—not among the Sabellian stocks merely, but even among the Latins—native sculpture and design were at this period only coming into existence. The most considerable works of art appear to have been executed abroad. We have just mentioned the statues of clay alleged to have been executed in Veii; and very recent excavations have shown that works in bronze made in Etruria, and furnished with Etruscan inscriptions, circulated in Praeneste at least, if not generally throughout Latium. The statue of Diana in the Romano-Latin federal temple on the Aventine, which was considered the oldest statue of a divinity in Rome,(21) exactly resembled the Massiliot statue of the Ephesian Artemis, and was perhaps manufactured in Velia or Massilia. The guilds, which from ancient times existed in Rome, of potters, coppersmiths, and goldsmiths,(22) are almost the only proofs of the existence of native sculpture and design there; respecting the position of their art it is no longer possible to gain any clear idea.

Artistic Relations and Endowments of the Etruscans and Italians

If we endeavour to obtain historical results from the archives of the tradition and practice of primitive art, it is in the first place manifest that Italian art, like the Italian measures and Italian writing, developed itself not under Phoenician, but exclusively under Hellenic influence. There is not a single one of the aspects of Italian art which has not found its definite model in the art of ancient Greece; and, so far, the legend is fully warranted which traces the manufacture of painted clay figures, beyond doubt the most ancient form of art in Italy, to the three Greek artists, the "moulder," "fitter," and "draughtsman," Eucheir, Diopos, and Eugrammos, although it is more than doubtful whether this art came directly from Corinth or came directly to Tarquinii. There is as little trace of any immediate imitation of oriental models as there is of an independently-developed form of art. The Etruscan lapidaries adhered to the form of the beetle or -scarabaeus-, which was originally Egyptian; but —-scarabaei— were also used as models for carving in Greece in very early times (e. g. such a beetle-stone, with a very ancient Greek inscription, has been found in Aegina), and therefore they may very well have come to the Etruscans through the Greeks. The Italians may have bought from the Phoenician; they learned only from the Greek.

To the further question, from what Greek stock the Etruscans in the first instance received their art-models, a categorical answer cannot be given; yet relations of a remarkable kind subsist between the Etruscan and the oldest Attic art. The three forms of art, which were practised in Etruria at least in after times very extensively, but in Greece only to an extent very limited, tomb-painting, mirror-designing, and graving on stone, have been hitherto met with on Grecian soil only in Athens and Aegina. The Tuscan temple does not correspond exactly either to the Doric or to the Ionic; but in the more important points of distinction, in the course of columns carried round the -cella-, as well as in the placing of a separate pedestal under each particular column, the Etruscan style follows the more recent Ionic; and it is this same Iono-Attic style of building still pervaded by a Doric element, which in its general design stands nearest of all the Greek styles to the Tuscan. In the case of Latium there is an almost total absence of any certain traces of intercourse bearing on the history of art. If it was—as is indeed almost self-evident—the general relations of traffic and intercourse that determined also the introduction of models in art, it may be assumed with certainty that the Campanian and Sicilian Hellenes were the instructors of Latium in art, as in the alphabet; and the analogy between the Aventine Diana and the Ephesian Artemis is at least not inconsistent with such an hypothesis. Of course the older Etruscan art also served as a model for Latium. As to the Sabellian tribes, if Greek architectural and plastic art reached them at all, it must, like the Greek alphabet, have come to them only through the medium of the more western Italian stocks.

If, in conclusion, we are to form a judgment respecting the artistic endowments of the different Italian nations, we already at this stage perceive—what becomes indeed far more obvious in the later stages of the history of art—that while the Etruscans attained to the practice of art at an earlier period and produced more massive and rich workmanship, their works are inferior to those of the Latins and Sabellians in appropriateness and utility no less than in spirit and beauty. This certainly is apparent, in the case of our present epoch, only in architecture. The polygonal wall-masonry, as appropriate to its object as it was beautiful, was frequent in Latium and in the inland country behind it; while in Etruria it was rare, and not even the walls of Caere are constructed of polygonal blocks. Even in the religious prominence—-remarkable also as respects the history of art—assigned to the arch(23) and to the bridge(24) in Latium, we may be allowed to perceive, as it were, an anticipation of the future aqueducts and consular highways of Rome. On the other hand, the Etruscans repeated, and at the same time corrupted, the ornamental architecture of the Greeks: for while they transferred the laws established for building in stone to architecture in wood, they displayed no thorough skill of adaptation, and by the lowness of their roof and the wide intervals between their columns gave to their temples, to use the language of an ancient architect, a "heavy, mean, straggling, and clumsy appearance." The Latins found in the rich stores of Greek art but very little that was congenial to their thoroughly realistic tastes; but what they did adopt they appropriated truly and heartily as their own, and in the development of the polygonal wall-architecture perhaps excelled their instructors. Etruscan art is a remarkable evidence of accomplishments mechanically acquired and mechanically retained, but it is, as little as the Chinese, an evidence even of genial receptivity. As scholars have long since desisted from the attempt to derive Greek art from that of the Etruscans, so they must, with whatever reluctance, make up their minds to transfer the Etruscans from the first to the lowest place in the history of Italian art.

Notes for Book I Chapter XV

1. I. XII. Priests

2. I. XIII. Handicrafts

3. Thus Cato the Elder (de R. R. 160) gives as potent against sprains the formula: -hauat hauat hauat ista pista sista damia bodannaustra-, which was presumably quite as obscure to its inventor as it is to us. Of course, along with these there were also formulae of words; e. g. it was a remedy for gout, to think, while fasting, on some other person, and thrice nine times to utter the words, touching the earth at the same time and spitting:—"I think of thee, mend my feet. Let the earth receive the ill, let health with me dwell" (-terra pestem teneto, salus hie maneto-. Varro de R. R. i. 2, 27).

4. Each of the first five lines was repeated thrice, and the call at the close five times. Various points in the interpretation are uncertain, particularly as respects the third line. —The three inscriptions of the clay vase from the Quirinal (p. 277, note) run thus: -iove sat deiuosqoi med mitat nei ted endo gosmis uirgo sied—asted noisi ope toilesiai pakariuois—duenos med faked (=bonus me fecit) enmanom einom dze noine (probably=die noni) med malo statod.-Only individual words admit of being understood with certainty; it is especially noteworthy that forms, which we have hitherto known only as Umbrian and Oscan, like the adjective -pacer-and the particle -einom with the value of -et, here probably meet us withal as old-Latin.

5. I. II. Art

6. The name probably denotes nothing but "the chant-measure," inasmuch as the -satura- was originally the chant sung at the carnival (*ii*. Art). The god of sowing, -Saeturnus- or -Saiturnus-, afterwards -Saturnus-, received his name from the same root; his feast, the Saturnalia, was certainly a sort of carnival, and it is possible that the farces were originally exhibited chiefly at this feast. But there are no proofs of a relation between the Satura and the Saturnalia, and it may be presumed that the immediate association of the -versus saturnius- with the god Saturn, and the lengthening of the first syllable in connection with that view, belong only to later times.

7. I. XII. Foreign Worships

8. I. XIV. Introduction of Hellenic Alphabets into Italy

9. The statement that "formerly the Roman boys were trained in Etruscan culture, as they were in later times in Greek" (Liv. ix. 36), is quite irreconcilable with the original character of the Roman training of youth, and it is not easy to see what the Roman boys could have learned in Etruria. Even the most zealous modern partizans of Tages-worship will not maintain that the study of the Etruscan language played

such a part in Rome then as the learning of French does now with us; that a non-Etruscan should understand anything of the art of the Etruscan -haruspices- was considered, even by those who availed themselves of that art, to be a disgrace or rather an impossibility (Muller, Etr. ii. 4). Perhaps the statement was concocted by the Etruscizing antiquaries of the last age of the republic out of stories of the older annals, aiming at a causal explanation of facts, such as that which makes Mucius Scaevola learn Etruscan when a child for the sake of his conversation with Porsena (Dionysius, v. 28; Plutarch, Poplicola, 17; comp. Dionysius, iii. 70). But there was at any rate an epoch when the dominion of Rome over Italy demanded a certain knowledge of the language of the country on the part of Romans of rank.

10. The employment of the lyre in ritual is attested by Cicero de Orat. iii. 51, 197; Tusc. iv. 2, 4; Dionysius, vii. 72; Appian, Pun. 66; and the inscription in Orelli, 2448, comp. 1803. It was likewise used at the -neniae- (Varro ap. Nonium, v. -nenia-and -praeficae-). But playing on the lyre remained none the less unbecoming (Scipio ap. Macrob. Sat. ii. 10, *et al.*). The prohibition of music in 639 exempted only the "Latin player on the pipe along with the singer," not the player on the lyre, and the guests at meals sang only to the pipe (Cato in Cic. Tusc. i. 2, 3; iv. 2, 3; Varro ap. Nonium, v. -assa voce-; Horace, Carm. iv. 15, 30). Quintilian, who asserts the reverse (Inst. i. 10, 20), has inaccurately transferred to private banquets what Cicero (de Orat. iii. 51) states in reference to the feasts of the gods.

11. The city festival can have only lasted at first for a single day, for in the sixth century it still consisted of four days of scenic and one day of Circensian sports (Ritschl, Parerga, i. 313) and it is well known that the scenic amusements were only a subsequent addition. That in each kind of contest there was originally only one competition, follows from Livy, xliv. 9; the running of five-and-twenty pairs of chariots in succession on one day was a subsequent innovation (Varro ap. Serv. Georg. iii. 18). That only two chariots—and likewise beyond doubt only two horsemen and two wrestlers—strove for the prize, may be inferred from the circumstance, that at all periods in the Roman chariot-races only as many chariots competed as there were so-called factions; and of these there were originally only two, the white and the red. The horsemanship-competition of patrician youths which belonged to the Circensian games, the so-called Troia, was, as is well known, revived by Cæsar; beyond doubt it was connected with the cavalcade of the boy-militia, which Dionysius mentions (vii. 72).

12. I. VII. Servian Wall

13. I. VI. Time and Occasion of the Reform

14. I. II. Religion

15. -Vates- probably denoted in the first instance the "leader of the singing" (for so the -vates- of the Salii must be understood) and thereafter in its older usage approximated to the Greek —propheiteis—; it was a word be longing to religious

ritual, and even when subsequently used of the poet, always retained the accessory idea of a divinely-inspired singer—the priest of the Muses.

16. We shall show in due time that the Atellanae and Fescenninae belonged not to Campanian and Etruscan, but to Latin art.

17. Literally "word-crisping," in allusion to the -calamistri Maecenatis-.

18. I. III. Alba

19. Of this character were the Servian walls. They consisted partly of a strengthening of the hill-slopes by facing them with lining-walls as much as 4 metres thick, partly—in the intervals, above all on the Viminal and Quirinal, where from the Esquiline to the Colline gate there was an absence of natural defence—of an earthen mound, which was finished off on the outside by a similar lining-wall. On these lining-walls rested the breastwork. A trench, according to trustworthy statements of the ancients 30 feet deep and 100 feet broad, stretched along in front of the wall, for which the earth was taken from this same trench.—The breastwork has nowhere been preserved; of the lining-walls extensive remains have recently been brought to light. The blocks of tufo composing them are hewn in longish rectangles, on an average of 60 centimetres (= 2 Roman feet) in height and breadth, while the length varies from 70 centimetres to 3 metres, and they are, without application of mortar, laid together in several rows, alternately with the long and with the narrow side outermost.

The portion of the Servian wall near the Viminal gate, discovered in the year 1862 at the Villa Negroni, rests on a foundation of huge blocks of tufo of 3 to 4 metres in height and breadth, on which was then raised the outer wall from blocks of the same material and of the same size as those elsewhere employed in the wall. The earthen rampart piled up behind appears to have had on the upper surface a breadth extending about 13 metres or fully 40 Roman feet, and the whole wall-defence, including the outer wall of freestone, to have had a breadth of as much as 15 metres or 50 Roman feet. The portions formed of peperino blocks, which are bound with iron clamps, have only been added in connection with subsequent labours of repair.—Essentially similar to the Servian walls are those discovered in the Vigna Nussiner, on the slope of the Palatine towards the side of the Capitol, and at other points of the Palatine, which have been declared by Jordan (Topographic, ii. 173), probably with reason, to be remnants of the citadel-wall of the Palatine Rome,

20. -Ratio Tuscanica,: cavum aedium Tuscanicum.-

21. When Varro (ap. Augustin. De Civ. Dei, iv. 31; comp. Plutarch Num. 8) affirms that the Romans for more than one hundred and seventy years worshipped the gods without images, he is evidently thinking of this primitive piece of carving, which, according to the conventional chronology, was dedicated between 176 and 219, and, beyond doubt, was the first statue of the gods, the consecration of which

was mentioned in the authorities which Varro had before him. Comp, above, *xiv.* Development of Alphabets in Italy.

22. I. XIII. Handicrafts

23. I. XII. Nature of the Roman Gods

24. I. XII. Pontifices

End of Book I

Table of calendar equivalents—A. U. C vs. B. C.

A.U.C.*	B.C.	B.C.	A.U.C.
000	753	753	000
025	728	750	003
050	703	725	028
075	678	700	053
100	653	675	078
125	628	650	103
150	603	625	128
175	578	600	153
200	553	575	178
225	528	550	203
250	503	525	228
275	478	500	253
300	453	475	278
325	428	450	303
350	303	425	328
375	378	400	353
400	353	375	378
425	328	350	403
450	303	325	428
475	278	300	453
500	253	275	478
525	228	250	503
550	203	225	528
575	178	200	553
600	153	175	578
625	128	150	603
650	103	125	628
675	078	100	653
700	053	075	678
725	028	050	703
750	003	025	728
753	000	000	753

A. U. C.—Ab Urbe Condi (from the founding of the City of Rome)

Made in the USA
Lexington, KY
11 February 2010